C-1395   CAREER EXAMINATION SERIES

This is your
PASSBOOK for...

Power Plant Operator

Test Preparation Study Guide
Questions & Answers

COPYRIGHT NOTICE

This book is SOLELY intended for, is sold ONLY to, and its use is RESTRICTED to individual, bona fide applicants or candidates who qualify by virtue of having seriously filed applications for appropriate license, certificate, professional and/or promotional advancement, higher school matriculation, scholarship, or other legitimate requirements of education and/or governmental authorities.

This book is NOT intended for use, class instruction, tutoring, training, duplication, copying, reprinting, excerption, or adaptation, etc., by:

1) Other publishers
2) Proprietors and/or Instructors of "Coaching" and/or Preparatory Courses
3) Personnel and/or Training Divisions of commercial, industrial, and governmental organizations
4) Schools, colleges, or universities and/or their departments and staffs, including teachers and other personnel
5) Testing Agencies or Bureaus
6) Study groups which seek by the purchase of a single volume to copy and/or duplicate and/or adapt this material for use by the group as a whole without having purchased individual volumes for each of the members of the group
7) Et al.

Such persons would be in violation of appropriate Federal and State statutes.

PROVISION OF LICENSING AGREEMENTS – Recognized educational, commercial, industrial, and governmental institutions and organizations, and others legitimately engaged in educational pursuits, including training, testing, and measurement activities, may address request for a licensing agreement to the copyright owners, who will determine whether, and under what conditions, including fees and charges, the materials in this book may be used them. In other words, a licensing facility exists for the legitimate use of the material in this book on other than an individual basis. However, it is asseverated and affirmed here that the material in this book CANNOT be used without the receipt of the express permission of such a licensing agreement from the Publishers. Inquiries re licensing should be addressed to the company, attention rights and permissions department.

All rights reserved, including the right of reproduction in whole or in part, in any form or by any means, electronic or mechanical, including photocopying, recording, or by any information storage and retrieval system, without permission in writing from the Publisher.

Copyright © 2025 by
National Learning Corporation

212 Michael Drive, Syosset, NY 11791
(516) 921-8888 • www.passbooks.com
E-mail: info@passbooks.com

PASSBOOK® SERIES

THE *PASSBOOK® SERIES* has been created to prepare applicants and candidates for the ultimate academic battlefield – the examination room.

At some time in our lives, each and every one of us may be required to take an examination – for validation, matriculation, admission, qualification, registration, certification, or licensure.

Based on the assumption that every applicant or candidate has met the basic formal educational standards, has taken the required number of courses, and read the necessary texts, the *PASSBOOK® SERIES* furnishes the one special preparation which may assure passing with confidence, instead of failing with insecurity. Examination questions – together with answers – are furnished as the basic vehicle for study so that the mysteries of the examination and its compounding difficulties may be eliminated or diminished by a sure method.

This book is meant to help you pass your examination provided that you qualify and are serious in your objective.

The entire field is reviewed through the huge store of content information which is succinctly presented through a provocative and challenging approach – the question-and-answer method.

A climate of success is established by furnishing the correct answers at the end of each test.

You soon learn to recognize types of questions, forms of questions, and patterns of questioning. You may even begin to anticipate expected outcomes.

You perceive that many questions are repeated or adapted so that you can gain acute insights, which may enable you to score many sure points.

You learn how to confront new questions, or types of questions, and to attack them confidently and work out the correct answers.

You note objectives and emphases, and recognize pitfalls and dangers, so that you may make positive educational adjustments.

Moreover, you are kept fully informed in relation to new concepts, methods, practices, and directions in the field.

You discover that you are actually taking the examination all the time: you are preparing for the examination by "taking" an examination, not by reading extraneous and/or supererogatory textbooks.

In short, this PASSBOOK®, used directedly, should be an important factor in helping you to pass your test.

POWER PLANT OPERATOR

DUTIES
Operates pumps, engines, blowers, generators, and related equipment at a sewage treatment and disposal plant; performs related duties as required.

SCOPE OF THE EXAMINATION
The multiple-choice test will cover knowledge, skills, and/or abilities in such areas as:
1. Reading comprehension and basic mathematics;
2. Tools, mechanical aptitude, and the reading of scales and gauges;
3. Operation, maintenance and repair of pumps, motors, valves, electrical and mechanical equipment
4. Elementary hydraulics and water pumping operations; and
5. Operation and maintenance of diesel engines.

HOW TO TAKE A TEST

I. YOU MUST PASS AN EXAMINATION

A. *WHAT EVERY CANDIDATE SHOULD KNOW*

Examination applicants often ask us for help in preparing for the written test. What can I study in advance? What kinds of questions will be asked? How will the test be given? How will the papers be graded?

As an applicant for a civil service examination, you may be wondering about some of these things. Our purpose here is to suggest effective methods of advance study and to describe civil service examinations.

Your chances for success on this examination can be increased if you know how to prepare. Those "pre-examination jitters" can be reduced if you know what to expect. You can even experience an adventure in good citizenship if you know why civil service exams are given.

B. *WHY ARE CIVIL SERVICE EXAMINATIONS GIVEN?*

Civil service examinations are important to you in two ways. As a citizen, you want public jobs filled by employees who know how to do their work. As a job seeker, you want a fair chance to compete for that job on an equal footing with other candidates. The best-known means of accomplishing this two-fold goal is the competitive examination.

Exams are widely publicized throughout the nation. They may be administered for jobs in federal, state, city, municipal, town or village governments or agencies.

Any citizen may apply, with some limitations, such as the age or residence of applicants. Your experience and education may be reviewed to see whether you meet the requirements for the particular examination. When these requirements exist, they are reasonable and applied consistently to all applicants. Thus, a competitive examination may cause you some uneasiness now, but it is your privilege and safeguard.

C. *HOW ARE CIVIL SERVICE EXAMS DEVELOPED?*

Examinations are carefully written by trained technicians who are specialists in the field known as "psychological measurement," in consultation with recognized authorities in the field of work that the test will cover. These experts recommend the subject matter areas or skills to be tested; only those knowledges or skills important to your success on the job are included. The most reliable books and source materials available are used as references. Together, the experts and technicians judge the difficulty level of the questions.

Test technicians know how to phrase questions so that the problem is clearly stated. Their ethics do not permit "trick" or "catch" questions. Questions may have been tried out on sample groups, or subjected to statistical analysis, to determine their usefulness.

Written tests are often used in combination with performance tests, ratings of training and experience, and oral interviews. All of these measures combine to form the best-known means of finding the right person for the right job.

II. HOW TO PASS THE WRITTEN TEST

A. NATURE OF THE EXAMINATION

To prepare intelligently for civil service examinations, you should know how they differ from school examinations you have taken. In school you were assigned certain definite pages to read or subjects to cover. The examination questions were quite detailed and usually emphasized memory. Civil service exams, on the other hand, try to discover your present ability to perform the duties of a position, plus your potentiality to learn these duties. In other words, a civil service exam attempts to predict how successful you will be. Questions cover such a broad area that they cannot be as minute and detailed as school exam questions.

In the public service similar kinds of work, or positions, are grouped together in one "class." This process is known as *position-classification*. All the positions in a class are paid according to the salary range for that class. One class title covers all of these positions, and they are all tested by the same examination.

B. FOUR BASIC STEPS

1) Study the announcement

How, then, can you know what subjects to study? Our best answer is: "Learn as much as possible about the class of positions for which you've applied." The exam will test the knowledge, skills and abilities needed to do the work.

Your most valuable source of information about the position you want is the official exam announcement. This announcement lists the training and experience qualifications. Check these standards and apply only if you come reasonably close to meeting them.

The brief description of the position in the examination announcement offers some clues to the subjects which will be tested. Think about the job itself. Review the duties in your mind. Can you perform them, or are there some in which you are rusty? Fill in the blank spots in your preparation.

Many jurisdictions preview the written test in the exam announcement by including a section called "Knowledge and Abilities Required," "Scope of the Examination," or some similar heading. Here you will find out specifically what fields will be tested.

2) Review your own background

Once you learn in general what the position is all about, and what you need to know to do the work, ask yourself which subjects you already know fairly well and which need improvement. You may wonder whether to concentrate on improving your strong areas or on building some background in your fields of weakness. When the announcement has specified "some knowledge" or "considerable knowledge," or has used adjectives like "beginning principles of…" or "advanced … methods," you can get a clue as to the number and difficulty of questions to be asked in any given field. More questions, and hence broader coverage, would be included for those subjects which are more important in the work. Now weigh your strengths and weaknesses against the job requirements and prepare accordingly.

3) Determine the level of the position

Another way to tell how intensively you should prepare is to understand the level of the job for which you are applying. Is it the entering level? In other words, is this the position in which beginners in a field of work are hired? Or is it an intermediate or advanced level? Sometimes this is indicated by such words as "Junior" or "Senior" in the class title. Other jurisdictions use Roman numerals to designate the level – Clerk I, Clerk II, for example. The word "Supervisor" sometimes appears in the title. If the level is not indicated by the title, check the description of duties. Will you be working under very close supervision, or will you have responsibility for independent decisions in this work?

4) Choose appropriate study materials

Now that you know the subjects to be examined and the relative amount of each subject to be covered, you can choose suitable study materials. For beginning level jobs, or even advanced ones, if you have a pronounced weakness in some aspect of your training, read a modern, standard textbook in that field. Be sure it is up to date and has general coverage. Such books are normally available at your library, and the librarian will be glad to help you locate one. For entry-level positions, questions of appropriate difficulty are chosen – neither highly advanced questions, nor those too simple. Such questions require careful thought but not advanced training.

If the position for which you are applying is technical or advanced, you will read more advanced, specialized material. If you are already familiar with the basic principles of your field, elementary textbooks would waste your time. Concentrate on advanced textbooks and technical periodicals. Think through the concepts and review difficult problems in your field.

These are all general sources. You can get more ideas on your own initiative, following these leads. For example, training manuals and publications of the government agency which employs workers in your field can be useful, particularly for technical and professional positions. A letter or visit to the government department involved may result in more specific study suggestions, and certainly will provide you with a more definite idea of the exact nature of the position you are seeking.

III. KINDS OF TESTS

Tests are used for purposes other than measuring knowledge and ability to perform specified duties. For some positions, it is equally important to test ability to make adjustments to new situations or to profit from training. In others, basic mental abilities not dependent on information are essential. Questions which test these things may not appear as pertinent to the duties of the position as those which test for knowledge and information. Yet they are often highly important parts of a fair examination. For very general questions, it is almost impossible to help you direct your study efforts. What we can do is to point out some of the more common of these general abilities needed in public service positions and describe some typical questions.

1) General information

Broad, general information has been found useful for predicting job success in some kinds of work. This is tested in a variety of ways, from vocabulary lists to questions about current events. Basic background in some field of work, such as sociology or economics, may be sampled in a group of questions. Often these are principles which have become familiar to most persons through exposure rather than through formal training. It is difficult to advise you how to study for these questions; being alert to the world around you is our best suggestion.

2) Verbal ability

An example of an ability needed in many positions is verbal or language ability. Verbal ability is, in brief, the ability to use and understand words. Vocabulary and grammar tests are typical measures of this ability. Reading comprehension or paragraph interpretation questions are common in many kinds of civil service tests. You are given a paragraph of written material and asked to find its central meaning.

3) Numerical ability

Number skills can be tested by the familiar arithmetic problem, by checking paired lists of numbers to see which are alike and which are different, or by interpreting charts and graphs. In the latter test, a graph may be printed in the test booklet which you are asked to use as the basis for answering questions.

4) Observation

A popular test for law-enforcement positions is the observation test. A picture is shown to you for several minutes, then taken away. Questions about the picture test your ability to observe both details and larger elements.

5) Following directions

In many positions in the public service, the employee must be able to carry out written instructions dependably and accurately. You may be given a chart with several columns, each column listing a variety of information. The questions require you to carry out directions involving the information given in the chart.

6) Skills and aptitudes

Performance tests effectively measure some manual skills and aptitudes. When the skill is one in which you are trained, such as typing or shorthand, you can practice. These tests are often very much like those given in business school or high school courses. For many of the other skills and aptitudes, however, no short-time preparation can be made. Skills and abilities natural to you or that you have developed throughout your lifetime are being tested.

Many of the general questions just described provide all the data needed to answer the questions and ask you to use your reasoning ability to find the answers. Your best preparation for these tests, as well as for tests of facts and ideas, is to be at your physical and mental best. You, no doubt, have your own methods of getting into an exam-taking mood and keeping "in shape." The next section lists some ideas on this subject.

IV. KINDS OF QUESTIONS

Only rarely is the "essay" question, which you answer in narrative form, used in civil service tests. Civil service tests are usually of the short-answer type. Full instructions for answering these questions will be given to you at the examination. But in case this is your first experience with short-answer questions and separate answer sheets, here is what you need to know:

1) Multiple-choice Questions

Most popular of the short-answer questions is the "multiple choice" or "best answer" question. It can be used, for example, to test for factual knowledge, ability to solve problems or judgment in meeting situations found at work.

A multiple-choice question is normally one of three types—

- It can begin with an incomplete statement followed by several possible endings. You are to find the one ending which *best* completes the statement, although some of the others may not be entirely wrong.
- It can also be a complete statement in the form of a question which is answered by choosing one of the statements listed.

- It can be in the form of a problem – again you select the best answer.

Here is an example of a multiple-choice question with a discussion which should give you some clues as to the method for choosing the right answer:

When an employee has a complaint about his assignment, the action which will *best* help him overcome his difficulty is to
    A. discuss his difficulty with his coworkers
    B. take the problem to the head of the organization
    C. take the problem to the person who gave him the assignment
    D. say nothing to anyone about his complaint

In answering this question, you should study each of the choices to find which is best. Consider choice "A" – Certainly an employee may discuss his complaint with fellow employees, but no change or improvement can result, and the complaint remains unresolved. Choice "B" is a poor choice since the head of the organization probably does not know what assignment you have been given, and taking your problem to him is known as "going over the head" of the supervisor. The supervisor, or person who made the assignment, is the person who can clarify it or correct any injustice. Choice "C" is, therefore, correct. To say nothing, as in choice "D," is unwise. Supervisors have and interest in knowing the problems employees are facing, and the employee is seeking a solution to his problem.

2) True/False Questions

The "true/false" or "right/wrong" form of question is sometimes used. Here a complete statement is given. Your job is to decide whether the statement is right or wrong.

SAMPLE: A roaming cell-phone call to a nearby city costs less than a non-roaming call to a distant city.

This statement is wrong, or false, since roaming calls are more expensive.

This is not a complete list of all possible question forms, although most of the others are variations of these common types. You will always get complete directions for answering questions. Be sure you understand *how* to mark your answers – ask questions until you do.

V. RECORDING YOUR ANSWERS

Computer terminals are used more and more today for many different kinds of exams.

For an examination with very few applicants, you may be told to record your answers in the test booklet itself. Separate answer sheets are much more common. If this separate answer sheet is to be scored by machine – and this is often the case – it is highly important that you mark your answers correctly in order to get credit.

An electronic scoring machine is often used in civil service offices because of the speed with which papers can be scored. Machine-scored answer sheets must be marked with a pencil, which will be given to you. This pencil has a high graphite content which responds to the electronic scoring machine. As a matter of fact, stray dots may register as answers, so do not let your pencil rest on the answer sheet while you are pondering the correct answer. Also, if your pencil lead breaks or is otherwise defective, ask for another.

Since the answer sheet will be dropped in a slot in the scoring machine, be careful not to bend the corners or get the paper crumpled.

The answer sheet normally has five vertical columns of numbers, with 30 numbers to a column. These numbers correspond to the question numbers in your test booklet. After each number, going across the page are four or five pairs of dotted lines. These short dotted lines have small letters or numbers above them. The first two pairs may also have a "T" or "F" above the letters. This indicates that the first two pairs only are to be used if the questions are of the true-false type. If the questions are multiple choice, disregard the "T" and "F" and pay attention only to the small letters or numbers.

Answer your questions in the manner of the sample that follows:

32. The largest city in the United States is
    A. Washington, D.C.
    B. New York City
    C. Chicago
    D. Detroit
    E. San Francisco

1) Choose the answer you think is best. (New York City is the largest, so "B" is correct.)
2) Find the row of dotted lines numbered the same as the question you are answering. (Find row number 32)
3) Find the pair of dotted lines corresponding to the answer. (Find the pair of lines under the mark "B.")
4) Make a solid black mark between the dotted lines.

VI. BEFORE THE TEST

Common sense will help you find procedures to follow to get ready for an examination. Too many of us, however, overlook these sensible measures. Indeed, nervousness and fatigue have been found to be the most serious reasons why applicants fail to do their best on civil service tests. Here is a list of reminders:

- Begin your preparation early – Don't wait until the last minute to go scurrying around for books and materials or to find out what the position is all about.
- Prepare continuously – An hour a night for a week is better than an all-night cram session. This has been definitely established. What is more, a night a week for a month will return better dividends than crowding your study into a shorter period of time.
- Locate the place of the exam – You have been sent a notice telling you when and where to report for the examination. If the location is in a different town or otherwise unfamiliar to you, it would be well to inquire the best route and learn something about the building.
- Relax the night before the test – Allow your mind to rest. Do not study at all that night. Plan some mild recreation or diversion; then go to bed early and get a good night's sleep.
- Get up early enough to make a leisurely trip to the place for the test – This way unforeseen events, traffic snarls, unfamiliar buildings, etc. will not upset you.
- Dress comfortably – A written test is not a fashion show. You will be known by number and not by name, so wear something comfortable.

- Leave excess paraphernalia at home – Shopping bags and odd bundles will get in your way. You need bring only the items mentioned in the official notice you received; usually everything you need is provided. Do not bring reference books to the exam. They will only confuse those last minutes and be taken away from you when in the test room.
- Arrive somewhat ahead of time – If because of transportation schedules you must get there very early, bring a newspaper or magazine to take your mind off yourself while waiting.
- Locate the examination room – When you have found the proper room, you will be directed to the seat or part of the room where you will sit. Sometimes you are given a sheet of instructions to read while you are waiting. Do not fill out any forms until you are told to do so; just read them and be prepared.
- Relax and prepare to listen to the instructions
- If you have any physical problem that may keep you from doing your best, be sure to tell the test administrator. If you are sick or in poor health, you really cannot do your best on the exam. You can come back and take the test some other time.

VII. AT THE TEST

The day of the test is here and you have the test booklet in your hand. The temptation to get going is very strong. Caution! There is more to success than knowing the right answers. You must know how to identify your papers and understand variations in the type of short-answer question used in this particular examination. Follow these suggestions for maximum results from your efforts:

1) Cooperate with the monitor

The test administrator has a duty to create a situation in which you can be as much at ease as possible. He will give instructions, tell you when to begin, check to see that you are marking your answer sheet correctly, and so on. He is not there to guard you, although he will see that your competitors do not take unfair advantage. He wants to help you do your best.

2) Listen to all instructions

Don't jump the gun! Wait until you understand all directions. In most civil service tests you get more time than you need to answer the questions. So don't be in a hurry. Read each word of instructions until you clearly understand the meaning. Study the examples, listen to all announcements and follow directions. Ask questions if you do not understand what to do.

3) Identify your papers

Civil service exams are usually identified by number only. You will be assigned a number; you must not put your name on your test papers. Be sure to copy your number correctly. Since more than one exam may be given, copy your exact examination title.

4) Plan your time

Unless you are told that a test is a "speed" or "rate of work" test, speed itself is usually not important. Time enough to answer all the questions will be provided, but this does not mean that you have all day. An overall time limit has been set. Divide the total time (in minutes) by the number of questions to determine the approximate time you have for each question.

5) Do not linger over difficult questions

If you come across a difficult question, mark it with a paper clip (useful to have along) and come back to it when you have been through the booklet. One caution if you do this – be sure to skip a number on your answer sheet as well. Check often to be sure that you have not lost your place and that you are marking in the row numbered the same as the question you are answering.

6) Read the questions

Be sure you know what the question asks! Many capable people are unsuccessful because they failed to *read* the questions correctly.

7) Answer all questions

Unless you have been instructed that a penalty will be deducted for incorrect answers, it is better to guess than to omit a question.

8) Speed tests

It is often better NOT to guess on speed tests. It has been found that on timed tests people are tempted to spend the last few seconds before time is called in marking answers at random – without even reading them – in the hope of picking up a few extra points. To discourage this practice, the instructions may warn you that your score will be "corrected" for guessing. That is, a penalty will be applied. The incorrect answers will be deducted from the correct ones, or some other penalty formula will be used.

9) Review your answers

If you finish before time is called, go back to the questions you guessed or omitted to give them further thought. Review other answers if you have time.

10) Return your test materials

If you are ready to leave before others have finished or time is called, take ALL your materials to the monitor and leave quietly. Never take any test material with you. The monitor can discover whose papers are not complete, and taking a test booklet may be grounds for disqualification.

VIII. EXAMINATION TECHNIQUES

1) Read the general instructions carefully. These are usually printed on the first page of the exam booklet. As a rule, these instructions refer to the timing of the examination; the fact that you should not start work until the signal and must stop work at a signal, etc. If there are any *special* instructions, such as a choice of questions to be answered, make sure that you note this instruction carefully.

2) When you are ready to start work on the examination, that is as soon as the signal has been given, read the instructions to each question booklet, underline any key words or phrases, such as *least, best, outline, describe* and the like. In this way you will tend to answer as requested rather than discover on reviewing your paper that you *listed without describing*, that you selected the *worst* choice rather than the *best* choice, etc.

3) If the examination is of the objective or multiple-choice type – that is, each question will also give a series of possible answers: A, B, C or D, and you are called upon to select the best answer and write the letter next to that answer on your answer paper – it is advisable to start answering each question in turn. There may be anywhere from 50 to 100 such questions in the three or four hours allotted and you can see how much time would be taken if you read through all the questions before beginning to answer any. Furthermore, if you come across a question or group of questions which you know would be difficult to answer, it would undoubtedly affect your handling of all the other questions.

4) If the examination is of the essay type and contains but a few questions, it is a moot point as to whether you should read all the questions before starting to answer any one. Of course, if you are given a choice – say five out of seven and the like – then it is essential to read all the questions so you can eliminate the two that are most difficult. If, however, you are asked to answer all the questions, there may be danger in trying to answer the easiest one first because you may find that you will spend too much time on it. The best technique is to answer the first question, then proceed to the second, etc.

5) Time your answers. Before the exam begins, write down the time it started, then add the time allowed for the examination and write down the time it must be completed, then divide the time available somewhat as follows:
    - If 3-1/2 hours are allowed, that would be 210 minutes. If you have 80 objective-type questions, that would be an average of 2-1/2 minutes per question. Allow yourself no more than 2 minutes per question, or a total of 160 minutes, which will permit about 50 minutes to review.
    - If for the time allotment of 210 minutes there are 7 essay questions to answer, that would average about 30 minutes a question. Give yourself only 25 minutes per question so that you have about 35 minutes to review.

6) The most important instruction is to *read each question* and make sure you know what is wanted. The second most important instruction is to *time yourself properly* so that you answer every question. The third most important instruction is to *answer every question*. Guess if you have to but include something for each question. Remember that you will receive no credit for a blank and will probably receive some credit if you write something in answer to an essay question. If you guess a letter – say "B" for a multiple-choice question – you may have guessed right. If you leave a blank as an answer to a multiple-choice question, the examiners may respect your feelings but it will not add a point to your score. Some exams may penalize you for wrong answers, so in such cases *only*, you may not want to guess unless you have some basis for your answer.

7) Suggestions
    a. Objective-type questions
        1. Examine the question booklet for proper sequence of pages and questions
        2. Read all instructions carefully
        3. Skip any question which seems too difficult; return to it after all other questions have been answered
        4. Apportion your time properly; do not spend too much time on any single question or group of questions

5. Note and underline key words – *all, most, fewest, least, best, worst, same, opposite,* etc.
6. Pay particular attention to negatives
7. Note unusual option, e.g., unduly long, short, complex, different or similar in content to the body of the question
8. Observe the use of "hedging" words – *probably, may, most likely,* etc.
9. Make sure that your answer is put next to the same number as the question
10. Do not second-guess unless you have good reason to believe the second answer is definitely more correct
11. Cross out original answer if you decide another answer is more accurate; do not erase until you are ready to hand your paper in
12. Answer all questions; guess unless instructed otherwise
13. Leave time for review

b. Essay questions
1. Read each question carefully
2. Determine exactly what is wanted. Underline key words or phrases.
3. Decide on outline or paragraph answer
4. Include many different points and elements unless asked to develop any one or two points or elements
5. Show impartiality by giving pros and cons unless directed to select one side only
6. Make and write down any assumptions you find necessary to answer the questions
7. Watch your English, grammar, punctuation and choice of words
8. Time your answers; don't crowd material

8) Answering the essay question

Most essay questions can be answered by framing the specific response around several key words or ideas. Here are a few such key words or ideas:

M's: manpower, materials, methods, money, management
P's: purpose, program, policy, plan, procedure, practice, problems, pitfalls, personnel, public relations

a. Six basic steps in handling problems:
1. Preliminary plan and background development
2. Collect information, data and facts
3. Analyze and interpret information, data and facts
4. Analyze and develop solutions as well as make recommendations
5. Prepare report and sell recommendations
6. Install recommendations and follow up effectiveness

b. Pitfalls to avoid
1. *Taking things for granted* – A statement of the situation does not necessarily imply that each of the elements is necessarily true; for example, a complaint may be invalid and biased so that all that can be taken for granted is that a complaint has been registered

2. *Considering only one side of a situation* – Wherever possible, indicate several alternatives and then point out the reasons you selected the best one
3. *Failing to indicate follow up* – Whenever your answer indicates action on your part, make certain that you will take proper follow-up action to see how successful your recommendations, procedures or actions turn out to be
4. *Taking too long in answering any single question* – Remember to time your answers properly

IX. AFTER THE TEST

Scoring procedures differ in detail among civil service jurisdictions although the general principles are the same. Whether the papers are hand-scored or graded by machine we have described, they are nearly always graded by number. That is, the person who marks the paper knows only the number – never the name – of the applicant. Not until all the papers have been graded will they be matched with names. If other tests, such as training and experience or oral interview ratings have been given, scores will be combined. Different parts of the examination usually have different weights. For example, the written test might count 60 percent of the final grade, and a rating of training and experience 40 percent. In many jurisdictions, veterans will have a certain number of points added to their grades.

After the final grade has been determined, the names are placed in grade order and an eligible list is established. There are various methods for resolving ties between those who get the same final grade – probably the most common is to place first the name of the person whose application was received first. Job offers are made from the eligible list in the order the names appear on it. You will be notified of your grade and your rank as soon as all these computations have been made. This will be done as rapidly as possible.

People who are found to meet the requirements in the announcement are called "eligibles." Their names are put on a list of eligible candidates. An eligible's chances of getting a job depend on how high he stands on this list and how fast agencies are filling jobs from the list.

When a job is to be filled from a list of eligibles, the agency asks for the names of people on the list of eligibles for that job. When the civil service commission receives this request, it sends to the agency the names of the three people highest on this list. Or, if the job to be filled has specialized requirements, the office sends the agency the names of the top three persons who meet these requirements from the general list.

The appointing officer makes a choice from among the three people whose names were sent to him. If the selected person accepts the appointment, the names of the others are put back on the list to be considered for future openings.

That is the rule in hiring from all kinds of eligible lists, whether they are for typist, carpenter, chemist, or something else. For every vacancy, the appointing officer has his choice of any one of the top three eligibles on the list. This explains why the person whose name is on top of the list sometimes does not get an appointment when some of the persons lower on the list do. If the appointing officer chooses the second or third eligible, the No. 1 eligible does not get a job at once, but stays on the list until he is appointed or the list is terminated.

X. HOW TO PASS THE INTERVIEW TEST

The examination for which you applied requires an oral interview test. You have already taken the written test and you are now being called for the interview test – the final part of the formal examination.

You may think that it is not possible to prepare for an interview test and that there are no procedures to follow during an interview. Our purpose is to point out some things you can do in advance that will help you and some good rules to follow and pitfalls to avoid while you are being interviewed.

What is an interview supposed to test?

The written examination is designed to test the technical knowledge and competence of the candidate; the oral is designed to evaluate intangible qualities, not readily measured otherwise, and to establish a list showing the relative fitness of each candidate – as measured against his competitors – for the position sought. Scoring is not on the basis of "right" and "wrong," but on a sliding scale of values ranging from "not passable" to "outstanding." As a matter of fact, it is possible to achieve a relatively low score without a single "incorrect" answer because of evident weakness in the qualities being measured.

Occasionally, an examination may consist entirely of an oral test – either an individual or a group oral. In such cases, information is sought concerning the technical knowledges and abilities of the candidate, since there has been no written examination for this purpose. More commonly, however, an oral test is used to supplement a written examination.

Who conducts interviews?

The composition of oral boards varies among different jurisdictions. In nearly all, a representative of the personnel department serves as chairman. One of the members of the board may be a representative of the department in which the candidate would work. In some cases, "outside experts" are used, and, frequently, a businessman or some other representative of the general public is asked to serve. Labor and management or other special groups may be represented. The aim is to secure the services of experts in the appropriate field.

However the board is composed, it is a good idea (and not at all improper or unethical) to ascertain in advance of the interview who the members are and what groups they represent. When you are introduced to them, you will have some idea of their backgrounds and interests, and at least you will not stutter and stammer over their names.

What should be done before the interview?

While knowledge about the board members is useful and takes some of the surprise element out of the interview, there is other preparation which is more substantive. It *is* possible to prepare for an oral interview – in several ways:

1) Keep a copy of your application and review it carefully before the interview

This may be the only document before the oral board, and the starting point of the interview. Know what education and experience you have listed there, and the sequence and dates of all of it. Sometimes the board will ask you to review the highlights of your experience for them; you should not have to hem and haw doing it.

2) Study the class specification and the examination announcement

Usually, the oral board has one or both of these to guide them. The qualities, characteristics or knowledges required by the position sought are stated in these documents. They offer valuable clues as to the nature of the oral interview. For example, if the job involves supervisory responsibilities, the announcement will usually indicate that knowledge of modern supervisory methods and the qualifications of the candidate as a supervisor will be tested. If so, you can expect such questions, frequently in the form of a hypothetical situation which you are expected to solve. NEVER go into an oral without knowledge of the duties and responsibilities of the job you seek.

3) Think through each qualification required

Try to visualize the kind of questions you would ask if you were a board member. How well could you answer them? Try especially to appraise your own knowledge and background in each area, *measured against the job sought*, and identify any areas in which you are weak. Be critical and realistic – do not flatter yourself.

4) Do some general reading in areas in which you feel you may be weak

For example, if the job involves supervision and your past experience has NOT, some general reading in supervisory methods and practices, particularly in the field of human relations, might be useful. Do NOT study agency procedures or detailed manuals. The oral board will be testing your understanding and capacity, not your memory.

5) Get a good night's sleep and watch your general health and mental attitude

You will want a clear head at the interview. Take care of a cold or any other minor ailment, and of course, no hangovers.

What should be done on the day of the interview?

Now comes the day of the interview itself. Give yourself plenty of time to get there. Plan to arrive somewhat ahead of the scheduled time, particularly if your appointment is in the fore part of the day. If a previous candidate fails to appear, the board might be ready for you a bit early. By early afternoon an oral board is almost invariably behind schedule if there are many candidates, and you may have to wait. Take along a book or magazine to read, or your application to review, but leave any extraneous material in the waiting room when you go in for your interview. In any event, relax and compose yourself.

The matter of dress is important. The board is forming impressions about you – from your experience, your manners, your attitude, and your appearance. Give your personal appearance careful attention. Dress your best, but not your flashiest. Choose conservative, appropriate clothing, and be sure it is immaculate. This is a business interview, and your appearance should indicate that you regard it as such. Besides, being well groomed and properly dressed will help boost your confidence.

Sooner or later, someone will call your name and escort you into the interview room. *This is it.* From here on you are on your own. It is too late for any more preparation. But remember, you asked for this opportunity to prove your fitness, and you are here because your request was granted.

What happens when you go in?

The usual sequence of events will be as follows: The clerk (who is often the board stenographer) will introduce you to the chairman of the oral board, who will introduce you to the other members of the board. Acknowledge the introductions before you sit down. Do not be surprised if you find a microphone facing you or a stenotypist sitting by. Oral interviews are usually recorded in the event of an appeal or other review.

Usually the chairman of the board will open the interview by reviewing the highlights of your education and work experience from your application – primarily for the benefit of the other members of the board, as well as to get the material into the record. Do not interrupt or comment unless there is an error or significant misinterpretation; if that is the case, do not hesitate. But do not quibble about insignificant matters. Also, he will usually ask you some question about your education, experience or your present job – partly to get you to start talking and to establish the interviewing "rapport." He may start the actual questioning, or turn it over to one of the other members. Frequently, each member undertakes the questioning on a particular area, one in which he is perhaps most competent, so you can expect each member to participate in the examination. Because time is limited, you may also expect some rather abrupt switches in the direction the questioning takes, so do not be upset by it. Normally, a board member will not pursue a single line of questioning unless he discovers a particular strength or weakness.

After each member has participated, the chairman will usually ask whether any member has any further questions, then will ask you if you have anything you wish to add. Unless you are expecting this question, it may floor you. Worse, it may start you off on an extended, extemporaneous speech. The board is not usually seeking more information. The question is principally to offer you a last opportunity to present further qualifications or to indicate that you have nothing to add. So, if you feel that a significant qualification or characteristic has been overlooked, it is proper to point it out in a sentence or so. Do not compliment the board on the thoroughness of their examination – they have been sketchy, and you know it. If you wish, merely say, "No thank you, I have nothing further to add." This is a point where you can "talk yourself out" of a good impression or fail to present an important bit of information. Remember, *you close the interview yourself*.

The chairman will then say, "That is all, Mr. _____, thank you." Do not be startled; the interview is over, and quicker than you think. Thank him, gather your belongings and take your leave. Save your sigh of relief for the other side of the door.

How to put your best foot forward

Throughout this entire process, you may feel that the board individually and collectively is trying to pierce your defenses, seek out your hidden weaknesses and embarrass and confuse you. Actually, this is not true. They are obliged to make an appraisal of your qualifications for the job you are seeking, and they want to see you in your best light. Remember, they must interview all candidates and a non-cooperative candidate may become a failure in spite of their best efforts to bring out his qualifications. Here are 15 suggestions that will help you:

1) **Be natural – Keep your attitude confident, not cocky**

If you are not confident that you can do the job, do not expect the board to be. Do not apologize for your weaknesses, try to bring out your strong points. The board is interested in a positive, not negative, presentation. Cockiness will antagonize any board member and make him wonder if you are covering up a weakness by a false show of strength.

2) **Get comfortable, but don't lounge or sprawl**

Sit erectly but not stiffly. A careless posture may lead the board to conclude that you are careless in other things, or at least that you are not impressed by the importance of the occasion. Either conclusion is natural, even if incorrect. Do not fuss with your clothing, a pencil or an ashtray. Your hands may occasionally be useful to emphasize a point; do not let them become a point of distraction.

3) **Do not wisecrack or make small talk**

This is a serious situation, and your attitude should show that you consider it as such. Further, the time of the board is limited – they do not want to waste it, and neither should you.

4) Do not exaggerate your experience or abilities

In the first place, from information in the application or other interviews and sources, the board may know more about you than you think. Secondly, you probably will not get away with it. An experienced board is rather adept at spotting such a situation, so do not take the chance.

5) If you know a board member, do not make a point of it, yet do not hide it

Certainly you are not fooling him, and probably not the other members of the board. Do not try to take advantage of your acquaintanceship – it will probably do you little good.

6) Do not dominate the interview

Let the board do that. They will give you the clues – do not assume that you have to do all the talking. Realize that the board has a number of questions to ask you, and do not try to take up all the interview time by showing off your extensive knowledge of the answer to the first one.

7) Be attentive

You only have 20 minutes or so, and you should keep your attention at its sharpest throughout. When a member is addressing a problem or question to you, give him your undivided attention. Address your reply principally to him, but do not exclude the other board members.

8) Do not interrupt

A board member may be stating a problem for you to analyze. He will ask you a question when the time comes. Let him state the problem, and wait for the question.

9) Make sure you understand the question

Do not try to answer until you are sure what the question is. If it is not clear, restate it in your own words or ask the board member to clarify it for you. However, do not haggle about minor elements.

10) Reply promptly but not hastily

A common entry on oral board rating sheets is "candidate responded readily," or "candidate hesitated in replies." Respond as promptly and quickly as you can, but do not jump to a hasty, ill-considered answer.

11) Do not be peremptory in your answers

A brief answer is proper – but do not fire your answer back. That is a losing game from your point of view. The board member can probably ask questions much faster than you can answer them.

12) Do not try to create the answer you think the board member wants

He is interested in what kind of mind you have and how it works – not in playing games. Furthermore, he can usually spot this practice and will actually grade you down on it.

13) Do not switch sides in your reply merely to agree with a board member

Frequently, a member will take a contrary position merely to draw you out and to see if you are willing and able to defend your point of view. Do not start a debate, yet do not surrender a good position. If a position is worth taking, it is worth defending.

14) Do not be afraid to admit an error in judgment if you are shown to be wrong

The board knows that you are forced to reply without any opportunity for careful consideration. Your answer may be demonstrably wrong. If so, admit it and get on with the interview.

15) Do not dwell at length on your present job

The opening question may relate to your present assignment. Answer the question but do not go into an extended discussion. You are being examined for a *new* job, not your present one. As a matter of fact, try to phrase ALL your answers in terms of the job for which you are being examined.

Basis of Rating

Probably you will forget most of these "do's" and "don'ts" when you walk into the oral interview room. Even remembering them all will not ensure you a passing grade. Perhaps you did not have the qualifications in the first place. But remembering them will help you to put your best foot forward, without treading on the toes of the board members.

Rumor and popular opinion to the contrary notwithstanding, an oral board wants you to make the best appearance possible. They know you are under pressure – but they also want to see how you respond to it as a guide to what your reaction would be under the pressures of the job you seek. They will be influenced by the degree of poise you display, the personal traits you show and the manner in which you respond.

ABOUT THIS BOOK

This book contains tests divided into Examination Sections. Go through each test, answering every question in the margin. We have also attached a sample answer sheet at the back of the book that can be removed and used. At the end of each test look at the answer key and check your answers. On the ones you got wrong, look at the right answer choice and learn. Do not fill in the answers first. Do not memorize the questions and answers, but understand the answer and principles involved. On your test, the questions will likely be different from the samples. Questions are changed and new ones added. If you understand these past questions you should have success with any changes that arise. Tests may consist of several types of questions. We have additional books on each subject should more study be advisable or necessary for you. Finally, the more you study, the better prepared you will be. This book is intended to be the last thing you study before you walk into the examination room. Prior study of relevant texts is also recommended. NLC publishes some of these in our Fundamental Series. Knowledge and good sense are important factors in passing your exam. Good luck also helps. So now study this Passbook, absorb the material contained within and take that knowledge into the examination. Then do your best to pass that exam.

EXAMINATION SECTION

EXAMINATION SECTION
TEST 1

DIRECTIONS: Each question or incomplete statement is followed by several suggested answers or completions. Select the one that BEST answers the question or completes the statement. *PRINT THE LETTER OF THE CORRECT ANSWER IN THE SPACE AT THE RIGHT.*

1. The heat energy required to evaporate 34.5 pounds of water per hour from and at 212°F is called

    A. the factor of evaporation
    B. mechanical horsepower
    C. boiler horsepower
    D. all of the above

2. The blowdown on a safety valve is the

    A. difference between the opening and closing pressures
    B. amount of steam blown down during its opening
    C. amount of condensation during its opening
    D. all of the above

3. Two safety valves are required on a boiler when the heating surface exceeds _____ square feet.

    A. 400   B. 500   C. 600   D. 700

4. An A.S.M.E. boiler has 750 sq.ft. of heating surface, the boiler Is built to operate at 150 pounds pressure, and the safety valve Is set to pop at 100 pounds. The first method of feeding water Is with a pump.
The SECOND method should be

    A. city water pressure
    B. a pump or injector
    C. an automatic feedwater device
    D. an air lift

5. A battery of ten boilers are operating with a maximum allowable working pressure of 100 pounds. Assuming all steam gauges are correct, one boiler shows 110 pounds with its safety valve blowing. The other boilers 80 pounds.
The problem is MOST likely that the

    A. spring in the safety valve is broken
    B. boiler is generating steam in excess of 100 pounds
    C. stop valve is closed or there is an obstruction in the dry pipe
    D. all of the above

6. Tensile strength is defined as the

    A. ability of a material to withstand pulling apart
    B. ultimate point before breaking under pressure
    C. point where the material breaks under tension
    D. all of the above

7. In a longitudinal drum type water tube boiler, the lower tubes in one drum show signs of overheating.
The trouble is MOST likely caused by

   A. scale deposits in the douncomers or circulating nipples, restricting the water
   B. low water level
   C. too much furnace heat
   D. flames licking

8. Internal corrosion or pitting in a boiler is caused by

   A. acid water
   B. organic matter in the feedwater
   C. corrosive scale
   D. all of the above

9. A heat exchange device consisting of tubes connected to headers and usually placed in the conversion area of boilers is a(n)

   A. air preheater   B. economizer
   C. superheater   D. all of the

10. A vibrating steam line attached to a boiler can cause

    A. fatigue leading to fracture or failure of the valve or connection to which the steam line is attached
    B. cracks In the boiler shell
    C. cracks in the furnace setting
    D. all of the above

11. Heat loss frequently occurs in steam boilers through

    A. air leakage
    B. excessive draft and gases leaving the boiler at high temperature
    C. uncovered or inefficiently covered shell and steam pipes
    D. all of the above

12. The basic principle of the draft gauge rests upon the

    A. venturi tube
    B. Bourdon gauge
    C. response of water in a U-tube to changes In draft pressure
    D. all of the above

13. A modification of the basic U-tube principle to permit easier readings of small changes in draft pressure led to the

    A. vacuum gauge   B. Inclined tube
    C. rectangular gauge   D. all of the avove

14. The Hays pointer gauge is termed a

    A. dry type
    B. diaphragm type
    C. non-liquid draft gauge
    D. all of the above

15. You are having combustion problems with one of your boilers that is not connected to the automatic analyzing section of your plant.
    Which of the following apparatus would you select in order to make a diagnosis?

    A. Tallow candles and a flue gas analyzer
    B. A sensitive differential draft gauge
    C. A high temperature thermometer or pyrometer
    D. All of the above

16. In the operation of a boiler plant, the elements that must be regulated are

    A. fuel supply in proportion to steam demand
    B. air supply
    C. ratio of air to fuel supply
    D. all of the above

17. A theoretically perfect CO_2 reading for fuel oil is 20.9%.
    The LOWEST acceptable percentage for good operation is

    A. 9-12 B. 13-14 C. 15-16 D. 17-18

18. If a furnace is panting or pulsating, the FIRST step to take is to raise the

    A. air supply
    B. fuel supply
    C. oil temperature
    D. all of the above

19. When the speed of burning, or flame propagation in a gas furnace EXCEEDS that of the gas issuing from the port, the flame

    A. grows larger and becomes bright orange
    B. becomes longer turns pale blue
    C. flashes back into the mixing tube
    D. all of the above

20. To prevent furnace accidents, the

    A. furnace must be purged properly before lighting
    B. furnace draft must be closed off
    C. burner must be lit from the fire walls
    D. all of the above

21. The weakness of natural draft is that it depends on many variables, such as the temperature of the atmosphere, height of the stack, direction in which the wind blows, etc.
    To improve draft by lessening these variables,

    A. make the stack higher
    B. install an air preheater
    C. install forced and/or induced draft
    D. all of the above

22. Which of the following can be classified as heat engines?

    A. Steam engines
    B. Steam and gas turbines
    C. Internal combustion engines
    D. All of the above

23. In many mechanical applications, it is necessary to convert straight line or reciprocating motion to rotating circular motion.
    The MOST efficient machine devised to perform this conversion is the

    A. piston
    B. slide valve
    C. connecting rod and crank
    D. all of the above

24. When a reciprocating engine Is in operation, TOP DEAD CENTER (TDC) and BOTTOM DEAD CENTER (BDC) are overcome with the use of the

    A. slide valve   B. piston
    C. fly wheel   D. all of the

25. An engine in which the speed is kept constant by a governor mounted on the crank shaft placed in one of the band wheels, is called a(n) _____ engine.

    A. compound   B. automatic   C. Corliss   D. gas

26. On a steam engine indicator card, the diagram length is 5.81 Inches, the spring scale is 50 pounds per square inch, and the average diagram height is .96 inches.
    The card mean Effective Pressure (MID) is _____ pounds per square inch,

    A. 12.9   B. 20,9   C. 48   D. 209

27. Turbines are erroneously classed as

    A. impulse and reaction
    B. high pressure and low pressure
    C. high speed and low speed
    D. all of the above

28. When the steam enters near the center of the turbine, and escapes toward the circumference, the flow is classed as

    A. parallel   B. radial
    C. axial   D. paradoxical

29. To insure safety in operation of a steam turbine, it must be assured that the

    A. main and emergency governors be tested to see that they are operating satisfactorily
    B. vacuum valve is in good working order
    C. atmospheric relief valve is in good working condition
    D. all of the above

30. In starting a turbine, it must be warmed-up SLOWLY by 30.____

    A. admitting steam by slightly opening the stop valve
    B. using electrical pre-heaters
    C. circulating hot oil through the system
    D. all of the above

31. If a turbine speed increases about 10% over its normal speed, a small centrifugal gover- 31.____
    nor releases a trigger arrangement which closes the throttle valve.
    This device is known as a(n)

    A. governor   B. speed control
    C. overspeed trip   D. speed sensitive device

32. The type of blading used for gas turbines is 32.____

    A. symmetrical   B. non-symmetrical
    C. expansion   D. all of the above

33. When taking over the watch in a diesel plant, you check the lube, fuel and cooling pres- 33.____
    sures, lube discharge, cooling discharge temperature, governor-oil level, crankcase oil
    level, shaft revolutions, examine the instrument readings on the control board, and look
    over the log sheet.
    An IMPORTANT item missed was the

    A. lube oil viscosity   B. pH of the water
    C. cylinder temperature   D. floor temperature

34. If a diesel engine is running away, you should 34.____

    A. cut off the air and fuel supply
    B. check the governor control mechanism
    C. not worry about it; the overspeed trip will take over
    D. all of the above

35. The following type of compressor used for gas turbines is the 35.____

    A. axial
    B. centrifugal
    C. combined axial-centrifugal
    D. all of the above

36. The MOST important caution areas around a jet engine are at the 36.____

    A. inlet and exhaust
    B. shaft coupling and fuel nozzle
    C. compressor and turbine
    D. all of the above

37. A pump is said to have a flooded suction when 37.____

    A. a pump is capable of lifting water
    B. a partial vacuum is created in the pump and suction pipe
    C. water flows into the pump by gravity
    D. all of the above

38. A boiler room has three reciprocating-type pumps. In the boiler feedwater pump,

    A. both cylinders are the same diameter
    B. the diameter of the steam cylinder is smaller than that of the water cylinder
    C. the diameter of the steam cylinder is larger than that of the water cylinder
    D. none of the above

39. An injector will NOT start if the steam pressure is *below* _____ lbs.

    A. 40   B. 50   C. 60   D. 80

40. The LOWEST temperature allowed for water entering a boiler is _____ degrees.

    A. 70   B. 90   C. 120   D. 200

41. In starting a boiler feed pump connected to a closed feedwater heater with no exhaust steam entering the heater, you open the drain and observe a flow of continuous water. This is an indication that

    A. everything is in order
    B. the steam trap is working
    C. there is a cracked or leaking tube or coil
    D. all of the above

42. A single pipe heating system is a system

    A. that has a pipe leaving and returning to the boiler
    B. where the condensed water returns through the pipe in which the steam rises
    C. used for hot water only
    D. all of the above

43. Moisture in the atmosphere affects water by

    A. *diminishing* its weight per cubic foot, thus making it more buoyant
    B. *increasing* its capacity for heat, making it more effective for either heating or cooling purposes
    C. *reducing* the amount of oxygen contained in a cubic foot, thus diminishing its value in respiration
    D. all of the above

44. The Copes feedwater regulator is a _____ type.

    A. thermostatic mechanical   B. thermostatic hydraulic
    C. float control   D. all of the above

45. The CORRECT installation of a reducing valve requires that

    A. there must be a by-pass around the valves
    B. a steam gauge be installed on the low pressure side
    C. a relief valve be installed on the low pressure side
    D. all of the above

46. A bucket type steam trap has ceased to operate.
It is POSSIBLE that there is a(n)

   A. hole in the bucket
   B. accumulation of mud or scale
   C. accumulation of heavy oil
   D. all of the above

47. Heat energy is ALWAYS

   A. potential   B. kinetic   C. atomic   D. mechanical

48. A Prony brake is a

   A. device for measuring power
   B. device for measuring negative acceleration
   C. tachometer for measuring revolutions per minute
   D. dynamometer

49. In ordering a thrust bearing to support a heavy load, the BEST type would be

   A. a babbit-lined sleeve bearing
   B. ball bearings in a specially designed outer race
   C. a roller bearing with modified cone-shaped rollers
   D. a roller bearing with cylindrical rollers

50. The volume of a given quantity of gas will be *increased* MOST If its

   A. temperature is increased and its pressure is decreased
   B. temperature is constant and its pressure is increased
   C. temperature is increased and its pressure is increased
   D. pressure and temperature are decreased

KEY (CORRECT ANSWERS)

1. C	11. D	21. C	31. C	41. C
2. A	12. C	22. D	32. D	42. B
3. B	13. B	23. C	33. C	43. D
4. B	14. D	24. C	34. A	44. A
5. C	15. D	25. B	35. D	45. D
6. D	16. D	26. C	36. A	46. D
7. A	17. B	27. A	37. C	47. B
8. D	18. A	28. B	38. C	48. A
9. C	19. C	29. D	39. A	49. C
10. A	20. A	30. A	40. B	50. A

TEST 2

DIRECTIONS: Each question or incomplete statement is followed by several suggested answers or completions. Select the one that BEST answers the question or completes the statement. *PRINT THE LETTER OF THE CORRECT ASSWER IN THE SPACE AT THE RIGHT.*

1. A bimetallic element is an essential component of NEARLY all   1.____

    A. optical pyrometers
    B. thermocouples
    C. thermostats
    D. thermels

2. Boiling occurs when   2.____

    A. any liquid attains a temperature of 212°F
    B. the critical temperature of a liquid is reached
    C. surface tension of a liquid is reduced to zero
    D. the vapor pressure of a liquid equals the atmospheric pressure above the liquid

3. Human comfort is MOST closely associated with   3.____

    A. temperature and relative humidity of the air
    B. carbon dioxide content of the air
    C. temperature and specific humidity of the air
    D. heat content and dew point of the air

4. An air conditioning cooling coil is actually the _____ of a refrigeration system.   4.____

    A. evaporator
    B. condenser
    C. expansion valve
    D. liquid received

5. In a typical commercial refrigeration system such as a cold storage warehouse or a walk-in freezer locker, the thermostat in the cooled spaces controls the action of the   5.____

    A. compressor motor starter switch
    B. high pressure cut-out switch
    C. solenoid valve in the liquid refrigerant line
    D. all of the above

6. A foot candle is a measure of   6.____

    A. intensity of illumination on a surface
    B. candle power of a light source
    C. power emitted by a source of light
    D. heat energy received from a standard candle

7. White ceiling and walls aid in Illumination of a room because of   7.____

    A. refraction
    B. absorption
    C. polarization
    D. diffused reflection

8. Which of the following is a measure of the time rate of flow of a quantity of electricity?   8.____

    A. Ampere   B. Coulomb   C. Oersted   D. Kilowatt

9. A wheatstone bridge is USUALLY used for determining

   A. currents
   B. potential differences
   C. resistance
   D. power

10. The volt is the unit used to measure

    A. potential difference
    B. quantity of electric charge
    C. resistance
    D. current

11. To measure the current being used by a light bulb, it is CORRECT to use a(n)

    A. watt-meter in series with it
    B. wheatstone bridge
    C. voltmeter in parallel with it
    D. ammeter in series with it

12. House lights are connected in parallel instead of series because

    A. the voltage must be the same across each lamp
    B. fewer amperes of current will flow through each lamp
    C. the current passing through one lamp will pass through each of the other lamps
    D. the resistance of each lamp is decreased

13. Direct current will NOT operate a(n)

    A. electric fan
    B. electromagnet
    C. transformer
    D. electric toaster

14. The impedance of an AC circuit containing resistance *only* is found by dividing

    A. amperes by volts
    B. volts by amperes
    C. coulombs by volts
    D. henries by volts

15. The CHIEF function of an electric generator in a closed circuit is to

    A. furnish electrons to the circuit
    B. furnish protons to the circuit
    C. maintain a potential difference
    D. give the electrons their negative charges

16. A direct current generator differs from an alternating current generator in that it has

    A. a commutator
    B. slip rings
    C. brushes
    D. an armature

17. Power companies charge the consumer according to the amount of electrical energy he has used in

    A. kilowatts
    B. volts
    C. ampere-hours
    D. kilowatt-hours

18. A rectifier is a device for changing

    A. electrical energy to mechanical energy
    B. high voltage to low voltage
    C. chemical energy to electrical energy
    D. alternating current to direct current

19. The commercial unit of electrical energy in the United States is

    A. volt-ampere   B. kilowatt
    C. watt-sec   D. kilowatt-hour

20. Electric power produced is USUALLY rated in

    A. kw-hr.   B. amp-sec   C. kva   D. kw

21. The direct current supplied to the field windings of an alternator is called the

    A. wye current   B. exciter current
    C. magnetic current   D. back emf

22. If an Industrial user is causing a low power factor on his lines, the power company will PROBABLY install

    A. ignitrons, to hold the voltage up
    B. indueers, to improve the phase angle
    C. capacitors, to improve phase angle
    D. a larger transformer, to handle the load more efficiently

23. The National Board of Boiler and Pressure Vessel Inspectors is comprised of

    A. the chief inspectors or other officials charged with the enforcement of boilers and pressure vessel with of their jurisdiction
    B. the manufacturers of boilers and pressure vessels
    C. a selected grorp of power engineers
    D. the commissioners from the state departments of labor

24. The PRIMCIPAL objective of the A.S.M.E. code is to

    A. provide minimum standards that will assure reasonable protection to life and property
    B. provide a margin, in construction, for deterioration
    C. assure a reasonably long and safe period of usefulness
    D. all of the above

25. The Uniform Boiler and Pressure Vessel Laws Society, Inc.

    A. recommends the A.S.M.E, Boiler and Pressure Vessel Code as the standard for construction
    B. tries to secure uniform rules and regulations among states, cities, and countries
    C. believes that all laws, rules, and regulations should follow nationally accepted codes and standards
    D. all of the above

26. An Act *to assure safe and healthful working conditions for working men and women, by authorising enfoTsenent of the standards developed under the Act, by assisting and enaouyaging the States in their efforts to assure safe and healthful working conditions* is known as

   A. The Occupational Safety and Health Act
   B. Public Law 91-596
   C. The Williams-Steiger Occupational Safety and Health Act
   D. all of the above

27. Freon is DANGEROUS because

   A. it displaces the oxygen in human body
   B. it decomposes into toxic products
   C. when exposed to a flame or hot surface about 1000°F it decomposes into products that are irritating and poisonous
   D. all of the above

28. Carbon tetrachlorlde CANNOT be used as a cleaning solvent because

   A. it evaporates rapidly and has a very toxic vapor
   B. the vapors rapidly overcome a worker
   C. it can harm the skin and vital body organs
   D. all of the above

29. What safety rule must every engineer and maintenance man know before working on machinery?

   A. Have a work order
   B. Lock the controls in off position with your own padlock
   C. Pull the switch
   D. Wear safety gloves

30. Assume that a fellow worker is in contact with an electrically changed wire.
    Of the following, the BAST reason for NOT grasping the victim's clothing with your bare hands in order to pull him off the wire is that

   A. his clothing may be damp with perspiration
   B. his clothing may be 100% wool
   C. you may be standing on a dry surface
   D. you may be wearing rubber-soled shoes

31. The use of the wrong lubricating oil in an air compressor can result in a breakdoun of the oil causing carbon deposit and a gas (CO).
    All that is needed for an explosion is

   A. a defective unloader   B. a dirty Intercooler
   C. ignition   D. frozen safety valve

32. Non-condeasables in a refrigeration system will

   A. *increase* water usage
   B. *lower* suction pressure
   C. *inarease* current draw of compressor
   D. all of the above

33. Bubbles in the liquid line sight glass of a refrigeration system could be caused by a(n)

    A. overcharge of oil
    B. leaking discharge valves in the compressor
    C. bad low pressure switch
    D. plugged drier

34. The causes of reduced condenser air quantity are
    I. dirty fan blades
    II. dirt on coil
    III. prevailing winds
    IV. lack of freon
    The CORRECT answer is:

    A. I, II
    B. II, III
    C. I, II, III
    D. II, III, IV

35. High suction pressure and low head pressure indicate the compressor is deficient in

    A. refrigerant gas
    B. pumping capacity
    C. oil charge
    D. size

36. Solenoid valves may hum due to

    A. low voltage
    B. a loose connection
    C. sticking plunger
    D. all of the above

37. The cost of operating an air conditioning plant is $320 a day for 100 days $435 a day for 265 days.
    what is the total annual cost for operating this plant?

    A. $300,000   B. $208,096   C. $147,275   D. $128,200

38. A power plant uses 70,000 gallons of No. 6 fuel oil per seven day week. How many gallons would be used in one day?

    A. 10,000   B. 7,000   C. 6,000   D. 3,500

39. Air contains 23 parts of oxygen and 77 parts of nitrogen approximately. what is the weight of the oxygen in 12 pounds of air?

    A. 12   B. 9.24   C. 2.76   D. 1.54

40. What is the area of a piston 7 inches in diameter?

    A. 70   B. 38.5   C. 32.2   D. 25.7

41. An engine has an Indicated horsepower of 31 and a brake horsepower of 27.466. what is its mechanical efficiency, usng the formula $M = \dfrac{Hn}{Hi}$

    A. 60%   B. 75.5%   C. 88.6%   D. 92.5%

42. A boiler requires 30,000 pounds of water per hour.
What size of feedpipe, in inches, is necessary if the rate is 360 feet per minute, using the formula $d = \sqrt{\dfrac{1830}{v}}$?

    A. 1 B. 2 C. 4 D. 6

43. A 200 H.P. package boiler operating on No, 5 oil uses 0.280 gallons per BHP per hour. If this boiler operates continuously at full capacity and 80% efficiency, how many gallons of fuel will this boiler use per a 24 hour day?

    A. 2,058 B. 1,562 C. 1,344 D. 1,228

44. A power plant has a total of 235 horsepower in electric motors.
How many kilowatt hours does this amount to if motors run 10 hours per day, using the formula 1 horsepower = 746 watt hours?

    A. 1,753 B. 17,531 C. 175,310 D. 1,753,100

45. A steam turbine turns at 3600 RPM and the diameter of Its largest rotor is 12 ft.
Find the linear velocity of a point on the tip of a rotor blade in ft/sec?

    A. 4200 B. 3600 C. 2260 D. 1200

46. In an alternating current circuit, the voltmeter and ammeter readings are 110 and 20, respectively.
What is the apparent power?

    A. 2,200 watts B. 4,400 watts
    C. 440 volts   D. 220 volts

47. If the angle oflog in the preceding question is 45°, what is the true power? (cos 45° = .707)

    A. 220 volts   B. 1000 watts
    C. 1555.4   D. 440 volts

48. An ice plant freezes ice in 300lb. blocks from water at 70°F. Each block is frozen in a galvanized steel *can* (specific head of steel = 0.115), whose weight is 120 lbs. The ice is at 10°F when the process is complete.
How many BTU's of cooling capacity are required to produce each 300 lb. block of ice?

    A. 580 B. 5,873 C. 58,730 D. 587,300

49. A cast Iron water pipe with an 8 Inch Inside diameter is to be subjected to an Internal pressure of 200 pounds per square inch.
What should the MINIMUM thickness of the pipe be, in inches, so that the stress does NOT exceed 3,500 pounds per square inch, using the formula $S = Pr/t$?
_____ inch.

    A. .228 B. .500 C. .728 D. .750

50. A plain butt weld joins two steel plates, which are each 1/2 inch thick and 8 inches wide. The allowable working stress is 13,000 pounds per square inch for a tensile loading of such a welded joint.
What is the ALLOWABLE tensile load, in pounds, that may be applied to the plates, using the formula P = SWbt?

A. 40,000 B. 52,000 C. 60,000 D. 65,000

50.____

KEY (CORRECT ANSWERS)

1. B	11. D	21. B	31. C	41. C
2. D	12. A	22. C	32. D	42. B
3. A	13. C	23. A	33. D	43. C
4. A	14. B	24. D	34. C	44. A
5. C	15. C	25. D	35. B	45. C
6. A	16. A	26. D	36. D	46. A
7. D	17. D	27. D	37. C	47. C
8. A	18. D	28. D	38. A	48. C
9. C	19. D	29. B	39. C	49. A
10. A	20. C	30. A	40. B	50. B

EXAMINATION SECTION

TEST 1

DIRECTIONS: Each question or incomplete statement is followed by several suggested answers or completions. Select the one that BEST answers the question or completes the statement. *PRINT THE LETTER OF THE CORRECT ANSWER IN THE SPACE AT THE RIGHT.*

1. The MAIN advantage of a rotary pump over a centrifugal pump is that it
    A. has more velocity
    B. has greater speed
    C. delivers more gallons per minute
    D. is self-priming and requires no valves

2. Pump efficiency can be termed
    I. hydraulic   II. volumetric   III. thermal   IV. mechanical

    The CORRECT answer is:
    A. I, II   B. I, III, IV   C. I, II, IV   D. I, II, III, IV

3. A superheater vent valve is installed on a boiler to
    A. insure a flow of steam through the superheater when steam is being raised on the boiler
    B. insure that some of the excess steam is released
    C. lower the steam temperature
    D. none of the above

4. Which of the following is a wearing ring on a centrifugal pump?
    A. Lantern   B. Turbine   C. Impeller   D. Thrust

5. Worn sealing rings can cause the
    A. capacity to increase
    B. discharge to flow back into the inlet
    C. priming to stop
    D. shaft to throw out of alignment

6. Vibration is caused by
    A. packing too tight   B. water hammer
    C. shaft alignment   D. worn bearings

7. A condensate pump helps to
    A. create vacuum in the system
    B. induce the steam to circulate rapidly
    C. return the condensate back to the boiler
    D. reduce the back pressure on the engine

8. Important pumps on a feedwater line are the
    I. rotary   II. vacuum   III. turbine   IV. centrifugal
    The CORRECT answer is:
    A. I, II   B. II, III, IV   C. I, II, III   D. I, II, III, IV

9. Which of the following is a reciprocating pump? 9._____
   A. Two stage
   B. Turbine
   C. Simplex
   D. All of the above

10. Which cylinder is larger on a duplex pump? 10._____
    A. Water
    B. Air
    C. Steam
    D. All are the same size

11. The FEWEST number of valves on a duplex pump is 11._____
    A. 4
    B. 8
    C. 12
    D. 16

12. A pump may fail to discharge when the 12._____
    A. pump is not properly primed
    B. inlet valve is stuck
    C. valve seats are in bad condition
    D. all of the above

13. A pump may pound and vibrate because of 13._____
    A. air in the liquid
    B. a leaky inlet line
    C. excessive speed
    D. all of the above

14. If a pump races while increasing its output, the cause may be 14._____
    A. a leaky plunger
    B. a broken or stuck water valve
    C. an air leak
    D. not enough steam to move the piston

15. If the piston strikes the head of the cylinder, the cause would MOST probably be 15._____
    A. improper adjustment of the cushion valve
    B. cylinder rings are worn
    C. too much lap on the valves
    D. none of the above

16. To adjust the cushion valve, you should 16._____
    A. run the pump at full speed
    B. cut down the steam supply
    C. run the pump with a full load
    D. run the pump without a water load

17. If the pump lacks a cushion valve, you should 17._____
    A. lower the steam pressure
    B. adjust the lost motion enough to permit the pump to make a full stroke without striking
    C. adjust the piston rings
    D. adjust the back pressure valve

18. What condition would cause a piston to stop on dead center?   18._____
    A. The slide valve is worn
    B. There is not enough steam pressure
    C. There is too high of a head
    D. The cylinder shoulders are worn

19. Positive suction head is a condition present when the   19._____
    A. pump is located below the liquid supply
    B. pump is located between the boiler and the feedwater tank
    C. pump is located above the liquid supply
    D. water pressure is greater than the suction pressure

20. A centrifugal pump will most likely fail if   20._____
    A. the suction side of the pump is defective
    B. the discharge valve is closed
    C. wearing rings are worn
    D. strainer is clogged

21. The pump may fail to discharge if there is   21._____
    A. not enough water pressure
    B. improper priming
    C. air trapped at the top of the casing causing the pump to lose its discharge
    D. too high of a head

22. The failure of a pump to discharge can be rectified by   22._____
    A. increasing the water pressure
    B. reducing the pipe size
    C. decreasing the water pressure
    D. repriming the pump

23. To prevent a pump from failing to discharge, you should   23._____
    A. install a lantern ring
    B. replace the impeller
    C. install a bigger motor
    D. remove some packing

24. Reduction in both capacity and head is caused by   24._____
    A. too much air leaking through the packing
    B. reverse rotation of the motor
    C. a closed suction valve
    D. a clogged strainer

25. Small by-pass lines are installed around a large gate valve in order to   25._____
    A. equalize the pressure on the globe valve
    B. balance the pressure on the gate valve when the valve is being opened
    C. increase the velocity of the steam
    D. eliminate the sudden change in temperature of the steam

KEY (CORRECT ANSWERS)

1. D	11. B
2. D	12. D
3. A	13. D
4. C	14. D
5. B	15. A
6. D	16. D
7. C	17. B
8. D	18. A
9. C	19. A
10. C	20. A

21. B
22. D
23. A
24. B
25. B

TEST 2

DIRECTIONS: Each question or incomplete statement is followed by several suggested answers or completions. Select the one that BEST answers the question or completes the statement. *PRINT THE LETTER OF THE CORRECT ANSWER IN THE SPACE AT THE RIGHT.*

1. The purpose of a volume casing on a centrifugal pump is to
    A. convert velocity into vacuum
    B. convert velocity into pressure
    C. prevent cavitation of the pump
    D. increase the velocity of the water

    1._____

2. How many type of feedwater heaters are currently in existence
    A. 1 B. 2 C. 4 D. 5

    2._____

3. Which of the following are types of feedwater heaters?
    A. Economizer B. Closed C. Deaerator D. All of the above

    3._____

4. When the temperature leaving the feedwater heater is too low, the MAIN problem is probably that
    A. steam pressure is too low
    B. back pressure is too low
    C. steam is of poor quality
    D. too much condensate is in the steam

    4._____

5. The advantage of a feedwater heater is:
    A. Hotter feedwater
    B. Less fuel consumption
    C. Less air in the feedwater
    D. All of the above

    5._____

6. To increase the back pressure, you should
    A. install a bigger back pressure valve
    B. put a heavier spring on the valve
    C. close the back pressure valve
    D. increase the line pressure

    6._____

7. Which of the following is NOT a use of a feedwater heater? To
    A. pre-heat the feedwater
    B. eliminate scale foaming substances by precipitation
    C. utilize some of the steam going to waste
    D. store generated steam

    7._____

8. In relation to the feedwater pump, the feedwater heater should be located in another part of the building
    A. in the basement of the plant
    B. about 10 or 12 feet above the pump

    8._____

19

9. An open feedwater heater is a heater
   A. open at one end
   B. with steam coils
   C. where water and steam are in actual contact
   D. with 2/3 steam space

10. The MAIN advantage of an open heater is that it
    A. can separate scale forming substances from the feed-water by precipitation
    B. produces hotter water
    C. can hold more steam
    D. is cheap to operate

11. How much steam supply is sufficient for an open heater?
    A. 3 to 5 lbs.   B. 5 to 7 lbs.   C. 8 to 10 lbs.   D. All of the above

12. _____ A(n)   should be installed on an open feedwater heater
    A. exhaust or vent pipe   B. oil separator
    C. steam gauge   D. all of the above

13. A closed feedwater heater is a heater in which
    A. steam travels through coils or tubes and water on the outside of the coils
    B. water runs through a tube with steam on the outside heating the water
    C. feedwater is heated and passed back to the deaerator
    D. none of the above

14. At what pressure should a feedwater heater operate?
    A. 1-15 lbs.   B. 15-20 lbs.   C. 20-25 lbs.   D. 25-30 lbs.

15. The safety device normally installed on a feedwater heater is a _____ valve.
    A. pneumatic   B. pressure relief
    C. safety   D. by-pass

16. The FIRST indication of a broken coil on a feedwater heater would be the
    A. heater filling up with water
    B. relief valve opening
    C. steam pressure increasing
    D. water pressure rising

17. On a double-acting reciprocating pump, what is installed on the discharge side of the pump? A(n)
    A. air chamber and gauge
    B. pressure gauge and relief valve.
    C. pressure gauge and safety valve
    D. air chamber and a gate valve

18. What types of lubricators are MOST commonly used today?
    I. Hydrokinetic   II. Force feed pump
    III. Splash system   IV. Gravity

    The CORRECT answer is:
    A. I, II   B. II, III, IV   C. I, III, IV   D. I, II, III, IV

19. What type of lubricant is used on piston rods and valve stems on a reciprocating pump?   19._____
    Mineral oil
    A. Compress oil
    B. Oil with high velocity
    C. Cylinder oil and graphite mixed together
    D. A reciprocating pump contains the following notation:

20. What is the diameter of the liquid cylinder? 7 x 6 x 4.   20._____
    A. 6"   B. 4"
    C. 7"   D. none of the above

21. What types of pumps are used in a heating system?   21._____
    I. Reciprocating   II. Condensate
    III. Centrifugal   IV. Vacuum

    The CORRECT answer is:
    A. I, II   B. I, III
    C. II, IV   D. III, IV

22. The purpose of a steam loop, or thermal pump, is to   22._____
    A. deliver steam to the engine
    B. protect water from entering the steam gauge
    C. return condensate back to the boiler
    D. trap steam from high pressure lines into a low-pressure line

23. What effect does a short stroke have on a reciprocating pump? It   23._____
    A. increases the pump capacity
    B. increases the steam capacity, and decreases the pump consumption
    C. increases the steam Consumption, and decreases the pump capacity
    D. relieves the pressure in the air chamber

24. A pump with two liquid cylinders, and one steam cylinder is called a ___ pump.   24._____
    A. triplex   B. duplex
    C. tandem   D. double tandem

25. The air chamber on a reciprocating pump is located on the   25._____
    A. discharge side of the feed pump
    B. discharge side of the reciprocating pump
    C. discharge side of all pumps
    D. suction side of a reciprocating pump

4 (#2)

KEY (CORRECT ANSWERS)

1. A
2. B
3. D
4. B
5. D

6. C
7. D
8. D
9. C
10. C

11. D
12. D
13. A
14. A
15. B

16. B
17. B
18. D
19. D
20. A

21. C
22. C
23. B
24. C
25. B

EXAMINATION SECTION
TEST 1

DIRECTIONS: Each question or incomplete statement is followed by several suggested answers or completions. Select the one that BEST answers the question or completes the statement. *PRINT THE LETTER OF THE CORRECT ANSWER IN THE SPACE AT THE RIGHT.*

1. Assume that an engine has a no-load speed of 1800 RPM and a full-load speed of 1650 RPM,
   The speed regulation of this engine is MOST NEARLY

   A. 12%.   B. 11%   C. 9.1%   D. 8.4%

2. The color of the third wire used for grounding portable electric power tools is generally

   A. black   B. white   C. red   D. green

3. A series circuit consists of a pure inductance and a pure resistance. When an AC voltage is impressed across such a circuit, the _____ the resistance by 90 degrees.

   A. current in the inductance lags the current in
   B. current in the inductance leads the current in
   C. voltage across the inductance lags the voltage across
   D. voltage across the inductance leads the voltage across

4. Of the following devices, the one which should be used for throttling of water going through it is the _____ valve.

   A. gate   B. globe   C. check   D. relief

5. If the line-to-line voltage of a wye-connected 3-phase system is 220 volts AC and the phase current is 10 amperes, then the total power delivered is MOST NEARLY _____ watts.

   A. 1270   B. 2200   C. 3800   D. 6600

6. The sensitivity of a meter movement is given as 50 microamperes. This is equivalent to a voltmeter rating of _____ ohms/volt.

   A. 50,000   B. 20,000   C. 50   D. 20

7. Doubling the number of turns of an inductor should _____ its original value.

   A. *reduce* the inductance to one-quarter of
   B. *reduce* the inductance to one-half of
   C. *increase* the inductance to twice
   D. *increase* the inductance to four times

8. Electrical fuses are rated in

   A. current and voltage   B. current and wattage
   C. ampere-hours   D. watt-hours

9. A 30-ohm resistor is placed in parallel with an inductor that has an inductive reactance of 40 ohms. If 120 volts AC is impressed across the parallel combination, the *total current* drawn from the 120-volt AC line is _____ amps.

   A. 1.7   B. 2.4   C. 3.0   D. 5.0

10. The symbol shown at the right, found in the schematic of a motor control circuit represents a

    A. silicon-controlled rectifier
    B. thyratron
    C. heat-sunk diode
    D. thermal overload

11. A device that can be used to check the condition of the electrolyte in a storage battery is the

    A. hygrometer   B. hydrometer
    C. hydrostat   D. aquastat

12. Of the following, the BEST device to use to check the condition of the insulation of a cable is the

    A. ohmmeter   B. wheatstone bridge
    C. voltmeter   D. megger

13. The decibel is a unit used in measuring the level of

    A. magnetization   B. acidity
    C. sound   D. contamination

14. A rectangular bus bar with a cross-section of 1.0 inch x .50 inch has a cross-sectional area MOST NEARLY equivalent to _____ circular mils.

    A. 250,000   B. 640,000
    C. 1,000,000   D. 1,280,000

15. The electrical conductivity of copper is lower than that of

    A. silver   B. gold   C. carbon   D. aluminum

16. A voltmeter has a ground connection and two terminals, one of which is used for 0-300 volts and the other for 0-750 volts. The scale is marked only for the 0-750 range. A scale reading of 200, when the 0-300 volt range is being used, corresponds to an actual voltage of _____ volts.

    A. 200   B. 160   C. 120   D. 80

17. When putting out a fire with a hand extinguisher, it is BEST to direct the discharge at the _____ the fire.

    A. base of   B. area behind
    C. area in front of   D. highest flames of

18. Someone suggests that the silver-plated main contacts of a circuit breaker be cleaned with fine sandpaper. This suggestion is

    A. *poor,* since the useful silver plating would be removed
    B. *good,* since you would be removing silver oxide which is a poor conductor
    C. *good,* since this will prevent overheating of the circuit breaker
    D. *poor,* since this will change the adjustment of the main contacts

19. If a multi-scale DC voltmeter reads downscale (goes below zero) when connected across two pins of an electrical connector, it is MOST likely that the

    A. meter is defective
    B. voltage across the pins is AC
    C. meter leads are reversed
    D. wrong scale is being used

20. Measurements of illumination in a work area are made with light meters which measure in units of

    A. foot-lamberts
    B. foot-candles
    C. lumens
    D. watts

21. Assume that new types of circuit breakers and controls are to be installed in the plant where you work. This equipment is to be operated and maintained by you. Of the following, the FIRST step you should take to become familiar with the new equipment is to

    A. read the instruction books for the equipment
    B. call in the manufacturer's field personnel for instructions
    C. read textbooks on the general theory of such equipment
    D. make trial disassemblies and reassemblies of the equipment

22. Of the following, the BEST way to lift a heavy object is to

    A. keep legs spread apart and straight, slowly bending at the waist to grasp the object
    B. place the feet about shoulder-width apart and slowly bend at the knees to reach down to the object
    C. keep legs straight and close together, slowly bending at the waist to grasp the object
    D. place feet close together, and with legs and back straight, bend at the waist to reach down and quickly lift the object

23. Sparks and open flames should be kept away from storage batteries that are being charged because of the high combustibility of the

    A. electrolytes in the batteries
    B. battery cases when hot
    C. gases being produced
    D. sulfuric acid fumes being generated

24. A 16-foot wood ladder is to be leaned against a wall. Of the following, the SAFEST distance at which the base of the ladder should be placed from the base of the wall is _____ feet.

    A. 4   B. 6   C. 8   D. 9

25. Of the following fittings, the one used to connect two lengths of conduit in a straight line is a(n)

    A. elbow   B. nipple   C. tee   D. coupling

26. If a nut is to be tightened to an exact specified value, the wrench that should be used is a(n) _____ wrench.

    A. torque   B. lock-jaw   C. alligator   D. spanner

27. Unloaders are generally found on

    A. centrifugal pumps
    B. air compressors
    C. flexible couplings
    D. surge suppressors

28. A compound gauge indicates

    A. pressures in lbs. and vacuums in inches of water
    B. both pressures and vacuums in lbs. per sq. inch
    C. pressures in lbs. per sq. inch and vacuums in inches of mercury
    D. pressures in lbs. and vacuums in inches of mercury per sq. inch

29. Of the following, the metal that is used for bearing linings is

    A. Muntz metal
    B. duraluminum
    C. naval brass
    D. babbitt

30. It has been discovered that the commutator of an electrical machine has developed a flat spot.
    To remove the flat spot, the

    A. entire commutator should be ground or turned down until the flat spot is removed
    B. brushes should be changed to a harder grade and the flat spot will eventually wear away
    C. entire commutator should be resurfaced with emery cloth attached to a wooden block which is then pressed against the turning commutator
    D. commutator bars that have the flat spot should be removed for repair or replacement, then reassembled back into the commutator

31. The FIRST operation performed on raw sewage as it comes into a sewage treatment plant is to

    A. add sufficient amounts of chlorine to kill any living organisms
    B. place it into settling tanks to allow sludge to settle to the bottom
    C. pass it through screens to remove or break up coarse material
    D. introduce selected bacteria to initiate biodegrada-tion

32. The MAIN function of diffusers in sewage treatment plants is to

    A. maintain a uniform distribution of non-solubles in the sewage
    B. release compressed air into the sewage
    C. pass the sewage through a fine filter
    D. disperse objectionable and toxic gases that are formed in the sewage

33. A comminutor at a sewage plant is used to

   A. shred sewage matter that is not removed by screens
   B. enable people in one building to talk to people in other buildings
   C. convert AC electric power to DC in the sewage plant
   D. reduce the level of noise in the sewage settling basin building

34. The pH of a substance is an indication of its

   A. resistance to corrosion
   B. magnetic properties
   C. transparency or translucency
   D. acidity or alkalinity

35. Assume that a vacuum gauge reads 15 inches of Hg. The equivalent in *absolute pressure* is MOST NEARLY _____ p.s.i.

   A. 2.0   B. 4.0   C. 7.5   D. 14.7

KEY (CORRECT ANSWERS)

1. C		16. D	
2. D		17. A	
3. D		18. A	
4. B		19. C	
5. C		20. B	
6. B		21. A	
7. D		22. B	
8. A		23. C	
9. D		24. A	
10. A		25. D	
11. B		26. A	
12. D		27. B	
13. C		28. C	
14. B		29. D	
15. A		30. A	

31. C
32. B
33. A
34. D
35. C

TEST 2

DIRECTIONS: Each question or incomplete statement is followed by several suggested answers or completions. Select the one that BEST answers the question or completes the statement. *PRINT THE LETTER OF THE CORRECT ANSWER IN THE SPACE AT THE RIGHT.*

1. An ADVANTAGE of a rotary pump over a centrifugal pump is that the rotary pump is

    A. self-priming and requires no valves
    B. better able to handle gritty water
    C. better suited for high pressures and high discharges
    D. quieter and has a pulseless discharge

2. A method used to eliminate water hammer in a water line is to

    A. increase the pressure in the line
    B. use slow-closing valves and faucets
    C. treat the water with a water softener
    D. increase the temperature of the water

3. A pipe nipple that is threaded over its entire length is called a _____ nipple.

    A. shoulder   B. long   C. close   D. short

4. A Stillson wrench is also called a _____ wrench.

    A. strap   B. pipe   C. monkey   D. crescent

5. In a piping diagram, the symbol shown at the right represents a

    A. pressure regulator   B. strainer
    C. check valve   D. drier

6. A shut-off valve is found to have the designation *WOG 300*. The letters WOG mean

    A. Water or Gas Valve
    B. Water, Oil or Gas Pressure
    C. Worthington Gate Valve
    D. Working Gauge Pressure

7. A plunger-type compressed-air-driven reciprocating water pump has a marking *3x4x7*. The number 7 refers to the

    A. diameter of the compressed air piston in inches
    B. diameter of the water piston in inches
    C. length of the stroke in inches
    D. compression ratio

8. Methane is a gas that

    A. has a smell like rotten eggs
    B. is heavier than air
    C. forms the major part of natural gas
    D. is non-combustible

9. As a cylinder in a diesel engine is going through its compression cycle, the air in the cylinder will _____ in pressure and _____ in temperature.

    A. decrease; decrease
    B. increase; increase
    C. decrease; increase
    D. increase; decrease

10. A specification for the installation of a storage tank indicates that a hydrostatic test should be made before placing the tank in service.
    A hydrostatic test consists of

    A. immersing the tank, with ports closed, in water and checking for water seeping in
    B. filling the tank with water under pressure and noting how well the pressure is held or whether water leaks out
    C. creating a vacuum in the interior of the tank and noting how well the vacuum is held or whether air leaks in
    D. filling the tank with compressed air and checking for leaks with soapy water

11. When the ignition characteristics of a fuel are represented by a cetane number, the fuel is one that is normally used in a

    A. gasoline engine
    B. gas turbine
    C. diesel engine
    D. steam boiler

12. Of the following, a characteristic of a wound-rotor AC induction motor is that it

    A. provides a wide range of speed control
    B. does not require slip-rings
    C. has a *squirrel cage* armature
    D. operates on single-phase power

13. Detergents are used in lubricating oils to

    A. reduce the S.A.E. number
    B. prevent oxidation of the oil
    C. keep insoluble matter in suspension
    D. combat corrosion

14. In a four-stroke diesel engine, each piston fires every _____ of the crankshaft.

    A. one-half revolution
    B. revolution
    C. two revolutions
    D. four revolutions

15. An electric motor with pressure grease fittings and relief plugs requires lubrication. A grease gun should be connected to each fitting and the grease gun should be pumped *until*

    A. grease oozes out along the shaft
    B. grease oozes out from the relief plug hole
    C. the handle becomes hard to move
    D. the handle starts to move freely

16. Of the following, the one which is NOT used for applying grease to a bearing is a(n)

    A. Alemite fitting
    B. grease cup
    C. Zerk fitting
    D. pressure plug

17. Of the following, the substance that should be used to melt ice on pavements and walkways is called

    A. calcium chloride
    B. trichloroethylene
    C. sodium hydroxide
    D. slaked lime

18. On a working drawing, the symbol (shading) given as shown at the right represents

    A. cast iron   B. concrete   C. glass   D. steel

19. A machine screw is indicated on a drawing as The head is the American Standard type called _____ head.

    A. flat   B. oval   C. fillister   D. round

20. The tool that is shown at the right is properly referred to as a(n) _____ tap.

    A. bottoming   B. acme   C. taper   D. plug

21. The tool indicated at the right is referred to as an arch punch.
    This tool should be used to

    A. cut holes in 1/16 inch steel
    B. cut large diameter holes in masonry
    C. run through a conduit prior to pulling a cable or wires
    D. make holes in rubber or leather gasket material

22. Before putting an aerosol container for garbage pickup, it is *good* practice to

    A. puncture it with a screwdriver
    B. use out the contents in normal manner
    C. put it out as is regardless of container contents
    D. remove the spray nozzle

23. A lantern ring is a type of

    A. optical illusion on a light source seen through a fine screen mesh
    B. sealing arrangement used to minimize air leakage between a rotating shaft and a sleeve
    C. piston ring which provides lubrication of the cylinder wall
    D. oil ring bearing lubrication

24. Monel metal is an alloy used for water heater tanks. It is a combination MAINLY of

    A. iron and lead
    B. chromium and zinc
    C. nickel and copper
    D. vanadium and tin

25. The plumbing fitting shown at the right is called a

   A. Street Elbow
   B. Return Bend
   C. Running Trap
   D. Reversing El

26. A galvanized steel plate is a plate with a coating of

   A. lead and tin alloy   B. tin
   C. zinc   D. brass

27. *If* the barrel of a standard micrometer is rotated through one complete revolution, the *gap* dimension is changed by _____ inch,

   A. .010   B. .025   C. .100   D. .250

28. Of the following, the indication that a fluorescent lamp is in need of replacement is that

   A. a very low level hum is produced by the ballast
   B. there is a slight delay before the lamp comes up to full brightness after the switch is turned on
   C. the lamp flashes on and off, and there are black coatings at the ends
   D. the lamp does not go off each time the switch is turned off

29. The one of the following that is recommended for prime-coating bare metals is

   A. varnish   B. zinc chromate
   C. shellac   D. linseed oil

30. *Dressing* a grinding wheel refers to

   A. replacing the wheel with a new one
   B. reducing the thickness of the wheel
   C. cleaning the grinding surface and making the wheel round
   D. repositioning the wheel on its shaft to eliminate *wobble*

31. A fusible metal plug is a protective device that

   A. melts when the electric current through it exceeds the rating
   B. melts when its temperature reaches a specific figure
   C. ruptures when the pressure behind it goes beyond a certain level
   D. ruptures when the *pull* on it exceeds a specified number of pounds

32. Of the following, the material that is beginning to be used for electrical conduits, plastic water pipes, and electrical insulation is

   A. trichloroethyline   B. polyvinylchloride
   C. carbontrichlorofluoride D. teflon

33. At certain conditions of speed, pressure, and temperature, centrifugal pumps can be made to cavitate.
    The conditions causing cavitation

    A. should be avoided since the impeller may become seriously pitted
    B. result in the highest pump efficiency
    C. produce *water hammer* and should be avoided
    D. also produce the quietest operation of the pump

34. A nut is turned on a 1/2" - 10 bolt.
    When the nut is turned through five complete turns on the bolt, the distance it moves longitudinally on the bolt is _____ inch.

    A. .100   B. .200   C. .375   D. .500

35. A growler is a device used for

    A. vibrating pipes carrying solid matter
    B. sounding an alarm when hazardous conditions develop
    C. detecting shorts in armatures
    D. chewing up solids in sewage

KEY (CORRECT ANSWERS)

1. A		16. D	
2. B		17. A	
3. C		18. D	
4. B		19. B	
5. C		20. A	
6. B		21. D	
7. C		22. B	
8. C		23. B	
9. B		24. C	
10. B		25. B	
11. C		26. C	
12. A		27. B	
13. C		28. C	
14. C		29. B	
15. B		30. C	

31. B
32. B
33. A
34. D
35. C

EXAMINATION SECTION
TEST 1

DIRECTIONS: Each question or incomplete statement is followed by several suggested answers or completions. Select the one that BEST answers the question or completes the statement. *PRINT THE LETTER OF THE CORRECT ANSWER IN THE SPACE AT THE RIGHT.*

1. Of the following diesel injection systems, the one which is SELDOM used, and then only for large engines using heavy viscous fuels, is the _____ system. 1.____

   A. common-rail
   B. individual-pump
   C. distributor
   D. air-injection

2. An engine indicator is an instrument that is used to determine the _____ engin 2.____

   A. operating speed of the
   B. temperature in an
   C. oil pressure in an
   D. performance of the

3. The MOST accurate method of determining whether there are cracks in the crankshafts of diesel engines is to use 3.____

   A. chalk and alcohol
   B. magnaflux
   C. electrolysis
   D. copper sulfate solution

4. The MAIN function of a mechanical clutch on a direct-drive propulsion diesel engine is to provide a means for 4.____

   A. disconnecting the engine from the propeller shaft
   B. reversing the direction of rotation of the propeller shaft
   C. reducing the operating speed
   D. obtaining a low propeller-shaft with a high engine speed

5. Of the following, the one which is NOT used to start a diesel engine in an emergency is compressed 5.____

   A. air
   B. nitrogen
   C. carbon dioxide
   D. oxygen

6. In comparing the exhaust temperatures of a two stroke-cycle diesel engine with that of a four-stroke-cycle diesel engine, the exhaust temperature of a two-stroke-cycle diesel engine is 6.____

   A. the same as that of the four-stroke-cycle engine
   B. lower than that of the four-stroke-cycle engine
   C. higher than that of the four-stroke-cycle engine
   D. either higher or lower than that of the four-stroke-cycle engine depending on the relative size of the engines

7. If the fluid level in a closed system cooling system expansion tank is low, it should be replenished with

   A. pure ethylene glycol
   B. sea water
   C. distilled water
   D. Zeolite

8. The differential needle valve injection nozzles of a diesel engine are opened by

   A. a spring force
   B. the cam mechanism
   C. the fuel oil pressure
   D. a solenoid mechanism

9. The MAIN reason for using filters in the fuel oil system of a diesel engine is to

   A. remove vanadium and sodium from the oil
   B. protect the injectors and the injection pumps
   C. protect the booster pumps
   D. remove water from the fuel oil

10. An oiler cleaning plugged diesel fuel injector orifices should use

    A. acetone
    B. music wire
    C. steam pressure
    D. hot water

11. In a common rail fuel injection system, timing is controlled by the

    A. injector cam only
    B. fuel pump only
    C. wedge only
    D. injector cam and the wedge

12. The MAIN bearings of a reciprocating engine are classified as _____ bearings.

    A. thrust
    B. angular
    C. radial
    D. guide

13. Proper vacuum will be maintained in the main condenser of a reciprocating steam engine propulsion plant when the condenser overboard discharge temperature is kept below the temperature corresponding to the vacuum by APPROXIMATELY _____ to _____ degrees F.

    A. 1; 3
    B. 5; 8
    C. 10; 12
    D. 12; 14

14. When propulsion reciprocating steam engines are fitted with forced lubrication and are not in operation or under repair, oil should be circulated through the lube oil system for at least 15 minutes

    A. daily
    B. every 2 days
    C. every 4 days
    D. weekly

15. On a multi-expansion counterflow reciprocating steam engine, by-passes to the receivers are used when

    A. warming-up the engine
    B. frequent stopping and reversing of the engine is expected
    C. taking a cylinder out of service
    D. securing the engine

16. A pyrometer is used for measuring

    A. pressure
    B. vacuum
    C. temperature
    D. viscosity

17. Clearance pocket valves on uniflow reciprocating steam engines are opened when

    A. the engine is running at maximum speed
    B. warming-up the engine
    C. boiler carryover has occurred
    D. there is a loss of vacuum

18. Of the following, the one that would cause a loss of vacuum in the main condenser of a multi-expansion counter-flow reciprocating steam engine installation is

    A. operating the main condenser circulating pump too fast
    B. excessively worn high pressure cylinder piston rod packing
    C. excessive use of cylinder lubrication
    D. operating the main condenser condensate pump too fast

19. The MAIN purpose of the oil groves in a reciprocating steam engine bearing is to

    A. promote destribution of lube oil in the bearing
    B. prevent pressure build-up in the bearing
    C. ensure proper flow of oil out of the bearing
    D. allow space for locating a thermometer well

20. Steam admission valves used in a propulsion uniflow reciprocating steam engine are of the _____ valve type.

    A. Corliss
    B. slide
    C. poppet
    D. piston

21. Cylinders of propulsion uniflow steam engines are lubricated from

    A. a gravity feed system
    B. the same system that lubricates the engine bearings
    C. a splash feed system
    D. mechanical lubricators

22. Steam admission valves installed on propulsion steam engines of the uniflow type are operated by

    A. one cam shaft
    B. two parallel cam shafts
    C. individual eccentric sheaves and rods
    D. individual eccentric sheaves and wristplates

23. Intercoolers and aftercoolers are fitted to most air compressor installations in order to

    A. cool the cylinder jacket water
    B. cool the air compressor lube oil
    C. condense the moisture from compressed air
    D. remove metal impurities from the compressor

24. The difference between an open and a closed feedwater heater is that

    A. the closed heater is vented and the open heater is uncovered
    B. the open heater is used with high temperatures and the closed heater is used with low temperatures
    C. steam and water are at different pressures in the open heater and are at the same pressure in closed heaters
    D. steam and water are directly mixed in the open heater and are not mixed in the closed heater

25. Of the following types of pumps, the one which does NOT have moving parts is the _____ pump.

    A. jet   B. propeller
    C. centrifugal   D. rotary

26. Of the following, the one which is NOT a common use for compressed air aboard ship is

    A. starting diesel engines
    B. operating automatic combustion control systems
    C. operating pneumatic tools
    D. supplying secondary air to the firebox

27. Marine centrifugal pumps have impellers which USUALLY rotate

    A. in the direction of the vane curvature (forward curved)
    B. in the direction opposite to the vane curvature (backward curved)
    C. in either direction
    D. at twice motor speed

28. Of the following methods, the one which is NOT used to allow for the expansion of condenser tubes is the use of

    A. ferrules   B. bowed tubes
    C. shell expansion joints   D. tube knuckles

29. Of the following fittings, the one which is NOT found on the steam side of a condenser is a

    A. drain well gage glass   B. sentinel valve
    C. zinc plate anode   D. vacuum gage

30. The operation of a condensate pump when the level of the water in the drain well is low will MOST probably result in

    A. too high a level in the heater
    B. excessive discharge pressure
    C. pump cavitation
    D. loss of condensate level

31. Pounding in the liquid end of a reciprocating steam pump would NOT be caused by

    A. tight packing in the liquid end
    B. improper adjustment of the steam cushioning valves
    C. a loose liquid piston
    D. loose water chest valves

32. The CORRECT procedure to lower the salinity of boiler water is to

    A. add boiler compound
    B. add chloride ions
    C. pass the boiler water through an ultraviolet purifier
    D. *blow down* the boiler

33. In an automatic packaged boiler, a condition which will NOT cause the fuel oil solenoid valve to close it

    A. low water level
    B. high oil pressure
    C. high steam pressure
    D. low voltage

34. Of the following, the one which is NOT a heat recovery unit is a(n)

    A. spark arrester
    B. exhaust boiler
    C. stack mounted hot water heater
    D. exhaust gas heated evaporator

35. Of the following materials, the one which is NOT used for water lubricated stern tube bearings is

    A. lignum vitae
    B. rubber
    C. babbitt
    D. laminated resin bonded composition

36. The pump used with an electro-hydraulic steering gear is a _____ pump.

    A. screw
    B. variable stroke
    C. gear
    D. lobe

37. The device that is used to change over hydraulic pumps on electro-hydraulic steering gears is a _____ valve.

    A. differential
    B. shuttle
    C. six-way
    D. check

38. The telemotor receiver signal of an electro-hydraulic steering gear is used

    A. to directly set the variable stroke pump
    B. to start or stop the pump motors
    C. to turn the six way valve
    D. as an imput signal to the differential follow-up control

39. Hot packing glands on a centrifugal pump are NOT caused by

    A. tight packing
    B. plugged lantern rings
    C. excessive water leakage
    D. a scored shaft

40. A *hunting* governor on an engine
    A. maintains a steady engine rpm
    B. maintains a lower rpm of the engine than required
    C. permits the engine to alternately race and slow down
    D. maintains a higher rpm of the engine than required

KEY (CORRECT ANSWERS)

1. D	11. D	21. D	31. A
2. D	12. A	22. B	32. D
3. B	13. B	23. C	33. B
4. A	14. A	24. D	34. A
5. D	15. A	25. A	35. C
6. B	16. C	26. D	36. B
7. C	17. D	27. B	37. B
8. C	18. C	28. D	38. D
9. B	19. A	29. C	39. C
10. B	20. C	30. C	40. C

TEST 2

DIRECTIONS: Each question or incomplete statement is followed by several suggested answers or completions. Select the one that BEST answers the question or completes the statement. *PRINT THE LETTER OF THE CORRECT ANSWER IN THE SPACE AT THE RIGHT.*

1. A centrifugal pump should be started with the suction

    A. and the discharge valves open
    B. and the discharge valves closed
    C. valve closed and the discharge valve open
    D. valve open and the discharge valve closed

    1.____

2. In a high pressure turbine installation, condenser vacuum is maintained by an air

    A. and condensate pump   B. injector
    C. ejector   D. eductor

    2.____

3. The MAIN reason why most reciprocating pumps are fitted with air chambers is to

    A. provide a steady discharge pressure
    B. prime the auction side of the pump
    C. seal the liquid end piston rod packing glands
    D. cushion the liquid piston

    3.____

4. Propeller thrust is GENERALLY absorbed by a(n) _____ bearing.

    A. Westinghouse type   B. antifriction
    C. Kingsbury type   D. Hele-Shaw type

    4.____

5. Gland sealing steam is provided on turbines exhausting to a condenser in order to prevent

    A. loss of vacuum   B. reduction of shaft speed
    C. overheating of seal   D. breakdown of carbon packing

    5.____

6. The MAXIMUM temperature at which a turbine bearing may satisfactorily operate is

    A. 120° F   B. 180° F   C. 220° F   D. 250° F

    6.____

7. The type of turbine governor which closes the throttle valve and stops the turbine when the turbine speed reaches 10% in excess of normal speed is called a(n) _____ governor.

    A. emergency   B. constant speed
    C. speed limiting   D. load limiting

    7.____

8. A turbo-generator lube oil cooler should be put into operation

    A. as soon as the turbine is started
    B. before the turbine is started
    C. when the sump oil temperature is at 140° F
    D. when the temperature of the hottest bearing reaches 100° F

    8.____

9. The suction and discharge valves of an air compressor should be cleaned with

   A. soap suds
   B. kerosene
   C. gasoline
   D. carbon tetrachloride

10. Lubrication for modern air compressors is supplied by

    A. a gravity feed
    B. grease cups
    C. a wick feed
    D. an oil pump attached to air compressor shaft

11. Sealed stern tube bearings are lubricated with

    A. water   B. lube oil   C. tallow   D. fish oil

12. Of the following hand operated valves, the one which is BEST suited for regulating or controlling fluid flow is the _____ valve.

    A. non-rising stem gate
    B. rising stem gate
    C. globe
    D. quick closing

13. It would be physically impossible to open the throttle valve when starting a turbo-generator set before the

    A. condensate pump is started
    B. circulating pump is started
    C. turbine casing and throttle drains are open
    D. hand lube oil pump is operated

14. Of the following types of Bourdon tube gages, the one which is commonly used for indicating the pressure drop between the inlet side and the outlet side of a lube oil strainer is the _____ type.

    A. simplex
    B. vacuum
    C. duplex
    D. compound

15. The function of a turbine feed pump governor is to hold the

    A. pump discharge pressure constant as the flow varies
    B. turbine speed constant as the load varies
    C. flow through the pump constant as the discharge pressure varies
    D. load constant as the turbine speed varies

16. Of the following, the BEST action to take if there is brush sparking on the commutator of an operating motor is to

    A. stop the motor
    B. change the motor speed
    C. reverse the direction of rotation
    D. report this condition to the marine engineer of the watch

17. The bearings installed in electric motors from 1 to 200 horsepower are, GENERALLY, _____ bearings.

    A. bronze bushing type
    B. ball or roller type

C. babbitt type
D. sleeve type

18. Turbine reduction gear surfaces receive lubricating oil

    A. from spray nozzles
    B. by splash lubrication
    C. by gears dipping in sump oil
    D. from oil rings

19. While under way, strainers used in forced feed lubrication systems should be cleaned EVERY _____ hours.

    A. 4   B. 12   C. 18   D. 24

20. A device used for deadening or silencing exhaust noises from a diesel engine is called a(n)

    A. air blower   B. exhaust manifold
    C. tail pipe   D. muffler

21. The API Service Classification *Service DM* pertains to a grease used for

    A. gasoline engines
    B. diesel engines
    C. direct current generators or motors
    D. reciprocating pumps

22. Of the following types of lubricating materials, the BEST type to use for modern machinery operating at high speeds and high temperatures is

    A. animal   B. vegetable
    C. water   D. mineral

23. Lubricating oil viscosities

    A. decrease with a temperature decrease
    B. decrease with a temperature increase
    C. increase with a temperature increase
    D. remain constant regardless of temperature changes

24. In order to clean a metal edge type filter, an oiler would

    A. operate the cleaner blades
    B. wash the filter in kerosene
    C. throw out the element
    D. change the basket

25. Detergents are used in lubricating oils to

    A. prevent rusting of ferrous surface
    B. prevent formation of sludge deposits
    C. prevent oxidation of oil
    D. control oil foaming

26. The designation SAE 30 of a lubricating oil refers to its

    A. ability to vaporize
    B. value as an anti-oxidant
    C. viscosity
    D. anti-corrosion additives

27. Of the following, the one which is NOT normally a cause of lube oil contamination in a diesel engine is

    A. fuel oil burning on the cylinder walls
    B. dust entering the air intake system
    C. leaky crankcase seals
    D. dilution by the fuel oil

28. Lube oil pressure regulator valves usually *dump* oil from the lube oil

    A. cooler inlet to lube oil cooler outlet
    B. pump discharge to filter
    C. header to sump
    D. cooler inlet to sump

29. Of the following, the one which is NOT a function of lubricating oils in diesel engines is to

    A. assist in sealing the piston-cylinder wall clearance
    B. act as a vibration absorber
    C. clean and carry away dirt or metal particles from bearing
    D. act as a cooling agent

30. Of the following fluids, the one that should be used to clean filtering bags of pressure type lube oil filters is

    A. gasoline
    B. carbon tetrachloride
    C. kerosene
    D. bunker c

31. The fluid used as a sealing agent in lube oil centrifuges is

    A. kerosene
    B. ethylene glycol
    C. magnesium sulfate brine
    D. water

32. A good surface film on the commutators and the slip rings of electrical generators is indicated when the surface film color appears

    A. gray
    B. brown
    C. jet black
    D. bright copper

33. Assume that you are an oiler on an engine room watch and you hear a continuous ringing of the general alarm bell for more than 10 seconds.
    Your FIRST action should be to

    A. see that water is supplied to the deck fire line
    B. leave the engine room
    C. go to the boat station
    D. assist in securing the propulsion unit

34. In disposing of a small amount of waste oil you should

    A. carefully pour it into the engine room bilge well
    B. put it into a 5 gallon container, seal, and drop it over the ship's side

C. pour it into the waste rag can
D. pour it into an oil slop tank

35. Assume that a fireman pulled a *live* burner.
The FIRST thing you as an oiler should do in this case is to

A. leave the fireroom
B. sound the alarm
C. shut off the oil supply
D. call the engineer

36. Assume that the CO_2 alarm sounded in a space where you are working.
You should

A. immediately leave the area
B. finish what you are doing and then leave the area
C. signal to the bridge that you heard the alarm
D. wait for a second alarm bell to ring before taking any action

37. Of the following, when extinguishing a burning liquid with a portable foam type extinguisher, the stream of foam should NOT be directed

A. against the back wall of the vat or tank just above the burning surface
B. into the burning liquid
C. on the floor just in front of the burning area
D. from far enough away to allow it to fall lightly upon the burning surface

Questions 38 - 40.

DIRECTIONS: Questions numbered from 38 to 40 inclusive refer to the sketch shown below of a main condenser circulating water system.

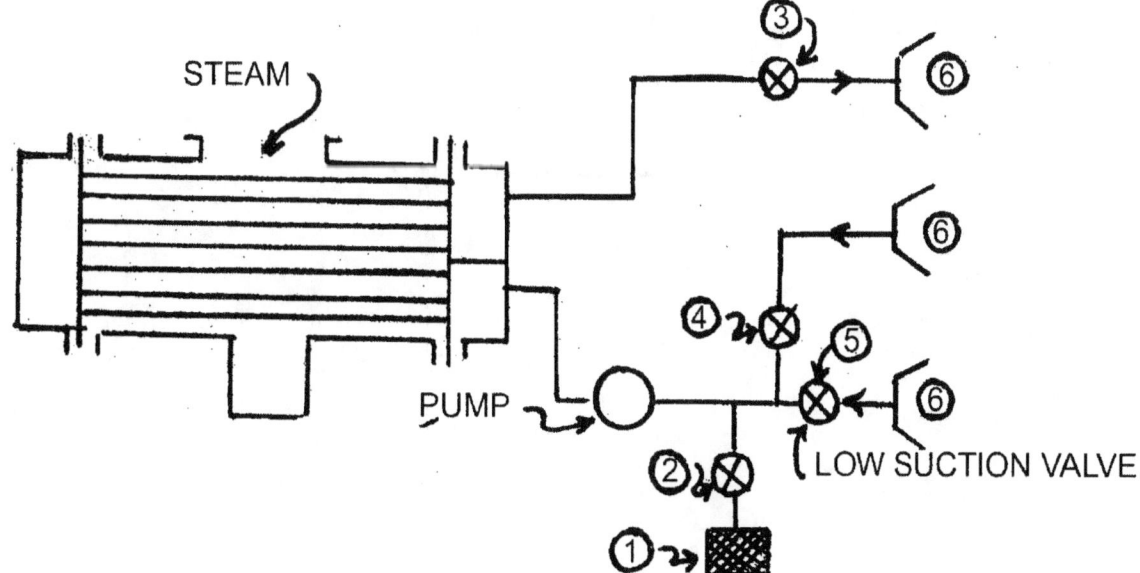

38. During normal operation of the systems shown above, valves

A. 3 and 5 should be open and valves 2 and 4 should be closed
B. 2 and 4 should be open and valves 3 and 5 should be closed
C. 2 and 3 should be open and valves 4 and 5 should be closed
D. 4 and 5 should be open and valves 2 and 3 should be closed

39. The valve which is usually installed at point 2 is a(n) _____ valve. 39.____

    A. automatic opening   B. glove check
    C. non-return   D. gate

40. The parts numbered 6 are 40.____

    A. sea chests   B. tanks
    C. manifolds   D. headers

KEY (CORRECT ANSWERS)

1. D	11. B	21. B	31. D
2. C	12. C	22. D	32. B
3. A	13. D	23. B	33. A
4. C	14. C	24. A	34. D
5. A	15. A	25. B	35. C
6. B	16. D	26. C	36. A
7. A	17. B	27. C	37. B
8. D	18. A	28. C	38. A
9. A	19. A	29. B	39. C
10. D	20. D	30. C	40. A

EXAMINATION SECTION
TEST 1

DIRECTIONS: Each question or incomplete statement is followed by several suggested answers or completions. Select the one that BEST answers the question or completes the statement. *PRINT THE LETTER OF THE CORRECT ANSWER IN THE SPACE AT THE RIGHT.*

1. The one of the following gases which will NOT be found in the flue gases produced by the complete combustion of fuel oil is

   A. oxygen
   B. hydrogen
   C. nitrogen
   D. carbon dioxide

   1.____

2. The amount of CO_2 in a flue gas sample is USUALLY stated in

   A. parts per million
   B. pounds
   C. percent
   D. pounds per mol

   2.____

3. A change in the efficiency of combustion in a boiler can USUALLY be determined by comparing the previously recorded readings with the current readings of the

   A. stack temperature and CO_2
   B. Ringelman chart and CO_2
   C. stack temperature and CO
   D. over-the-fire draft and CO

   3.____

4. The tube-metal temperature is appreciably higher in a superheater tube than in a boiler tube when they are both subjected to the same temperatures because the superheater tube

   A. outside gas film conductivity is higher than that of the boiler tube
   B. outside gas film conductivity is lower than that of the boiler tube
   C. inside vapor film conductivity is lower than the water film conductivity in the boiler tube
   D. inside vapor film conductivity is higher than the water film conductivity in the boiler tube

   4.____

5. In a balanced draft furnace, the

   A. draft changes from positive to negative in the furnace
   B. breeching contains a barometric damper
   C. draft reading is negative at the furnace inlet
   D. draft reading is positive at the furnace outlet

   5.____

6. The heating of a #6 fuel oil in an oil burner to a temperature higher than necessary solely for proper atomization is

   A. *desirable* because it can increase the burner capacity by increasing the specific volume of the oil
   B. *desirable* because it can increase the flame stability when vaporization occurs intermittently in the supply line to the burner

   6.____

45

C. *undesirable* because it can decrease the burner capacity by decreasing the specific volume of the oil
D. *undesirable* because it can decrease the burner capacity by increasing the specific volume of the oil

7. In a cylindrical boiler drum, the ratio of the force tending to burst a longitudinal seam to the force tending to burst a circumferential seam is MOST NEARLY

   A. 1:1   B. 2:1   C. 3:1   D. 4:1

8. The one of the following actions an operator should NOT take to stop or decrease carry-over caused by foaming in a boiler is to

   A. lower the water level in the drum
   B. blow down the boiler
   C. increase the rate of chemical feed to the boiler
   D. reduce the steam output

9. The PRIMARY reason for treating de-aerated feedwater with sodium sulphite is to

   A. remove dissolved oxygen   B. control scale
   C. prevent carry-over   D. increase alkalinity

10. In accordance with recommended practice, a sample of boiler water for pH analysis should be taken

    A. immediately after chemicals are added to the feedwater
    B. just before bottom blowdown
    C. when the steaming rate is high
    D. prior to putting the boiler on the line

11. Of the following oil burner types, the one in which the return oil passes through the atomizer body is the

    A. rotary cup
    B. steam atomizing
    C. mechanical pressure atomizing
    D. air atomizing

12. One advantage that the mechanical pressure atomizing oil burner has over the steam atomizing oil burner is that, with the mechanical pressure atomizing oil burner, the

    A. required oil temperature is lower
    B. required pump pressure is lower
    C. range of capacity available is wider
    D. fuel is more accurately and uniformly metered

13. Of the following, the LEAST likely cause of faulty atomization of fuel oil in a rotary cup burner is

    A. too low an oil temperature
    B. carbon formation on the rotary cup
    C. too low an oil pressure
    D. insufficient secondary air

14. The device which senses the presence of the burner flame in a rotary cup oil burner is

    A. mercury tube
    B. lead sulfide cell
    C. vaporstat
    D. selenium rectifier

15. The component present, in GREATEST amount by weight, in #6 fuel oil is

    A. carbon   B. hydrogen   C. nitrogen   D. oxygen

16. The explosion hazard in an oil-fired boiler is usually GREATEST when

    A. lighting off
    B. securing the boiler
    C. firing at 75% of rated load
    D. firing at 100% of rated load

17. Of the following, the one which is the MOST complete and correct statement of the function of an F and T steam trap is that it removes

    A. only condensate from a steam line
    B. both condensate and non-condensable gases from a steam line
    C. only non-condensable gases from a steam line
    D. both sediment and rust particles from a steam line

18. Fire actuated fusible plugs on boilers should be renewed AT LEAST once every _____ months.

    A. 12   B. 18   C. 24   D. 30

19. A safety valve on a boiler must reach its full lift when the pressure is no GREATER than _____ above its set pressure.

    A. 3%   B. 5%   C. 7%   D. 8%

20. A device used to calibrate a steam pressure gauge is the _____ tester.

    A. spring-scale
    B. dead-weight
    C. live-load
    D. in-line

21. The one of the following statements that is NOT correct concerning feedwater injectors is that they are

    A. inefficient pumping units
    B. practical only on large boilers
    C. highly efficient thermally
    D. unreliable when subjected to varying loads and pressures

22. A steam pressure gauge is located 10 feet below the point where the connection is made to the top of a boiler water column. If the absolute pressure in the steam drum is 125 psi, the pressure at the gauge will be MOST NEARLY _____ psig.

    A. 102   B. 116   C. 119   D. 148

23. When comparing the operation and maintenance of a Stirling boiler with that of an equivalent horizontal straight tube boiler, the one of the following statements that is MOST complete and accurate is:

A. It is much harder to get to the tubes of a Stirling boiler for maintenance work than to a straight tube boiler with box headers
B. A Stirling boiler will steam at a lower rate than a straight tube boiler
C. Leaks occur more frequently in a Stirling boiler than in a straight tube boiler
D. The water and steam circulation rates are greater in a Stirling boiler than in a straight tube boiler

24. A supplier quotes a list price of $68.00 less discounts of 25 and 20 percent for a replacement part.
    The actual cost of this item is MOST NEARLY

    A. $31   B. $34   C. $37   D. $41

25. The MAIN reason for maintaining an air dome in a pressurized house tank is to

    A. increase the tank pressure above the pump pressure
    B. avoid frequent start-and-stop pump operation
    C. force the water up to the top floor
    D. aerate the water

26. In a magnetic across-the-line starter for a 10 hp motor connected to a 4-wire, 3-phase circuit with grounded neutral, the MINIMUM required number of over-current devices is

    A. one, in the neutral conductor
    B. two, in any two conductors except the neutral
    C. three, in all conductors except the neutral
    D. four, in all four conductors

27. In order to select the correct heaters for the equipment described in Question 26 from the controller manufacturer's chart, the MOST important information needed is the

    A. power factor   B. line voltage
    C. full-load motor current D. motor horsepower

28. An electric motor, which is direct-connected to a centrifugal pump on an integral machined base, is to be replaced. In order to minimize the labor involved in replacing the motor, the specifications should include

    A. end bell size   B. serial number
    C. NEMA frame size   D. shaft size

29. A squirrel cage induction motor is rated at 5 hp when connected to a 220-volt, 3-phase, 60-cycle service.
    If this motor is connected to a 208-volt, 3-phase, 60-cycle circuit, the horsepower rating would

    A. remain constant
    B. be increased by approximately 5%
    C. be decreased by approximately 10%
    D. be decreased by approximately 30%

30. A 20 hp, 230-volt DC motor operates at 75% efficiency. The full-load current, in amperes, is MOST NEARLY

    A. 45   B. 65   C. 85   D. 115

31. In a cooling tower, the water is cooled MAINLY by

   A. condensation
   B. conduction
   C. convection
   D. evaporation

32. An economizer is used with a steam boiler in order to raise the temperature of the

   A. boiler feedwater by utilizing some of the heat in the exit flue gases
   B. boiler feedwater by utilizing exhaust steam from the turbines or steam engines
   C. air used for combustion of the fuel utilizing some of the heat in the exit flue gases
   D. air used for combustion of the fuel utilizing exhaust steam from the turbines or steam engines

33. A centrifugal boiler feed pump requires 5 hp to drive it at a certain speed, total head and quantity of water delivered.
   If the speed and the quantity of water delivered are doubled and the total head quadrupled, the horsepower required will be APPROXIMATELY

   A. 10   B. 20   C. 30   D. 40

34. In a centrifugal pump installation, the available net positive suction head is NOT affected by the

   A. suction piping size and length
   B. level of the liquid supply
   C. temperature of the liquid being pumped
   D. cavitation in the pump

35. In operating a closed water circulating system, it is good practice to

   A. treat the water chemically for corrosion control
   B. drain and flush the system regularly to control corrosion
   C. leave the system undisturbed because it is sealed and needs no maintenance
   D. replace the pump shaft seals every three months

36. The function of an unloader on an electric motor-driven air compressor is to

   A. release the pressure in the cylinders in order to reduce the starting load
   B. reduce the speed of the motor when the maximum pressure is reached
   C. prevent excess pressure in the receiver
   D. drain the condensate from the cylinder head

37. The MOST highly toxic of the following refrigerants is

   A. sulphur dioxide
   B. ammonia
   C. methyl chloride
   D. freon 12

38. The MOST important objective of a safety training program should be to motivate the worker to

   A. avoid tripping hazards
   B. use hand tools properly
   C. write a clear concise accident report
   D. be constantly alert to safety hazards

39. An automatically controlled circulating water pump in a domestic hot water system is started by a device when it senses a

    A. drop in the water pressure in the circulating line
    B. drop in the water temperature in the return line
    C. rise in the water pressure in the circulating line
    D. rise in the temperature in the return line

40. In performing a hydrostatic test on an existing power boiler, the required test pressure must be controlled so that it is NOT exceeded by more than

    A. 2% B. 4% C. 6% D. 8%

41. A preventive maintenance program in a boiler room should provide for routine periodic replacement of

    A. programmer electronic tubes
    B. badly leaking boiler tubes
    C. electric motors
    D. safety valve springs

42. The FIRST step to take in planning a preventive maintenance program is to

    A. replace all electric wiring
    B. make an equipment inventory
    C. replace all pump seals
    D. repair all equipment which is not in operation

43. The MOST important consideration in a fire prevention program is to

    A. train the staff to place flammables in fireproof containers
    B. know how to attack fires regardless of size
    C. see that halls, corridors, and exits are not blocked
    D. detect and eliminate every possible fire hazard

44. The type of portable fire extinguisher recommended as MOST effective for putting out oil fires is the _____ type.

    A. pump tank   B. cartridge actuated
    C. soda acid   D. foam

45. Inspecting and testing of mechanical equipment is done periodically MAINLY to

    A. help the men become more familiar with the equipment
    B. keep the men busy during slack periods
    C. encourage the men to take better care of the equipment
    D. discover minor equipment faults before they develop into major breakdowns

46. During the first stage of the high air pollution alert, plans must be made in public buildings to discontinue on-site incineration and to provide personnel and space to store the quantity of refuse that could accumulate during a period of _____ day(s).

    A. 1 B. 2 C. 5 D. 7

47. The four stages of the warning system designated by the high air pollution alert warning system are:　　47.____

　　A. initial, chronic, acute, penetrating
　　B. forecast, alert, warning, emergency
　　C. light, medium, heavy, extra heavy
　　D. early, moderate, severe, toxic

48. Unless a sulphur exemption certificate is obtained, the amount of sulphur in residual fuel oil burned for heating purposes is restricted to NOT MORE than　　48.____

　　A. 0.2%　　B. 0.3%　　C. 0.55%　　D. 0.7%

49. Refuse burning equipment in public buildings other than central municipal incinerators may NOT be operated except during the hours between　　49.____

　　A. 7 A.M. and 12 Noon　　　　B. 7 A.M. and 5 P.M.
　　C. 9 A.M. and 3 P.M.　　　　　D. 8 P.M. and 11 P.M.

50. The air contaminant detector required in a boiler installation must be adjusted to cause an audible and/or visible signal upon the emission of an air contaminant whose density, on the standard smoke chart, is GREATER than　　50.____

　　A. No. 1　　B. No. 2　　C. No. 3　　D. No. 4

KEY (CORRECT ANSWERS)

1. B	11. C	21. B	31. D	41. A
2. C	12. D	22. B	32. A	42. B
3. A	13. D	23. D	33. D	43. D
4. C	14. B	24. D	34. D	44. D
5. A	15. A	25. B	35. A	45. D
6. D	16. A	26. B	36. A	46. C
7. B	17. B	27. C	37. A	47. B
8. C	18. A	28. C	38. D	48. B
9. A	19. A	29. C	39. B	49. B
10. B	20. B	30. C	40. A	50. A

TEST 2

DIRECTIONS: Each question or incomplete statement is followed by several suggested answers or completions. Select the one that BEST answers the question or completes the statement. *PRINT THE LETTER OF THE CORRECT ANSWER IN THE SPACE AT THE RIGHT.*

1. The one of the following grades of fuel oil that contains the GREATEST heating value in BTU per gallon is 1.____

   A. #2 B. #4 C. #5 D. #6

2. When we say that a fuel oil has a high viscosity, we mean MAINLY that the fuel oil will 2.____

   A. evaporate easily
   B. burn without smoke
   C. flow slowly through pipes
   D. have a low specific gravity

3. The type of fuel oil pump GENERALLY used with a rotary cup oil burner system is the 3.____

   A. propeller pump   B. internal pump
   C. centrifugal pump   D. piston

4. No. 6 fuel oil flowing to a mechanical atomizing burner should be preheated to APPROXIMATELY 4.____

   A. 185° F B. 115° F C. 100° F D. 80° F

5. The flame of an industrial rotary cup oil burner should be adjusted so that the flame 5.____

   A. has a yellow color with blue spots
   B. strikes all sides of the combustion chamber
   C. has a light brown color
   D. does not strike the rear of the combustion chamber

6. The location of the oil burner *remote control switch* should GENERALLY be 6.____

   A. at the boiler room entrance
   B. on the boiler shell
   C. on the oil burner motor
   D. on a wall nearest the boiler

7. With forced draft, the approximate wind box pressure in a single-retort underfeed stoker is NORMALLY 7.____

   A. 2" B. 5" C. 7" D. 9"

8. The pressure over the fire in a coal-fired steam boiler with a balanced-draft system and natural draft is MOST NEARLY 8.____

   A. +.60" B. +.50" C. -.02" D. -.70"

9. Three tons of coal with an ash content of 10% will yield a weight of ash of MOST NEARLY _____ lbs. 9.____

   A. 400 B. 500 C. 600 D. 700

10. To clean and spread the coal over the grates of a coal-fired boiler, you would use a tool known as a(n)

    A. hoe   B. extractor   C. lance   D. slice bar

11. To burn the volatile matter in coal MORE efficiently, one should

    A. mix peat with the coal
    B. supply overfire draft
    C. mix it with a lower grade of coal
    D. add moisture to the coal

12. The one of the following that lists the size classifications of anthracite coal in proper order ranging from the smallest to the largest is:

    A. Chestnut, culm, pea, birdseye, egg
    B. Egg, stove, pea, broken, culm
    C. Stove, egg, birdseye, culm, broken
    D. Birdseye, pea, chestnut, stove, egg

13. The fire in a hand-fired furnace can be cleaned by a method known as

    A. ashpit to grate   B. bottom to top
    C. side to side   D. grate to crown

14. Coal is normally *tempered* when operating a chain-grate stoker for the purpose of

    A. increasing coking   B. preventing clinking
    C. collecting particles D. promoting uniform burning

15. The one of the following coals that can legally be burned in power plants is

    A. anthracite   B. sub-bituminous
    C. non-coking   D. bituminous

16. The one of the following that is known as *rice coal* is _____ coal.

    A. pea   B. buckwheat #2   C. egg   D. culm

17. A MAJOR cause of air pollution resulting from the burning of fuel oils is _____ dioxide.

    A. sulphur   B. silicon   C. nitrous   D. hydrogen

18. The CO_2 percentage in the flue gas of a power plant is indicated by a

    A. Doppler meter   B. Ranarex indicator
    C. microtector   D. hygrometer

19. The MOST likely cause of black smoke exhausting from the chimney of an oil-fired boiler is

    A. high secondary air flow   B. low stack emission
    C. low oil temperature   D. high chimney draft

20. The diameter of the steam piston in a steam-driven duplex vacuum pump whose dimensions are given as 3 by 2 by 4 is

    A. 2   B. 3   C. 4   D. 6

21. An induced draft fan is GENERALLY connected between the

   A. condenser and the first pass
   B. stack and the breeching
   C. feedwater heater and the boiler feed pump
   D. combustion chamber and fuel oil tanks

22. The PURPOSE of an air chamber on a reciprocating water pump is to

   A. maintain a uniform flow
   B. reduce the amount of steam expansion
   C. create a pulsating flow
   D. vary the amount of steam admission

23. *Flash point* is the temperature at which oil will

   A. change completely to vapor
   B. safely fire in a furnace
   C. flash into flame if a lighted match is passed just above the top of the oil
   D. burn intermittently when ignited

24. A *sounding box* would NORMALLY be found

   A. on top of the boiler
   B. next to a compressed air tank
   C. in a fuel oil tank
   D. in a steam condenser

25. An *intercooler* is GENERALLY found on a(n)

   A. steam pump
   B. air compressor
   C. steam engine
   D. rotary oil pump

26. The instrument used to measure atmospheric pressure is a

   A. capillary tube
   B. venturi
   C. barometer
   D. calorimeter

27. The control which starts or stops the operation of the oil burner at a pre-determined steam pressure is the

   A. pressuretrol
   B. air flow interlock
   C. transformer
   D. magnetic oil valve

28. In a closed feedwater heater, the water and the steam

   A. come into direct contact
   B. are kept apart from each other
   C. are under negative pressure
   D. mix and exhaust to the atmosphere

29. A *knocking* noise in steam lines is GENERALLY the result of

   A. superheated steam expansion
   B. high steam pressure

C. condensation in the line
D. rapid steam expansion

30. An electrical component known as a step-up transformer operates by

    A. raising voltage and decreasing amperage
    B. decreasing amperage and raising resistance
    C. raising amperage and decreasing resistance
    D. raising voltage and amperage at the same time

31. A monometer is an instrument that is used to measure

    A. heat radiation   B. air volume
    C. eondensate water level   D. air pressure

32. Three 75-gallon per hour mechanical pressure type oil burners operating together are to burn 150,000 gallons of No. 6 fuel oil.
    The number of hours they would take to burn this amount of oil is MOST NEARLY

    A. 665   B. 760   C. 870   D. 1210

33. The sum of 10 1/2, 8 3/4, 5 1/2, and 2 1/4 is

    A. 23   B. 25   C. 26   D. 27

34. A water tank measures 50 feet long, 16 feet wide, and 12 feet high. Assume that water weighs 60 pounds per cubic foot and that one gallon of water weighs 8 pounds.
    The number of gallons the tank can hold when it is half full is

    A. 21,500   B. 28,375   C. 33,410   D. 36,000

35. Assuming 70 gallons of oil cost $42.00, then 110 gallons of oil at the same rate will cost

    A. $66.00   B. $84.00   C. $96.00   D. $152.00

Questions 36-40.

DIRECTIONS: Questions 36 through 40, inclusive, are to be answered in accordance with the information contained in the following paragraph.

Fuel is conserved when a boiler is operating near its most efficient load. The efficiency of a boiler will change as the output varies. Large amounts of air must be used at low ratings and so the heat exchanger is inefficient. As the output increases, the efficiency decreases due to an increase in flue gas temperature. Every boiler has an output rate for which its efficiency is highest. For example, in a water-tube boiler, the highest efficiency might occur at 120 percent of rated capacity while in a vertical fire-tube boiler highest efficiency might be at 70% of rated capacity. The type of fuel burned and cleanliness affects the maximum efficiency of the boiler. When a power plant contains a battery of boilers, a sufficient number should be kept in operation so as to maintain the output of individual units near their points of maximum efficiency. One of the boilers in the battery can be used as a regulator to meet the change in demand for steam while the other boilers could still operate at their most efficient rating. Boiler performance is expressed as the number of pounds of steam generated per pound of fuel.

36. According to the above paragraph, the number of pounds of steam generated per pound of fuel is a measure of boiler   36.____

    A. size
    B. performance
    C. regulator input
    D. by-pass

37. According to the above paragraph, the HIGHEST efficiency of a vertical fire-tube boiler might occur at   37.____

    A. 70% of rate capacity
    B. 80% of water tube capacity
    C. 95% of water tube capacity
    D. 120% of rated capacity

38. According to the above paragraph, the MAXIMUM efficiency of a boiler is affected by   38.____

    A. atmospheric temperature
    B. atmospheric pressure
    C. cleanliness
    D. fire brick material

39. According to the above paragraph, a heat exchanger uses large amounts of air at low   39.____

    A. fuel rates
    B. ratings
    C. temperatures
    D. pressures

40. According to the above paragraph, one boiler in a battery of boilers should be used as a   40.____

    A. demand   B. stand by   C. regulator   D. safety

KEY (CORRECT ANSWERS)

1. D	11. B	21. B	31. D
2. C	12. D	22. A	32. A
3. B	13. C	23. C	33. D
4. A	14. D	24. C	34. D
5. D	15. A	25. B	35. A
6. A	16. B	26. C	36. B
7. A	17. A	27. A	37. A
8. C	18. B	28. B	38. C
9. C	19. C	29. C	39. B
10. A	20. B	30. A	40. C

TEST 3

DIRECTIONS: Each question or incomplete statement is followed by several suggested answers or completions. Select the one that BEST answers the question or completes the statement. *PRINT THE LETTER OF THE CORRECT ANSWER IN THE SPACE AT THE RIGHT.*

1. The bottom blowdown on a boiler is used to

    A. remove mud drum water impurities
    B. increase boiler priming
    C. reduce steam pressure in the header
    D. increase the boiler water level

2. The term *spalling* refers to a boiler

    A. flue gas content   B. soot blower
    C. combustion chamber   D. mud leg

3. The wrench that would NORMALLY be used on hexagonally-shaped screwed valves and fittings is the _____ wrench.

    A. adjustable pipe   B. tappet
    C. monkey   D. open-end

4. The designated size of a boiler tube is GENERALLY based upon its

    A. internal diameter   B. external diameter
    C. wall thickness   D. weight per foot of length

5. A fusible plug on a boiler is made PRIMARILY of

    A. selenium   B. tin   C. zinc   D. iron

6. The range of *Ph* values for boiler feed water is NORMALLY

    A. 1 to 2   B. 4 to 6   C. 9 to 10   D. 12 to 15

7. The *boiler horsepower* is defined as the evaporation of _____ lbs. of water from and at 212° F.

    A. 900   B. 400   C. 345   D. 34.5

8. A low pressure air-atomizing oil burner has an operating air pressure range of _____ lbs.

    A. 25 to 35   B. 16 to 20   C. 6 to 10   D. 1 to 2

9. A superheater is installed in a Stirling boiler MAINLY for the purpose of raising the temperature of the

    A. secondary air
    B. steam leaving the steam drum
    C. boiler feed water
    D. primary air

57

10. The function of a counterflow economizer in a power plant is to

   A. use flue gases to heat feed water
   B. raise flue gas temperatures
   C. recirculate exhaust steam
   D. pre-heat combustion air

11. A fire due to spontaneous combustion would MOST easily occur in a pile of

   A. asbestos sheathing   B. loose lumber
   C. oil drums   D. oily waste rags

12. A *damper regulator,* used for combustion control, is operated by

   A. steam pressure   B. the water column
   C. the boiler pump   D. a pitot tube

13. The packing of an expansion joint in a firebrick wall of a combustion chamber is GENERALLY made of

   A. silica   B. brick cement
   C. silicon carbide   D. asbestos

14. An open-ended steam pipe, called a steam lance, is USUALLY used on a boiler to

   A. remove soot   B. bleed the steam header
   C. clean the mud drum   D. clean chimneys

15. A high vacuum reading on the fuel oil gauge would indicate

   A. an empty oil tank   B. high oil temperature
   C. a clogged strainer   D. worn pump gears

16. The one of the following boilers that is classified as an internally-fired boiler is the _____ boiler.

   A. cross-drum straight tube
   B. vertical tubular
   C. Stirling
   D. cross-drum horizontal box-header

17. Try-cocks are used on a boiler PRIMARILY to

   A. check the gauge glass reading
   B. release steam pressure
   C. drain the water column
   D. blow down the gauge glass

18. Scale deposits on the tubes and shell of a high-pressure boiler are UNDESIRABLE because the deposits cause

   A. protrusions or roughness   B. suction
   C. foaming   D. concentrates

19. The function of a radiation pyrometer is to measure

   A. boiler water height   B. boiler pressure
   C. furnace temperature   D. boiler drum stresses

20. An engine indicator is GENERALLY used to measure

   A. steam temperature
   B. heat losses
   C. errors in gauge readings
   D. steam cylinder pressures

21. A goose-neck is installed in the line connecting a steam gauge to a boiler to

   A. maintain constant steam flow
   B. prevent steam knocking
   C. maintain steam pressure
   D. protect the gauge element

22. A boiler steam gauge should have a range of AT LEAST

   A. one-half the working steam pressure
   B. the working steam pressure
   C. 1 1/2 times the maximum allowable working pressure
   D. twice the maximum allowable working pressure

23. A disconnected steam pressure gauge is USUALLY calibrated with a(n)

   A. Orsat instrument
   B. air pump
   C. tuyeres
   D. dead-weight tester

24. The recommended size joint for repairing firebrick wall is MOST NEARLY

   A. 1/64"   B. 1/16"   C. 1/4"   D. 1/2"

25. The acidity of boiler water is USUALLY determined by a _____ test.

   A. Rockwell
   B. soap hardness
   C. paper
   D. alkalinity

26. Electrostatic precipitators are used in power plants to

   A. remove fly ash from flue gases
   B. measure smoke conditions
   C. collect boiler impurities
   D. disperse minerals in feed water

27. Fly ash from the flue gases in a power plant is collected by a

   A. soot blower
   B. gas separator
   C. stack regulator
   D. mechanical separator

28. The installation of four new split packing rings in a stuffing box requires that the joints of the packing rings be placed _____ apart.

   A. 180°   B. 90°   C. 60°   D. 30°

29. In power plants, boiler feed water is chemically treated in order to

   A. prevent scale formation
   B. increase water foaming
   C. increase oxygen formation
   D. increase the temperature of the water

30. The soot in a fire tube boiler GENERALLY settles on the

    A. bridgewall
    B. inside tube surface
    C. combustion chamber sides
    D. outside tube surface

31. The one of the following classifications of fuel oil strainers that is generally NOT used with the heavier industrial fuel oils is a _____ strainer.

    A. wire mesh   B. metallic disc
    C. filter cloth   D. perforated metal cylinder

32. The temperature of the fuel oil leaving a pre-heater is controlled by a(n)

    A. potentiometer   B. relay
    C. low water cut-off D. aquastat

33. A pneumatic tool is GENERALLY powered by

    A. natural gas   B. steam   C. a battery   D. air

34. The maximum steam pressure permitted in the steam coils used for heating the oil in a submerged oil storage tank is MOST NEARLY _____ psi.

    A. 40   B. 35   C. 25   D. 10

35. The water pressure used in a hydrostatic test on a boiler is GENERALLY _____ maximum working pressure.

    A. 4 times   B. 2 times the
    C. 1 1/2 times the   D. the same as

36. The one of the following valves that should be used in a steam line to throttle the flow is the _____ valve.

    A. plug   B. check   C. gate   D. globe

37. The CO (carbon monoxide) content in the flue gas from an efficiently fired boiler should be APPROXIMATELY

    A. 0% to 1%   B. 4% to 6%
    C. 8% to 10%   D. 12% to 13%

38. The CO_2 (carbon dioxide) percentage in the flue gas of an efficiently fired boiler should be APPROXIMATELY

    A. 1%   B. 12%   C. 18%   D. 25%

39. When the temperature of stack gases rises considerably above the normal operating stack temperature, it GENERALLY indicates

    A. a low boiler water level
    B. a heavy smoke condition in the stack
    C. that the boiler is operating efficiently
    D. that the boiler tubes are dirty

40. A boiler safety valve is USUALLY set above the maximum working pressure by an amount equal to _____ of the maximum working pressure.   40.____

    A. 6%   B. 10%   C. 12%   D. 14%

KEY (CORRECT ANSWERS)

1.	A	11.	D	21.	D	31.	C
2.	C	12.	A	22.	C	32.	D
3.	D	13.	D	23.	D	33.	D
4.	B	14.	A	24.	B	34.	D
5.	B	15.	C	25.	D	35.	C
6.	C	16.	B	26.	A	36.	D
7.	D	17.	A	27.	D	37.	A
8.	D	18.	A	28.	B	38.	B
9.	B	19.	C	29.	A	39.	D
10.	A	20.	D	30.	B	40.	A

EXAMINATION SECTION
TEST 1

DIRECTIONS: Each question or incomplete statement is followed by several suggested answers or completions. Select the one that BEST answers the question or completes the statement. *PRINT THE LETTER OF THE CORRECT ANSWER IN THE SPACE AT THE RIGHT.*

1. The MAIN function of a *steam separator* in a steam power plant is to 1.____

    A. reduce steam pressure
    B. remove excess oil vapors from the steam
    C. increase steam quality
    D. reduce back-pressure on the steam-driven equipment

2. The MAIN purpose of a *dip tube* in a low-pressure hot water system is to 2.____

    A. prevent air from entering the main
    B. determine the level of water in the boiler
    C. reduce air pollution
    D. eliminate condensation when starting up

3. The rating of a unit ventilator is USUALLY determined by a(n) 3.____

    A. anemometer   B. hydrometer
    C. psychrometer   D. ammeter

4. Of the following devices, the one that is used to record the air-flow-steam-flow relationship of a boiler in a steam plant is a 4.____

    A. Orsat analyzer   B. manometer
    C. steam-flow meter   D. heat meter

5. Of the following types of gas fuels, the one which has the HIGHEST BTU content per cubic foot is _____ gas. 5.____

    A. manufactured   B. coke oven
    C. liquid petroleum   D. natural

6. Of the following gasket materials, the one which is BEST to use when oil at 300° F is being carried in a pipe is 6.____

    A. fiber and paper   B. synthetic rubber
    C. asbestos composition   D. corrugated copper

7. A monolithic repair of a slightly damaged sectional magnesia insulation covering is BEST made by 7.____

    A. wiring in a *Dutchman* and filling the voids with magnesia cement
    B. covering the damaged area with asbestos laminations
    C. filling in the broken portion with glass-fiber insulating cement
    D. replacing the entire section

8. Of the following piping materials, the one that should NOT be used in a fuel-oil piping system is

   A. galvanized iron
   B. type K copper tubing
   C. brass pipe
   D. steel pipe

9. A valve is marked *300 WOG.*
   This valve could NOT be properly used in a pipe conveying _____ pounds gage maximum.

   A. oil at 300
   B. air at 100
   C. water at 150
   D. steam at 300

10. A steam gage connection for a large boiler is connected to the top of the water column and is then brought down to the operating level 24 feet below. The gage actually reads 605 psi.
    The ACTUAL gage pressure in the boiler is MOST NEARLY _____ psi.

    A. 590 B. 595 C. 610 D. 620

11. Of the following types of industrial oil burners, the one that is COMPLETELY adaptable to fully automatic operation or wide variations in firing rate is the _____ burner.

    A. mechanical-pressure type
    B. air-atomizing
    C. steam-atomizing
    D. horizontal rotary-cup

12. A full backward curve type centrifugal fan is being used in a coal-fired power plant for forced draft. Assume that after adjusting the speed of the fan, it is still too high, resulting in more pressure than is necessary to overcome the resistance of the fuel bed and boiler. To correct this situation, it would be BEST to replace the fan with one of a _____ diameter, running at _____ rpm and with a _____ wheel.

    A. *smaller;* greater; wider
    B. *larger;* less; wider
    C. *larger;* greater; smaller
    D. *smaller;* less; smaller

13. Short stroking in a steam-driven reciprocating pump results in both a(n) _____ in steam consumption and a(n) _____ in pumping capacity.

    A. *decrease;* decrease
    B. *increase;* increase
    C. *decrease;* increase
    D. *increase;* decrease

14. Caustic embrittlement is the weakening of boiler steel as the result of inner crystalline cracks.
    This condition is caused by BOTH long exposure to

    A. a combination of stress and highly acidic water
    B. stress in the presence of free oxygen and highly acidic water
    C. a combination of stress and water with a pH of 7
    D. a combination of stress and highly alkaline water

15. Of the following statements pertaining to feedwater injectors, the one which is MOST nearly correct is that the injectors

    A. are very efficient pumping units
    B. are practical only on small boilers
    C. are very reliable in operation on all types of boilers
    D. can handle 250 to 300 degree water

16. In reference to power plant pumps, the letters N.P.S.H. are an abbreviation for

    A. Non Positive Static Head
    B. Net Position Static Head
    C. Non Positive Standard Head
    D. Net Positive Suction Head

17. A pump's maintenance is based on a preventive maintenance schedule. This means that the schedule should GENERALLY be determined by the

    A. actual time lapse between maintenance checks
    B. actual number of pump-operating hours
    C. pump's actual operating performance
    D. operating performance of the equipment connected to the pump

18. Periodic inspection and testing of mechanical equipment by the staff at a plant is done MAINLY to

    A. help the men to better understand the operation of the equipment
    B. keep the men busy during slack times
    C. encourage the men to better understand each others' working capabilities
    D. discover minor equipment faults before they develop into major breakdowns

19. In planning a preventive maintenance program, the FIRST step to be taken is to

    A. repair all equipment that is not in service
    B. check all fuel oil burner tips
    C. make an inventory of all plant equipment
    D. check all electrical wiring to motors

20. An electric motor having class A insulation has been permitted to operate continuously at rated load even though the internal insulation temperature reads 10C above the allowable maximum internal temperature. Operating at this excessive temperature WOULD

    A. require frequent lubrication of the motor bearings
    B. reduce the life expectancy of the electric motor
    C. require an increase in voltage
    D. reduce the power factor to one-half of its normal value

21. The synchronous speed of a three-phase squirrel cage induction motor operating from a fixed frequency system can ONLY be changed by altering the

    A. rated locked-rotor torque
    B. rheostat position of the unloaded machine
    C. brush holder position
    D. number of poles in the stator

22. A thermal overload relay on an electric motor has been frequently tripping out. Of the following actions, the BEST one to take first to correct this problem would be to

    A. bypass the relay
    B. block the relay on a closed position
    C. clean the relay contacts
    D. arbitrarily readjust the relay setting

23. An air heater for a steam generator providing combustion air at temperatures ranging upward from 300F will often effect savings in fuel ranging from

    A. 1 to 3%   B. 5 to 10%   C. 12 to 15%   D. 17 to 20%

24. You have been asked to make an inspection of the superheater of a steam generator for external corrosion. You should be aware that if the direction of gas flow perpendicular to a tangent to the superheater tube is considered to be the 12 o'clock position, the GREATEST metal loss due to external corrosion usually occurs on the _____ o'clock and _____ o'clock sectors of the tube.

    A. 12; 6   B. 10; 2   C. 8; 3   D. 7; 5

25. In the steam generating plant to which you are assigned, the starting-up time and the shutting-down time for the boiler is determined by the time required to limit the thermal stresses in the drums and headers. The drums and headers have rolled tube joints. The temperature change in saturated temperature per hour for limit controlled heating and cooling rates for this boiler is established at _____ change.

    A. 50° F   B. 75° F   C. 100° F   D. 200° F

KEY (CORRECT ANSWERS)

1. C		11. D	
2. A		12. B	
3. A		13. D	
4. C		14. D	
5. C		15. B	
6. C		16. D	
7. A		17. B	
8. A		18. D	
9. D		19. C	
10. B		20. B	

21. D
22. C
23. B
24. B
25. C

TEST 2

DIRECTIONS: Each question or incomplete statement is followed by several suggested answers or completions. Select the one that BEST answers the question or completes the statement. *PRINT THE LETTER OF THE CORRECT ANSWER IN THE SPACE AT THE RIGHT.*

1. Assume that the optimum pH level of boiler feedwater for a boiler installation ranges between 8.0 and 9.5.
   The alkalizer used in the feedwater treatment to maintain this optimum pH level SHOULD introduce

   A. an average amount of iron and copper corrosion products into the steam cycle
   B. an increase of partial pressure of the carbon dioxide in the steam
   C. the least amount of iron and copper corrosion products into the boiler cycle
   D. a control of corrosion rates by forming a coating on the surfaces contacted by the steam

   1.____

2. The ppm of sodium sulfite that can be *safely* used for the chemical scavenging of oxygen in boiler feedwater is DEPENDENT upon the

   A. steam output of the boiler
   B. boiler operating pressure
   C. number of boiler steam drums
   D. construction of the boiler

   2.____

3. Of the following piping materials, the one which is NOT generally used for pneumatic temperature control systems is

   A. copper   B. plastic
   C. steel   D. galvanized iron

   3.____

4. In accordance with recommended maintenance practice, thermostats used in a pneumatic temperature control system SHOULD be checked

   A. weekly   B. bi-monthly
   C. monthly   D. once a year

   4.____

5. Of the following, the BEST method to use to determine the moisture level in a refrigeration system is to

   A. weigh the drier after it has been in the system for a period of time
   B. visually check the sight glass for particles of corrosion
   C. use a moisture indicator
   D. test a sample of lubricating oil with phosphorus pentoxide

   5.____

6. A full-flow drier is USUALLY recommended to be used in a hermetic refrigeration compressor system to keep the system dry and to

   A. prevent the products of decomposition from getting into the evaporator in the event of a motor burn-out
   B. condense cut liquid refrigerant during compressor off cycles and compressor start-up
   C. prevent the compressor unit from decreasing in capacity
   D. prevent the liquid from dumping into the compressor crankcase

   6.____

7. An economizer in a steam boiler is used to raise the temperature of the

    A. combustion air for firing fuel oil utilizing some of the heat in the exit flue gases
    B. combustion air for firing fuel oil utilizing some of the heat in the exhaust steam from the turbines of steam engines
    C. boiler feedwater by utilizing some of the heat in the exit flue gases
    D. boiler feedwater by utilizing some of the heat in the exhaust steam from the turbines or steam engines

8. A mixed-base grease is a grease that is prepared by mixing lubricating oil with

    A. one metallic soap   B. two metallic soaps
    C. a synthetic lubricant   D. heavy gear oil

9. Of the following lubricants, the one which is classified as a circulating oil is _____ oil.

    A. turbine   B. gear
    C. machine   D. steam-cylinder

10. You are supervising the installation of a steam-driven reciprocating pump. The pump's air chamber is missing and you have to replace it with one with several salvaged ones. The salvaged air chamber selected should have a volume equal to MOST NEARLY _____ the piston displacement of the pump.

    A. half of   B. 1 1/2 times
    C. 2 times   D. 2 1/2 times

11. Economical partial-load operation of steam turbines is obtained by minimizing throttling losses.
    This is accomplished by

    A. reducing the boiler pressure and temperature
    B. throttling the steam flow into the uncontrolled set of nozzles
    C. dividing the first-stage nozzles into several groups and providing a steam control valve for each group
    D. controlling the fuel flow to the steam generator

12. You are ordering two pump wearing rings for a centrifugal pump.
    These rings are GENERALLY identified as

    A. two wearing rings
    B. one drive wearing ring and one casing wearing ring
    C. one casing wearing ring and one impeller wearing ring
    D. one first-stage wearing ring and one drive wearing ring

13. A thermo-hydraulic feedwater regulator is used to regulate the flow of water to a drum-type boiler. The amount of water input to the boiler is controlled *in proportion to* the

    A. boiler load
    B. setting of the feed pump relief valve
    C. amount of water in the outer tube that flashes into steam
    D. water level in the drum

14. The standard capacity rating conditions for any refrigeration compressor is _____ psig for the suction and _____ psig for the discharge.

    A. 5° F, 19.6; 86° F, 154.5
    B. 5° F, 9.6; 96° F, 154.5
    C. 10° F, 9.6; 96° F, 144.5
    D. 10° F, 19.6; 96° F, 134.5

14.____

15. Of the following, the MAIN purpose of a subcooler in a refrigerant piping system for a two-stage system is to

    A. reduce the total power requirements and total heat rejection to the second stage
    B. reduce total power requirements and return oil to the compressor
    C. improve the flow of evaporator gas per ton and increase the temperature
    D. increase the heat rejection per ton and avoid system shutdown

15.____

16. In large refrigeration systems, the USUAL location for charging the refrigeration system is into the

    A. suction line
    B. liquid line between the receiver shut-off valve and the expansion valve
    C. line between the condenser and the compressor
    D. line between the high pressure cut-off switch and the expansion valve

16.____

17. The effect of a voltage variation to 90 percent of normal voltage, for a compound wound DC motor, on the FULL load current is

    A. an increase in the full load current of approximately 10%
    B. a decrease in the full load current of approximately 10%
    C. zero
    D. a decrease in the full load current 20%

17.____

18. The purpose of a current-limiting reactor is to place an upper limit on the available short-circuit current that can occur under fault conditions.
    The reactor accomplishes this by contributing _____ to the circuit.

    A. additional capacitance
    B. reduced inductive reactance
    C. reduced capacitance
    D. additional inductive reactance

18.____

19. Alternating current electric motors are usually guaranteed to operate satisfactorily and to deliver their full horsepower PROVIDED the electrical power delivered to the motor is at the rated

    A. voltage and at plus or minus 5 percent frequency variation
    B. frequency and at a voltage 15 percent above or below rating
    C. voltage and at plus or minus 10 percent frequency variation
    D. frequency and at a voltage 20 percent above or below rating

19.____

20. A three-phase AC motor is connected to a 230 volt, three-phase, alternating current line. With this motor running at full load, the line current is found to be 20 amperes, with a power factor of 0.75.
    Under these conditions, the power, in kilowatts, supplied to this motor will be MOST NEARLY

    A. 3.5   B. 6.0   C. 10.5   D. 18.0

20.____

21. In accordance with the air pollution control code, no person shall cause or permit the emission of air contaminants from a boiler with a capacity of 500 million BTU per hour or more, if the air contaminant emitted has a sulfur dioxide content of MORE than _____ parts per million by volume of undiluted emissions measured at _____ percent excess air.

    A. 300; 15   B. 200; 10   C. 200; 15   D. 300; 10

22. Of the following statements concerning the requirements of the air pollution control code, the one which is the MOST complete and correct is that the owner of equipment

    A. and apparatus shall maintain such equipment and apparatus in good operating order by regular inspection and cleaning and by promptly making repairs
    B. shall maintain the equipment in good operating condition by making inspections and repairs on a regular basis
    C. and apparatus shall maintain the equipment and apparatus in operating condition by regular inspection and cleaning
    D. shall maintain such equipment in good working order by regular inspection and cleaning and by making repairs on a scheduled basis

23. Assume that one of your assistants was near the Freon 11 refrigeration system when a liquid Freon line ruptured. Some of the liquid Freon 11 has gotten into your assistant's right eye.
    Of the following actions, the one which you should NOT take is to

    A. immediately call for an eye specialist (medical doctor)
    B. gently and quickly rub the Freon 11 out of the eye
    C. use a boric-acid solution to clean out the Freon 11 from his eye
    D. wash the eye by gently blowing the Freon 11 out of his eye with air

24. Assume that a fire breaks out in an electrical control panel board.
    Of the following types of portable fire extinguishers, the BEST one to use to put out this fire would be a _____ type.

    A. dry-chemical   B. soda-acid
    C. foam   D. water-stream

25. Assume that you are checking the water level in a boiler which is on the line in a power plant. Upon opening the gage cocks, you determine that the water level was above the top gage cock.
    Of the following actions, the BEST one to take FIRST in this situation would be to

    A. shut off the fuel and air supply
    B. surface-blow the boiler
    C. close the steam-outlet valve from the boiler
    D. increase the speed of the feedwater pump

KEY (CORRECT ANSWERS)

1. C
2. B
3. C
4. D
5. C

6. A
7. C
8. B
9. A
10. D

11. C
12. C
13. D
14. A
15. A

16. B
17. A
18. D
19. A
20. B

21. B
22. A
23. B
24. A
25. C

EXAMINATION SECTION
TEST 1

DIRECTIONS: Each question or incomplete statement is followed by several suggested answers or completions. Select the one that BEST answers the question or completes the statement. *PRINT THE LETTER OF THE CORRECT ANSWER IN THE SPACE AT THE RIGHT.*

1. Fly ash from the flue gases in a power plant is collected by a
   A. soot blower
   B. gas separator
   C. stack regulator
   D. mechanical separator

2. The installation of four new split packing rings in a stuffing box requires that the joints of the packing rings be placed _____ ° apart.
   A. 180   B. 90   C. 60   D. 30

3. In power plants, boiler feed water is chemically treated in order to
   A. prevent scale formation
   B. increase water foaming
   C. increase oxygen formation
   D. increase water temperature

4. The soot in a fire tube boiler GENERALLY settles on the
   A. bridgewall
   B. inside tube surface
   C. combustion chamber sides
   D. outside tube surfaces

5. The one of the following classifications of fuel oil strainers that is generally NOT used with the heavier industrial fuel oils is a _____ strainer.
   A. wire mesh
   B. metallic disc
   C. filter cloth
   D. perforated metal cylinder

6. The temperature of the fuel oil leaving a pre-heater is controlled by a(n)
   A. potentiometer
   B. relay
   C. low water cut-off
   D. aquastat

7. A pneumatic tool is GENERALLY powered by
   A. natural gas
   B. steam
   C. a battery
   D. air

8. The maximum steam pressure permitted in the steam coils used for heating the oil in a submerged oil storage tank is MOST NEARLY _____ psi.
   A. 40   B. 35   C. 25   D. 10

73

2 (#1)

9. The water pressure used in a hydrostatic test on a boiler is GENERALLY _____ the maximum working pressure.

   A. 4 times
   B. 2 times
   C. 1 1/2 times
   D. the same as

10. The one of the following valves that should be used in a steam line to throttle the flow is the _____ valve.

    A. plug
    B. check
    C. gate
    D. globe

11. The CO (carbon monoxide) content in the flue gas from an efficiently fired boiler should be APPROXIMATELY

    A. 0-1%
    B. 4-6%
    C. 8-10%
    D. 12-13%

12. The CO_2 (carbon dioxide) percentage in the flue gas of an efficiently fired boiler should be APPROXIMATELY

    A. 1%
    B. 12%
    C. 18%
    D. 25%

13. When the temperature of stack gases rises considerably above the normal operating stack temperature, it GENERALLY indicates

    A. a low boiler water level
    B. a heavy smoke condition in the stack
    C. that the boiler is operating efficiently
    D. that the boiler tubes are dirty

14. A boiler safety valve is usually set ABOVE the maximum working pressure by an amount equal to _____% of the maximum working pressure.

    A. 3
    B. 10
    C. 12
    D. 14

15. The one of the following grades of fuel oil that contains the GREATEST heating value in BTU per gallon is #

    A. 2
    B. 4
    C. 5
    D. 6

16. When we say that a fuel oil has a *high viscosity*, we mean MAI1ILY that the fuel oil will

    A. evaporate easily
    B. burn without smoke
    C. flow slowly through pipes
    D. have a low specific gravity

17. The type of fuel oil pump GENERALLY used with a rotary cup oil burner system is the _____ pump.

    A. propeller
    B. integral
    C. centrifugal
    D. piston

18. No. 6 fuel oil flowing to a mechanical atomizing burner should be preheated to APPROXIMATELY _____ °F.

    A. 185
    B. 115
    C. 100
    D. 80

19. The flame of an industrial rotary cup oil burner should be adjusted so that the flame 19.____

    A. has a yellow color with blue spots
    B. strikes all sides of the combustion chamber
    C. has a light brown color
    D. does not strike the rear of the combustion chamber

20. The location of the oil burner *remote control switch* should generally be 20.____

    A. at the boiler room entrance
    B. on the boiler shell
    C. on the oil burner motor
    D. on the wall nearest the boiler

21. With forced draft, the APPROXIMATE wind box pressure in a single-retort underfeed stoker is normally _____ inches. 21.____

    A. 2   B. 5   C. 7   D. 9

22. The pressure over the fire in a coal-fired steam boiler with a balanced-draft system and natural draft is MOST NEARLY _____ inches. 22.____

    A. +.60   B. +.50   C. -.02   D. -.70

23. Three tons of coal with an ash content of 10% will yield a weight of ash of MOST NEARLY _____ lbs. 23.____

    A. 400   B. 500   C. 600   D. 700

24. To clean and spread the coal over the grates of a coal-fired boiler, a stationary fireman would use a tool known as a(n) 24.____

    A. hoe   B. extractor
    C. lance   D. slice bar

25. To burn the volatile matter in coal more efficiently, one should 25.____

    A. mix peat with the coal
    B. supply overfire draft
    C. mix it with a lower grade of coal
    D. add moisture to the coal

KEY (CORRECT ANSWERS)

1. D
2. B
3. A
4. B
5. C

6. D
7. D
8. D
9. C
10. D

11. A
12. B
13. D
14. A
15. D

16. C
17. C
18. A
19. D
20. A

21. A
22. C
23. C
24. A
25. B

TEST 2

DIRECTIONS: Each question or incomplete statement is followed by several suggested answers or completions. Select the one that BEST answers the question or completes the statement. *PRINT THE LETTER OF THE CORRECT ANSWER IN THE SPACE AT THE RIGHT.*

1. The term *spalling* refers to a boiler's

    A. flue gas content
    B. soot blower
    C. combustion chamber
    D. mud leg

    1.____

2. The wrench that would normally be used on hexagonally-shaped screwed valves and fittings is the _____ wrench.

    A. adjustable pipe
    B. tappet
    C. monkey
    D. open-end

    2.____

3. The designated size of a boiler tube is GENERALLY based upon its

    A. internal diameter
    B. external diameter
    C. wall thickness
    D. weight per foot of length

    3.____

4. A fusible plug on a boiler is made PRIMARILY of

    A. selenium
    B. tin
    C. zinc
    D. iron

    4.____

5. The range of pH values for boiler feed water is NORMALLY

    A. 1 to 2
    B. 4 to 6
    C. 9 to 10
    D. 12 to 15

    5.____

6. The *boiler horsepower* is defined as the evaporation of _____ lbs. of water from and at 212F.

    A. 900
    B. 400
    C. 345
    D. 34.5

    6.____

7. A low-pressure air-atomizing oil burner has an operating air pressure range of _____ lbs.

    A. 25 to 34
    B. 16 to 20
    C. 6 to 10
    D. 1 to 2

    7.____

8. A superheater is installed in a Stirling boiler MAINLY for the purpose of raising the temperature of the

    A. secondary air
    B. steam leaving the steam drum
    C. boiler feed water
    D. primary air

    8.____

9. The function of a counterflow economizer in a power plant is to

    A. use flue gases to heat feedwater
    B. raise flue gas temperatures
    C. recirculate exhaust steam
    D. pre-heat combustion air

    9.____

10. A fire due to spontaneous combustion would MOST easily occur in a pile of

    A. asbestos sheathing
    B. loose lumber
    C. oil drums
    D. oily waste rags

11. A *damper regulator*, used for combustion control, is operated by

    A. steam pressure
    B. the water column
    C. the boiler pump
    D. a pitot tube

12. The packing of an expansion joint in a firebrick wall of a combustion chamber is GENERALLY made of

    A. silica
    B. brick cement
    C. silicon carbide
    D. asbestos

13. An open-ended steam pipe, called a steam lance, is USUALLY used on a boiler to

    A. remove soot
    B. bleed the steam header
    C. clean the mud drum
    D. clean chimneys

14. A HIGH vacuum reading on the fuel oil gauge would indicate

    A. an empty oil tank
    B. high oil temperature
    C. a clogged strainer
    D. worn pump gears

15. The one of the following boilers that is classified as an internally fired boiler is the _____ boiler.

    A. cross-drum straight tube
    B. vertical tubular
    C. Stirling
    D. cross-drum horizontal box-header

16. Try-cocks are used on a boiler PRIMARILY to

    A. check the gauge glass reading
    B. release steam pressure
    C. drain the water column
    D. blow down the gauge glass

17. Scale deposits on the tubes and shell of a high-pressure boiler are undesirable because the deposits cause

    A. protrusions or roughness
    B. suction
    C. foaming
    D. concentrates

18. The function of a radiation pyrometer is to measure

    A. boiler water height
    B. boiler pressure
    C. furnace temperature
    D. boiler drum stresses

19. An engine indicator is GENERALLY used to measure   19._____

    A. steam temperature
    B. heat losses
    C. errors in gauge readings
    D. steam cylinder pressures

20. A goose-neck is installed in the line connecting a steam gauge to a boiler to   20._____

    A. maintain constant steam flow
    B. prevent steam knocking
    C. maintain steam pressure
    D. protect the gauge element

21. A boiler steam gauge should have a range of AT LEAST _____ pressure.   21._____

    A. one-half the working steam
    B. the working steam
    C. 1 1/2 times the maximum allowable working
    D. twice the maximum allowable working

22. A disconnected steam pressure gauge is USUALLY calibrated with a(n)   22._____

    A. Orsat instrument   B. air pump
    C. tuyeres   D. dead-weight tester

23. The recommended size joint for repairing firebrick wall is MOST NEARLY _____ inch.   23._____

    A. 1/64   B. 1/16   C. 1/4   D. 1/2

24. The acidity of boiler water is USUALLY determined by a(n) _____ test.   24._____

    A. Rockwell   B. soap hardness
    C. paper   D. alkalinity

25. Electrostatic precipitators are used in power plants to   25._____

    A. remove fly ash from flue gases
    B. measure smoke conditions
    C. collect boiler impurities
    D. disperse minerals in feed water

KEY (CORRECT ANSWERS)

1. C
2. D
3. B
4. B
5. C

6. D
7. D
8. B
9. A
10. D

11. A
12. D
13. A
14. C
15. B

16. A
17. A
18. C
19. D
20. D

21. C
22. D
23. A
24. D
25. A

TEST 3

DIRECTIONS: Each question or incomplete statement is followed by several suggested answers or completions. Select the one that BEST answers the question or completes the statement. *PRINT THE LETTER OF THE CORRECT ANSWER IN THE SPACE AT THE RIGHT.*

1. A boiler plant operates with induced draft and short divergent (larger at top) stack. The induced draft fan acts to replace the

    A. forced draft fan
    B. natural draft
    C. barometric damper
    D. long chimney

    1.____

2. A barometric damper is one which

    A. opens to relieve pressure on a condensing turbine when vacuum fails
    B. dampens the movement of mercury in a mercury barometer
    C. opens and closes to maintain constant exhaust pressure on a steam engine
    D. opens and closes so as to maintain a uniform draft at breeching of a boiler

    2.____

3. When comparing forced draft and induced draft fans, the MOST CORRECT statement is:

    A. The volume of air and gas handled by both is the same
    B. The induced draft fan handles a greater volume of air and gas
    C. The forced draft fan handles a greater volume of air and gas
    D. Output for both varies directly as the speed squared

    3.____

4. By increasing the outside lap on a *D* slide valve,

    A. compression changes
    B. expansion starts later and continues longer
    C. admission starts later
    D. exhaust occurs later

    4.____

5. The distinguishing characteristic of steam-engine cylinder oil is

    A. a high flash point
    B. a low flash point
    C. its color
    D. its oiliness

    5.____

6. The purpose of the arch in front of a boiler is to

    A. help ignite the coal
    B. create a draft
    C. support the grates
    D. help keep the gas in the boiler longer

    6.____

7. The unit of measurement used in the United States to determine the heating value of a fuel is the

    A. BTU
    B. calorie
    C. saybolt second
    D. degree

    7.____

8. The *calorific value* of coal is accurately determined by the use of a(n)

    A. Orsat apparatus
    B. calorimeter
    C. *Fyrite* instrument
    D. pyrometer

    8.____

9. The amount of heat liberated when a pound of carbon is burned to CO is MOST NEARLY _____ BTU.

   A. 4,500　　　B. 6,500　　　C. 8,500　　　D. 10,500

10. The amount of heat liberated when a pound of carbon is burned to CO_2 is MOST NEARLY _____ BTU.

    A. 10,000　　　B. 12,000　　　C. 14,000　　　D. 15,000

11. The heat content (BTU) in coal is PRIMARILY due to

    A. volatile matter and sulphur
    B. volatile matter, sulphur, and ash
    C. carbon
    D. volatile matter and carbon

12. A proximate analysis would include

    A. fixed carbon, volatile matter, moisture, and ash
    B. fixed carbon, volatile matter, and sulphur
    C. fixed carbon, moisture, and ash
    D. volatile matter, moisture, ash, and oxygen

13. A boiler is equipped with 5 steam atomizing oil burners and operates at a normal rating of 100,000 lbs. of steam per hour.
    A reduction in rating to 80,000 lbs. per hour would be accomplished by

    A. reducing the pressure of the oil
    B. reducing the temperature of the oil
    C. cutting out one of the burners
    D. closing in on the secondary air damper

14. A steam atomizing fuel oil burner

    A. makes very little noise when in operation
    B. is noisy in operation
    C. uses equal amounts of air and steam for atomization
    D. must always have negative draft in the wind box

15. The register of an oil burner is installed to

    A. measure air flow
    B. provide air for atomization
    C. provide air for combustion
    D. regulate air for combustion

16. Flame impingement upon sidewalls of a furnace in an oil fired boiler is eliminated by

    A. increasing the draft
    B. resetting the atomizer and diffuser
    C. adjusting the oil pressure and temperature
    D. adjusting the register

17. An oil fired boiler is equipped with a below-the-water-line heater and an electric pre-heater.
    When starting the boiler cold,

    A. the electric preheater is started first
    B. the below-the-water-line heater is started first
    C. no heater is required to start
    D. both heaters are started together

18. When a change is made by conversion from steam to mechanical atomization in an oil burning plant, of the following, the MOST appropriate action would be to _____ the oil _____.

    A. reduce; pressure
    B. reduce; temperature
    C. increase; pressure
    D. increase; temperature

19. Draft will vary from the highest positive pressure to the lowest negative pressure in a boiler in the following order:

    A. At top of stack, at bottom of stack, over fire, under fire
    B. Over fire, under fire, in second pass, in first pass, at base of stack
    C. At breeching, in second pass, in first pass, over fire, under fire
    D. under fire, over fire, in first pass, in second pass, at breeching

20. A forced draft fan delivers 15,000 cubic feet of air per minute when operating at 750 rpm. How much air will it deliver when operating at 500 rpm? _____ c.f.m.

    A. 8,000   B. 12,000   C. 10,000   D. 13,000

21. A forced draft fan turns 650 rpm and discharges 13,000 cfm of air.
    If the fan is slowed to 400 rpm, the air discharged, in cfm, would be

    A. 8000   B. 7500   C. 5000   D. 4000

22. An I.D. fan driven by a 30 H.P. motor runs at a speed of 1000 rpm and exhausts 20,000 cfm of gases.
    If the motor speed is increased to 2000 rpm, it would INCREASE the fan output to _____ cfm.

    A. 30,000   B. 160,000   C. 80,000   D. 40,000

23. A fan delivers 20,000 cfm at a speed of 1500 rpm.
    If the speed was raised to 3000 rpm and the efficiency dropped 10%, the delivery, in cfm, would MOST NEARLY be

    A. 30,000   B. 36,000   C. 40,000   D. 80,000

24. A forced draft fan turns 1000 rpm and delivers 150,000 cfm at a static pressure of 10".
    If the speed is reduced to 800 rpm, the capacity, in cfm, will be

    A. 150,000   B. 120,000   C. 90,000   D. 75,000

25. In the question above, the static pressure at the new speed will be _____ inches.

    A. 10   B. 8   C. 6.4   D. 7

KEY (CORRECT ANSWERS)

1. D
2. D
3. B
4. C
5. A

6. A
7. A
8. B
9. A
10. D

11. C
12. A
13. C
14. A
15. C

16. B
17. A
18. C
19. D
20. C

21. A
22. D
23. B
24. B
25. C

MECHANICAL APTITUDE TOOLS AND THEIR USE

EXAMINATION SECTION
TEST 1

Questions 1-16.

DIRECTIONS: Questions 1 through 16 refer to the tools shown below. The numbers in the answers refer to the numbers beneath the tools.
NOTE: These tools are NOT shown to scale

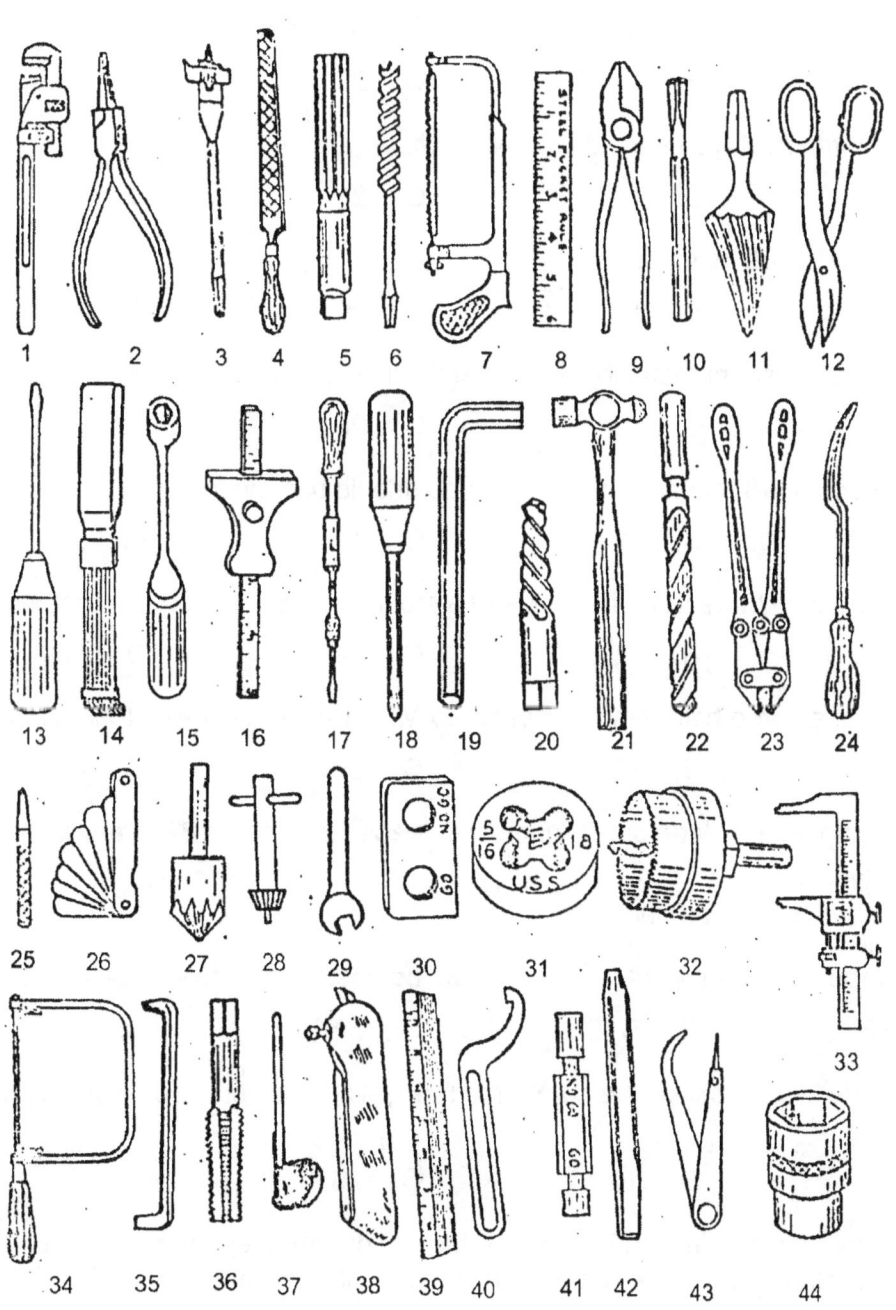

2 (#1)

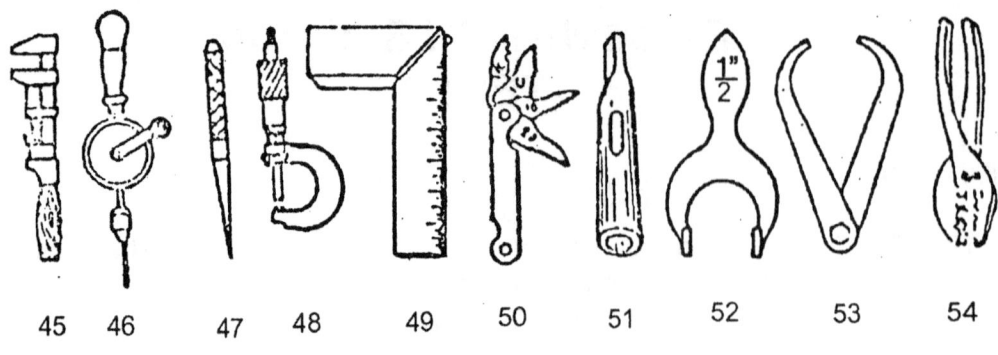

45 46 47 48 49 50 51 52 53 54

1. A 1" x 1" x 1/8" angle iron should be cut by using tool number
   A. 7   B. 12   C. 23   D. 42

2. To peen an iron rivet, you should use tool number
   A. 4   B. 7   C. 21   D. 43

3. The star "drill" is tool number
   A. 5   B. 10   C. 20   D. 22

4. To make holes in sheet metal for sheet metal screws, you should use tool number .
   A. 6   B. 10   C. 36   D. 46

5. To cut through a 3/8" diameter wire rope, you should use tool number
   A. 12   B. 23   C. 42   D. 54

6. To remove cutting burrs from the inside of a steel pipe, you should use tool number
   A. 5   B. 11   C. 14   D. 20

7. The depth of a bored hole may be measured MOST accurately with tool number
   A. 8   B. 16   C. 26   D. 41

8. If the marking on the blade of tool number 7 reads:12"-32", the 32 refers to the
   A. length   B. thickness   C. weight
   D. number of teeth per inch

9. If tool number 6 bears the mark "5", it should be used to drill holes having a diameter of
   A. 5/32"   B. 5/16"   C. 5/8"   D. 5"

10. To determine MOST quickly the number of threads per inch on a bolt, you should use tool number
    A. 8   B. 16   C. 26   D. 50

11. Wood screws, located in positions where the headroom does not permit the use of an ordinary screwdriver, may be removed by using tool number
    A. 17   B. 28   C. 35   D. 46

12. To remove a broken-off piece of 1/2" diameter pipe from a fitting, you should use tool number   12._____
    A. 5   B. 11   C. 20   D. 36

13. The outside diameter of a bushing may be measured MOST accurately with tool number   13._____
    A. 8   B. 26   C. 33   D. 43

14. To re-thread a stud hole in the casting of an elevator motor, you should use tool number   14._____
    A. 5   B. 20   C. 22   D. 36

15. To enlarge slightly a bored hole in a steel plate, you should use tool number   15._____
    A. 5   B. 11   C. 20   D. 36

16. The term "16 oz." should be applied to tool number   16._____
    A. 1   B. 12   C. 21   D. 42

KEYS (CORRECT ANSWERS)

1. A
2. C
3. B
4. D
5. B
6. B
7. B
8. D
9. B
10. D
11. C
12. C
13. C
14. D
15. A
16. C

TEST 2

Questions 1-11.

DIRECTIONS: Questions 1 through 11 refer to the instruments listed below. Each instrument is listed with an identifying number in front of it.

1 - Hygrometer
2 - Ammeter
3 - Voltmeter
4 - Wattmeter
5 - Megger
6 - Oscilloscope
7 - Frequency meter
8 - Micrometer
9 - Vernier calliper
10 - Wire gage
11 - 6-foot folding rule
12 - Architect's scale
13 - Planimeter
14 - Engineer's scale
15 - Ohmmeter

1. The instrument that should be used to *accurately* measure the resistance of a 4,700-ohm resistor is number
   A. 3   B. 4   C. 7   D. 15

2. To measure the current in an electrical circuit, the instrument that should be used is number
   A. 2   B. 7   C. 8   D. 15

3. To measure the insulation resistance of a rubber-covered electrical cable, the instrument that should be used is number
   A. 4   B. 5   C. 8   D. 15

4. An AC motor is hooked up to a power distribution box. In order to check the voltage at the motor terminals, the instrument that should be used is number
   A. 2   B. 3   C. 4   D. 7

5. To measure the shaft diameter of a motor *accurately* to one-thousandth of an inch, the instrument that should be used is number
   A. 8   B. 10   C. 11   D. 14

6. The instrument that should be used to determine whether 25 Hz. or 60 Hz. is present in an electrical circuit is number
   A. 4   B. 5   C. 7   D. 8

7. Of the following, the *proper* instrument to use to determine the diameter of the conductor of a piece of electrical hookup wire is number
   A. 10   B. 11   C. 12   D. 14

8. The amount of electrical power being used in a balanced three-phase circuit should be measured with number
   A. 2   B. 3   C. 4   D. 5

9. The electrical wave form at a given point in an electronic circuit can be observed with number
   A. 2   B. 3   C. 6   D. 7

10. The *proper* instrument to use for measuring the width of a door is number 10.____

　　A. 11　　　　　B. 12　　　　　C. 13　　　　　D. 14

11. A one-inch hole with a tolerance of plus or minus three-thousandths is reamed in a steel 11.____
    block. The *proper* instrument to accurately check the diameter of the hole is number

　　A. 8　　　　　B. 9　　　　　C. 11　　　　　D. 14

12. An oilstone is LEAST likely to be used correctly to sharpen a 12.____

　　A. scraper　　　B. chisel　　　C. knife　　　D. saw

13. To cut the ends of a number of lengths of wood at an angle of 45 degrees, it would be 13.____
    BEST to use a

　　A. mitre-box　　B. protractor　　C. triangle　　D. wooden rule

14. A gouge is a tool used for 14.____

　　A. planing wood smooth　　　　B. grinding metal
　　C. drilling steel　　　　　　　　D. chiseling wood

15. Holes are usually countersunk when installing 15.____

　　A. carriage bolts　　　　　　　B. lag screws
　　C. flat-head screws　　　　　　D. square nuts

16. A tool that is *generally* used to slightly elongate a round hole in scrap-iron is a 16.____

　　A. rat-tail file　　B. reamer　　C. drill　　D. rasp

17. When the term "10-24" is used to specify a machine screw, the number 24 refers to the 17.____

　　A. number of screws per pound　　B. diameter of the screw
　　C. length of the screw　　　　　　D. number of threads per inch

18. If you were unable to tighten a nut by means of a ratchet wrench because, although the 18.____
    nut turned on with the forward movement of the wrench, it turned off with the backward
    movement, you should

　　A. make the nut hand-tight before using the wrench
　　B. reverse the ratchet action
　　C. put a few drops of oil on the wrench
　　D. use a different socket in the handle

19. If you were installing a long wood screw and found you were unable to drive this screw 19.____
    more than three-quarters of its length by the use of a properly-fitting straight-handled
    screwdriver, the *proper* SUBSEQUENT action would be for you to

　　A. take out the screw and put soap on it
　　B. change to the use of a screwdriver-bit and brace
　　C. take out the screw and drill a shorter hole before redriving
　　D. use a pair of pliers on the blade of the screwdriver

20. Good practice requres that the end of a pipe to be installed in a plumbing system be reamed to remove the inside burr after it has been cut to length. The *purpose* of this reaming is to

    A. restore the original inside diameter of the pipe at the end
    B. remove loose rust
    C. make the threading of the pipe easier
    D. finish the pipe accurately to length

20.____

KEYS (CORRECT ANSWERS)

1.	D	11.	B
2.	A	12.	D
3.	B	13.	A
4.	B	14.	D
5.	A	15.	C
6.	C	16.	A
7.	A	17.	D
8.	C	18.	A
9.	C	19.	A
10.	A	20.	A

READING COMPREHENSION
UNDERSTANDING AND INTERPRETING WRITTEN MATERIAL
EXAMINATION SECTION
TEST 1

DIRECTIONS: Each question or incomplete statement is followed by several suggested answers or completions. Select the one that BEST answers the question or completes the statement. *PRINT THE LETTER OF THE CORRECT ANSWER IN THE SPACE AT THE RIGHT.*

Questions 1-8.

DIRECTIONS: Questions 1 through 8, inclusive, are to be answered in accordance with the following information.

In his 2017 annual report to the Mayor, the Public Works Commissioner stated that the city's basic water pollution control program begun in 1981 and costing $425 million so far would be completed in five or six years at a cost of $275 million more. However, he said, the city must spend an additional $175 million more on its marginal pollution control program to protect present and proposed beaches. Under the basic program, the city will have eliminated the last major discharges of raw sewage into the harbor. Over 800 million gallons, two-thirds of the city's spent water each day, is now treated at 12 plants, to which six new plants will be added, enabling the city to treat the estimated 1.8 billion gallons that will be discharged daily in 2050. The department had about $200 million worth of municipal construction under way in 2017, and completed $85.5 millions' worth.

1. According to the above, the city will add _____ new plants.
   A. 18   B. 12   C. 6   D. 4

2. The amount of municipal construction under way in 2017 was _____ million.
   A. $85.5   B. $175   C. $200   D. $425

3. It is estimated that in 2050 the city will treat daily _____ gallons.
   A. 700 million   B. 800 million   C. 900 million   D. 1.8 billion

4. According to the above article, the total cost of the water pollution program begun in 1981 will be _____ million.
   A. $275   B. $425   C. $700   D. $815

5. According to the above article, to protect present and proposed beaches, the city must spend an additional _____ million.
   A. $175   B. $275   C. $425   D. $450

6. The above article concerns the statements of the Commissioner of Public Works in his _____ annual report to the Mayor.
   A. 1981   B. 2050   C. 2017   D. 2018

7. The word *discharged* as used in the above article means MOST NEARLY   7.____

   A. emitted   B. erased   C. refuted   D. repelled

8. The word *pollution* as used in the above article means MOST NEARLY   8.____

   A. condensation   B. purification
   C. contamination   D. distillation

Questions 9-15.

DIRECTIONS: Questions 9 through 15, inclusive, are to be answered in accordance with the following information.

At sea level the atmosphere can exert a pressure of 14.7 pounds per square inch. This pressure is capable of sustaining a column of water having a height equal to 14.7 pounds multiplied by 2.304 (the height of water in feet which will exert one pound per square inch pressure). No pump built can produce a perfect vacuum. The atmospheric pressure exerting its force on the surface of the water from which suction is being taken forces the water up through the suction to the pump. From this, it is evident that the maximum height which a water pump of this type can lift water is determined ultimately by the atmospheric pressure. The tightness of the pump and its ability to create a vacuum also have a bearing.

9. The meaning of the word *vacuum* as used in the above article is a   9.____

   A. space entirely devoid of matter
   B. sealed tube filled with gas
   C. bottle-shaped vessel with a double wall
   D. cleaning device

10. With reference to the above article, if a pump could produce a perfect vacuum, the MAXIMUM height, in feet, that it could lift water at sea level is MOST NEARLY   10.____

    A. 33.9   B. 29.4   C. 23.3   D. 14.7

11. With reference to the above article, a column of water having a height of 4.6 feet at sea level will exert a pressure of MOST NEARLY _____ pounds per square inch.   11.____

    A. 3   B. 2   C. 1   D. $\frac{1}{2}$

12. The word *atmosphere* as used in the above article means   12.____

    A. the pull of gravity
    B. perfect vacuum
    C. the whole mass of air surrounding the earth
    D. the weight of water at sea level

13. The word *bearing* as used in the above article means MOST NEARLY   13.____

    A. direction   B. connection
    C. divergence   D. convergence

14. The word *evident* as used in the above article means MOST NEARLY 14.____

    A. disconcerting B. obscure
    C. equivocal D. manifest

15. The word *maximum* as used in the above article means MOST NEARLY 15.____

    A. best B. median C. adjacent D. greatest

Questions 16-19.

DIRECTIONS: Questions 16 through 19, inclusive, are to be answered in accordance with the following paragraph.

One of the categories of nuisance is a chemical one and relates to the dissolved oxygen of the watercourse. The presence in sewage and industrial wastes of materials capable of undergoing biochemical oxidation and resulting in reduction of oxygen in the watercourse leads to a partial or complete depletion of this oxygen. This, in turn, leads to the subsequent production of malodorous products of decomposition, to the destruction of aquatic plant life and major fish life, and to conditions offensive to sight and smell.

16. The word *malodorous* as used in the above paragraph means MOST NEARLY 16.____

    A. fragrant B. fetid C. wholesome D. redolent

17. From the above paragraph, because of pollution the amount of dissolved oxygen in the waterways is 17.____

    A. released B. multiplied
    C. lessened D. saturated

18. The word *categories* as used in the above paragraph means MOST NEARLY 18.____

    A. divisions B. clubs C. symbols D. products

19. The word *offensive* as used in the above paragraph means MOST NEARLY 19.____

    A. pliable B. complaint
    C. deferential D. disagreeable

Questions 20-22.

DIRECTIONS: Questions 20 through 22, inclusive, are to be answered in accordance with the following paragraph.

Thermostats should be tested in hot water for proper opening. A bucket should be filled with sufficient water to cover the thermostat and fitted with a thermometer suspended in the water so that the sensitive bulb portion does not rest directly on the bucket. The water is then heated on a stove. As the temperature of the water passes the 160-165° range, the thermostat should start to open and should be completely opened when the temperature has risen to 185-190°. Lifting the thermostat into the air should cause a pronounced closing action, and the unit should be closed entirely within a short time.

20. The thermostat described above is a device which opens and closes with changes in the 20.____

    A. position
    B. pressure
    C. temperature
    D. surroundings

21. According to the above paragraph, the closing action of the thermostat should be tested 21.____
    by

    A. working the thermostat back and forth
    B. permitting the water to cool gradually
    C. adding cold water to the bucket
    D. removing the thermostat from the bucket

22. The bulb of the thermometer should NOT rest directly on the bucket because 22.____

    A. the bucket gets hotter than the water
    B. the thermometer might be damaged in that position
    C. it is difficult to read the thermometer in that position
    D. the thermometer might interfere with operation of the thermostat

Questions 23-25.

DIRECTIONS: Questions 23 through 25, inclusive, are to be answered in accordance with information given in the paragraph below.

All idle pumps should be turned daily by hand and should be run under power at least once a week. Whenever repairs are made on a pump, a record should be kept so that it will be possible to judge the success with which the pump is performing its functions. If a pump fails to deliver liquid, there may be an obstruction in the suction line, the pump's parts may be badly worn, or the packing defective.

23. According to the above paragraph, pumps 23.____

    A. in use should be turned by hand every day
    B. which are not in use should be run under power every day
    C. which are in daily use should be run under power several times a week
    D. which are not in use should be turned by hand every day

24. According to the above paragraph, the reason for keeping records of repairs made on 24.____
    pumps is to

    A. make certain that proper maintenance is being performed
    B. discover who is responsible for improper repairs
    C. rate the performance of the pumps
    D. know when to replace worn parts

25. The one of the following causes of pump failure which is NOT mentioned in the above 25.____
    paragraph is

    A. excessive suction lift
    B. clogged lines
    C. bad packing
    D. worn parts

KEY (CORRECT ANSWERS)

1.	C	11.	B
2.	C	12.	C
3.	D	13.	B
4.	C	14.	D
5.	A	15.	D
6.	C	16.	B
7.	A	17.	C
8.	C	18.	A
9.	A	19.	D
10.	A	20.	C

21. D
22. A
23. D
24. C
25. A

TEST 2

DIRECTIONS: Each question or incomplete statement is followed by several suggested answers or completions. Select the one that BEST answers the question or completes the statement. *PRINT THE LETTER OF THE CORRECT ANSWER IN THE SPACE AT THE RIGHT.*

Questions 1-2.

DIRECTIONS: Questions 1 and 2 are to be answered in accordance with the information given in the following paragraph.

   A sludge lagoon is an excavated area in which digested sludge is desired. Lagoon depths vary from six to eight feet. There are no established criteria for the required capacity of a lagoon. The sludge moisture content is reduced by evaporation and drainage. Volume reduction is slow, especially in cold and rainy weather. Weather and soil conditions affect concentration. The drying period ranges from a period of several months to several years. After the sludge drying period has ended, a bulldozer or tractor can be used to remove the sludge. The dried sludge can be used for fill of low ground. A filled dried lagoon can be developed into a lawn. Lagoons can be used for emergency storage when the sludge beds are full. Lagoons are popular because they are inexpensive to build and operate. They have a disadvantage of being unsightly. A hazard to lagoon operation is the possibility of draining partly digested sludge to the lagoon that creates a fly and odor nuisance.

1. In accordance with the given paragraph, sludge lagoons have the disadvantage of being   1._____

    A. unsightly   B. too deep
    C. concentrated   D. wet

2. In accordance with the given paragraph, moisture content is reduced by   2._____

    A. digestion   B. evaporation
    C. oxidation   D. removal

Questions 3-5.

DIRECTIONS: Questions 3 through 5, inclusive, should be answered in accordance with the following paragraph.

   Sharpening a twist drill by hand is a skill that is mastered only after much practice and careful attention to the details. Therefore, whenever possible, use a tool grinder in which the drills can be properly positioned, clamped in place, and set with precision for the various angles. This machine grinding will enable you to sharpen the drills accurately. As a result, they will last longer and will produce more accurate holes.

3. According to the above paragraph, one reason for sharpening drills accurately is that the drills   3._____

    A. can then be used in a hand drill as well as a drill press
    B. will last longer
    C. can then be used by unskilled persons
    D. cost less

4. According to the above paragraph, 4.____

   A. it is easier to sharpen a drill by machine than by hand
   B. drills cannot be sharpened by hand
   C. only a skilled mechanic can learn to sharpen a drill by hand
   D. a good mechanic will learn to sharpen drills by hand

5. As used in the above paragraph, the word *precision* means MOST NEARLY 5.____

   A. accuracy   B. ease   C. rigidity   D. speed

Questions 6-9.

DIRECTIONS: Questions 6 through 9, inclusive, should be answered in accordance with the following paragraph.

Centrifugal pumps have relatively fewer moving parts than reciprocating pumps, and no valves. While reciprocating pumps when new are usually more efficient than centrifugal pumps, the latter retain their efficiency longer. Most rotary pumps are also without valves, but they have closely meshing parts between which high pressures may be set up after they begin to wear. In general, centrifugal pumps can be made much smaller than reciprocating pumps giving the same result. There is an exception in that positive displacement pumps delivering small volumes at high heads are smaller than equivalent centrifugal pumps. Centrifugal pumps cost less when first purchased than other comparable pumps. The original outlay may be as little as one-third or one-half that of a reciprocating pump suitable for the same purpose.

6. The type of pump NOT mentioned in the above paragraph is the _____ type. 6.____

   A. rotary   B. propeller
   C. reciprocating   D. centrifugal

7. According to the above paragraph, the type of pump that sometimes has valves and sometimes does NOT is the 7.____

   A. rotary   B. propeller
   C. reciprocating   D. centrifugal

8. According to the above paragraph, centrifugal pumps are 8.____

   A. *always* smaller than reciprocating pumps
   B. *smaller* than reciprocating pumps only when designed to deliver small quantities at low pressures
   C. *larger* than reciprocating pumps only when designed to deliver small quantities at high pressures
   D. *larger* than reciprocating pumps only when designed to deliver large quantities at low pressures

9. The advantage of centrifugal pumps that is NOT mentioned in the above paragraph is that 9.____

   A. the centrifugal pump retains its efficiency longer
   B. it is impossible to create an excessive pressure when using a centrifugal pump

C. there are fewer parts to wear out in a centrifugal pump
D. the centrifugal pump is cheaper

Questions 10-12.

DIRECTIONS: Questions 10 through 12, inclusive, should be answered in accordance with the following paragraph.

Gaskets made of relatively soft materials are placed between the meeting surfaces of hydraulic fittings in order to increase the tightness of the seal. They should be composed of materials that will not be affected by the liquid to be enclosed, nor by the conditions under which the system operates, including maximum pressure and temperature. They should be able to maintain the amount of clearance required between meeting surfaces. One of the materials most widely used in making gaskets is neoprene. Since neoprene is flexible, it is often used in sheet form at points where a gasket must expand enough to allow air to accumulate, as with cover plates on supply tanks. Over a period of time, oil tends to deteriorate the material used in making neoprene gaskets. The condition of the gasket must, therefore, be checked whenever the unit is disassembled. Since neoprene gasket material is soft and flexible, it easily becomes misshapen, scratched or torn. Great care is therefore necessary in handling neoprene. Shellac, gasket sealing compounds or *pipe dope* should never be used with sheet neoprene, unless absolutely necessary for satisfactory installation.

10. Of the following, the one that is NOT mentioned in the above paragraph as a requirement for a good gasket material is that the material must be

    A. cheap
    B. unaffected by heat developed in a system
    C. relatively soft
    D. capable of maintaining required clearances

11. According to the above paragraph, neoprene will be affected by

    A. air   B. temperature   C. pressure   D. oil

12. According to the above paragraph, care is necessary in handling neoprene because

    A. its condition must be checked frequently
    B. it tears easily
    C. pipe dope should not be used
    D. it is difficult to use

Questions 13-15.

DIRECTIONS: Questions 13 through 15, inclusive, are to be answered in accordance with the information given in the paragraph below.

Some gases which may be inhaled have an irritant effect on the respiratory tract. Among them are ammonia fumes, hydrogen sulfide, nitrous fumes, and phosgene. Persons who have been exposed to irritant gases must lie down at once and keep absolutely quiet until the dotor arrives. The action of some of these gases may be delayed, and at first the victim may show few or no symptoms.

13. According to the above paragraph, the part of the body that is MOST affected by irritant gases is the   13._____

    A. heart   B. lungs   C. skin   D. nerves

14. According to the above paragraph, a person who has inhaled an irritant gas should be   14._____

    A. given artificial respiration
    B. made to rest
    C. wrapped in blankets
    D. made to breathe smelling salts

15. A person is believed to have come in contact with an irritant gas but he does not become sick immediately.   15._____
    According to the above paragraph, we may conclude that the person

    A. did not really come in contact with the gas
    B. will become sick later
    C. came in contact with a small amount of gas
    D. may possibly become sick later

Questions 16-22.

DIRECTIONS: Questions 16 through 22, inclusive, are to be answered in accordance with the following paragraph.

At 2:30 P.M. on Monday, October 25, Mr. Paul Jones, a newly appointed sewage treatment worker, started on a routine inspectional tour of the settling tanks and other sewage treatment works installations of the plant to which he was assigned. At 2:33 P.M., Mr. Jones discovered a co-worker, Mr. James P. Brown, lying unconscious on the ground. Mr. Jones quickly reported the facts to his immediate superior, Mr. Jack Rota, who immediately telephoned for an ambulance. Mr. Rota then rushed to the site and placed a heavy woolen blanket over the victim. Mr. Brown was taken to the Ave. H hospital by an ambulance driven by Mr. Dave Smith, which arrived at the sewage disposal plant at 3:02 P.M. Patrolman Robert Daly, badge number 12520, had arrived before the ambulance and recorded all the details of the incident, including the statements of Mr. Jones, Mr. Rota, and Mr. Nick Nespola, a Stationary Engineer (Electric), who stated that he saw the victim when he fell to the ground.

16. The time which elapsed between the start of the sewage treatment worker's routine inspection and the arrival of the ambulance was MOST NEARLY _____ minutes.   16._____

    A. 3   B. 28   C. 29   D. 32

17. The name of the sewage treatment worker's immediate superior was   17._____

    A. James P. Brown   B. Jack Rota
    C. Paul Jones   D. Robert Daly

18. The name of the patrolman was   18._____

    A. James P. Brown   B. Jack Rota
    C. Paul Jones   D. Robert Daly

19. Referring to the above, the incident occurred on 19.____

    A. Monday, Oct. 25   B. Monday, Oct. 26
    C. Tuesday, Oct. 25   D. Tuesday, Oct. 26

20. The victim was found at exactly 20.____

    A. 2:30 A.M.   B. 2:33 P.M.   C. 2:33 A.M.   D. 2:30 P.M.

21. The sewage treatment worker's name was 21.____

    A. James P. Brown   B. Jack Rota
    C. Paul Jones   D. Dave Smith

22. The man named Nick Nespola was the 22.____

    A. Stationary Engineer (Electric)
    B. patrolman
    C. victim
    D. ambulance driver

Questions 23-25.

DIRECTIONS: Questions 23 through 25, inclusive, are to be answered in accordance with the information given in the paragraph below.

The bearings of all electrical equipment should be subjected to careful inspection at scheduled periodic intervals in order to secure maximum life. The newer type of sleeve bearings requires very little attention since the oil does not become contaminated and oil leakage is negligible. Maintenance of the correct oil level is frequently the only upkeep required for years of service with this type of bearing.

23. According to the above paragraph, the MAIN reason for making periodic inspections of electrical equipment is to 23.____

    A. reduce waste of lubricants
    B. prevent injury to operators
    C. make equipment last longer
    D. keep operators *on their toes*

24. According to the above paragraph, the bearings of electrical equipment should be inspected 24.____

    A. whenever the equipment isn't working properly
    B. whenever there is time for inspections
    C. at least once a year
    D. at regular times

25. According to the above paragraph, when using newer type of sleeve bearings, 25.____

    A. oil leakage is slight
    B. the oil level should be checked every few years
    C. oil leakage is due to carelessness
    D. oil soon becomes dirty

KEY (CORRECT ANSWERS)

1. A
2. B
3. B
4. A
5. A

6. B
7. A
8. C
9. B
10. A

11. D
12. B
13. B
14. B
15. D

16. D
17. B
18. D
19. A
20. B

21. C
22. A
23. C
24. D
25. A

TEST 3

DIRECTIONS: Each question or incomplete statement is followed by several suggested answers or completions. Select the one that BEST answers the question or completes the statement. *PRINT THE LETTER OF THE CORRECT ANSWER IN THE SPACE AT THE RIGHT.*

Questions 1-2.

DIRECTIONS: Questions 1 and 2 are to be answered on the basis of the paragraph below.

When summers are hot and dry, much water will be used for watering lawns. Domestic use will be further increased by more bathing, while public use will be affected by much street sprinkling and use in parks and recreation fields for watering grass and for ornamental fountains. Variations in the weather may cause variations in water consumption. A succession of showers in the summer could significantly reduce water consumption. High temperatures may also lead to high water use for air conditioning purposes. On the other hand, in cold weather water may be wasted at the faucets to prevent freezing of pipes, thereby greatly increasing consumption.

1. According to the above passage, water consumption

    A. will not be affected by the weather to any appreciable extent
    B. will always increase in the warm weather and decrease in cold weather
    C. will increase in cold weather and decrease in warm weather
    D. may increase because of high or low temperatures

2. The MAIN subject of the above passage is

    A. climatic conditions affecting water consumption
    B. water consumption in arid regions
    C. conservation of water
    D. weather variations

Questions 3-4.

DIRECTIONS: Questions 3 and 4 are to be answered on the basis of the paragraph below.

The efficiency of the water works management will affect con-sumption by decreasing loss and waste. Leaks in the water mains and services and unauthorized use of water can be kept to a minimum by surveys. A water supply that is both safe and attractive in quality will be used to a greater extent than one of poor quality. In this connection, it should be recognized that improvement of the quality of water supply will probably be followed by an increase in consumption. Increasing the pressure will have a similar effect. Changing the rates charged for water will also affect consumption. A study found that consumption decreases about five percent for each ten percent increase in water rates. Similarly, water consumption increases when the water rates are decreasing.

3. According to the above passage, an increase in the quality of water would MOST LIKELY

    A. cause an increase in water consumption
    B. decrease water consumption by about 10%

C. cause a decrease in water consumption
D. have no effect on water consumption

4. According to the above passage, a ten percent decrease in water rates would MOST LIKELY result in a _____ in the water consumption.

   A. five percent decrease
   B. five percent increase
   C. ten percent decrease
   D. ten percent increase

4.____

Questions 5-6.

DIRECTIONS: Questions 5 and 6 are to be answered on the basis of the paragraph below.

While the average domestic use of water may be expected to be about 35 gallons per person daily, wide variations are found. These are largely dependent upon the economic status of the consumers and will differ greatly in various sections of the city. In the high value residential districts of a city or in a suburban community of similar type population, the water consumption per person will be high. In apartment houses, which may be considered as representing the maximum domestic demand to be expected, the average consumption should be about 60 gallons per person. In an area of high value single residences, even higher consumption may be expected since to the ordinary domestic demand there will be added amount for watering lawns. The slum districts of large cities will show a consumption per person of about 20 gallons daily. The lowest figures of all will be found in low value districts where sewerage is not available and where perhaps a single faucet serves one or several households.

5. According to the above passage, domestic water consumption per person

   A. would probably be lowest for persons in an area of high value single residences
   B. would probably be lowest for persons in an apartment house
   C. would probably be lowest for persons in a slum area
   D. does not depend at all upon area or income

5.____

6. According to the above passage, the water consumption in apartment houses as compared to slum houses is about _____ times as much.

   A. $1\frac{1}{2}$
   B. 2
   C. $2\frac{1}{2}$
   D. 3

6.____

Questions 7-9.

DIRECTIONS: Questions 7 through 9 are to be answered in accordance with the paragraph below.

A connection for commercial purposes may be made from a metered fire or sprinkler line of 4 inches or larger in diameter, provided a meter is installed on the commercial branch line. Such connection shall be taken from the inlet side of the fire meter control valve, and the method of connection shall be subject to the approval of the department. On a 4-inch fire line, the connection shall not exceed inches in diameter. On a fire line 6 inches or larger in diameter, the size of the connection shall not exceed 2 inches. Fire lines shall not be cross-connected with any system of piping within the building.

7. According to the above paragraph, a connection for commercial purposes may be made to a metered sprinkler line provided that the diameter of the sprinkler line is AT LEAST

   A. $1\frac{1}{2}$"   B. 2"   C. 4"   D. 6"

7.____

8. According to the above paragraph, the connection for commercial purposes is taken from the

   A. inlet side of the main control valve
   B. outlet side of the wet connection
   C. inlet side of the fire meter control valve
   D. outlet side of the Siamese

8.____

9. According to the above paragraph, the MAXIMUM size permitted for the connection for commercial purposes depends on the

   A. location of the fire meter valve
   B. use to which the commercial line is to be put
   C. method of connection to the sprinkler line
   D. size of the sprinkler line

9.____

Questions 10-11.

DIRECTIONS: Questions 10 and 11 are to be answered in accordance with the paragraph below.

Meters shall be set or reset so that they may be easily examined and read. In all premises where the supply of water is to be fully metered, the meter shall be set within three feet of the building or vault wall at. point of entry of service pipe. The service pipe between meter control valve and meter shall be kept exposed. When a building is situated back of the building line or conditions exist in a building that prevent the setting of the meter at a point of entry, meter may be set outside of the building in a proper watertight and frost-proof pit or meter box, or at another location approved by the Deputy Commissioner, Assistant to Commissioner, or the Chief Inspector.

10. According to the above paragraph, a meter should be set

    A. at a point in the building convenient to the owner
    B. within 3 feet of the building wall
    C. in back of the building
    D. where the district inspector thinks is best

10.____

11. According to the above paragraph, one of the conditions imposed when a meter is permitted to be installed outside of a building is that the meter must be installed

    A. between the service pipe and the meter control valve
    B. within 3 feet of the point of entry of the service pipe
    C. in a watertight enclosure
    D. above ground in a frost-proof box

11.____

Questions 12-15.

DIRECTIONS: Questions 12 through 15 are to be answered in accordance with the paragraphs below.

No individual or collective air conditioning system installed on any premises for a single consumer shall be permitted to waste annually more than the equivalent of a continuous flow of five gallons of city water per minute.

All individual or collective air conditioning systems installed on any premises for a single consumer using city water annually in excess of the equivalent of five gallons per minute shall be equipped with a water conserving device such as economizer, evaporative condenser, water cooling tower, or other similar apparatus, which device shall not consume for makeup purposes in excess of 15% of the consumption that would normally be used without such device.

Any individual or collective group of such units installed on any premises for a single consumer with a rated capacity of 25 tons or more, or water consumption of 50 gallons or more per minute, shall be equipped, where required by the department, with a water meter to separately register the consumption of such unit or groups of units.

This rule shall also apply to all air conditioning equipment now in service.

12. The rules described in the above paragraphs apply

    A. *only* to new installations of air conditioning equipment
    B. *only* to air conditioning systems which waste more than 5 gallons of city water per minute
    C. *only* to new installations of air conditioning equipment which waste more than 5 gallons of city water per minute
    D. to all air conditioning systems, whether existing ones or new installations

13. According to the above paragraphs, one of the acceptable methods of reducing wasting of water in an air conditioning system is by means of a

    A. cooling tower   B. water meter
    C. check valve   D. collective system

14. According to the above paragraphs, the department may require that an air conditioning system have a separate water meter when the system

    A. wastes more than 5 gallons of city water per minute
    B. uses more than 15% make-up water
    C. is equipped with an economizer
    D. has a rated capacity of 25 tons or more

15. According to the above paragraphs, the MAXIMUM quantity of make-up water permitted where an air conditioning system uses 50 gallons of water per minute is _____ gallons/minute.

    A. 7   B. $7\frac{1}{2}$ C. 8   D. $8\frac{1}{2}$

Questions 16-17.

DIRECTIONS: Questions 16 and 17 are to be answered in accordance with the paragraph below.

Where flushometers, suction tanks, other fixtures or piping are equipped with quick closing valves and are supplied by direct street pressure in excess of 70 pounds, an air chamber of an approved type shall be installed within two feet of the house control valve or meter in the service near the point of entry. Where water hammer conditions exist in any installation, regardless of the pressure obtaining, an air chamber of an approved type shall be installed where and as directed by the Chief Inspector or Engineer.

16. According to the above paragraph, air chambers are required when or wherever   16._____

   A. there are flushometers
   B. piping is supplied at a direct street pressure in excess of 70 lbs. per sq. in.
   C. a quick closing valve is used
   D. water hammer can occur in any piping

17. According to the above paragraph, air chambers should be installed   17._____

   A. within two feet of the house control valve or meter
   B. in a water system regardless of operating pressure
   C. on the fixture side of the quick closing valve
   D. on the suction side of the service meter

Questions 18-23.

DIRECTIONS: Questions 18 through 23 are to be answered in accordance with the paragraph below.

The acceptor's responsibility—The purpose of commercial standards is to establish for specific commodities, nationally *recognized* grades or consumer *criteria* and the benefits therefrom will be measurable in direct proportion to their general recognition and actual use. Instances will occur when it may be necessary to deviate from the standard, and the signing of an acceptance does not *preclude* such departures; however, such signature indicates an *intention* to follow the commercial standard where practicable, in the production, distribution, or consumption of the article in question.

18. The advantage which may be gained from the establishment of commercial standards is dependent upon the   18._____

   A. degree of consumer and manufacturer acceptance
   B. improvement of product quality
   C. degree of change required in the manufacturing process
   D. establishment and use of the highest standards

19. Nationally respected and adopted commercial standards are   19._____

   A. *undesirable;* as they are a direct benefit to unscrupulous manufacturers
   B. *desirable;* as they serve as a yardstick for consumers
   C. *undesirable;* as they tend to lower quality
   D. *desirable;* as they tend to reduce manufacturing costs

20. The word *preclude,* as used in this paragraph, means MOST NEARLY 20.____
    A. permit   B. allow   C. include   D. prevent

21. The word *intention,* as used in this paragraph, means MOST NEARLY 21.____
    A. agreement   B. impulse   C. objection   D. obstinance

22. The word *recognized,* as used in this paragraph, means MOST NEARLY 22.____
    A. desirable   B. stable   C. branded   D. accepted

23. The word *criteria,* as used in this paragraph, means MOST NEARLY 23.____
    A. efforts   B. standards   C. usage   D. costs

Questions 24-25.

DIRECTIONS: Questions 24 and 25 are to be answered in accordance with the paragraph below.

Sewage treatment plants are designed so that the sewage flow reaches the plant by gravity. In some instances, a small percentage of the sewerage system may be below the planned level of the plant. Economy in construction and other factors may indicate that the raising of that lower portion of the flow by means of pumps, to the desired plant elevation, is more desirable than lowering the plant structure. Some plants operate with this feature.

24. According to the above paragraph, 24.____

    A. a small percentage of the sewage reaches the plant by means of gravity
    B. all sewage reaches the plant by means of gravity
    C. where sewage cannot reach the plant by gravity, it is pumped
    D. pumping is used so that all sewage can reach the plant

25. According to the above paragraph, the reason that some plants are built above the level 25.____
    of the sewerage system is that

    A. these plants operate more efficiently this way
    B. gravity will naturally bring the sewage in at a lower level
    C. pumping of the sewage is more expensive
    D. these plants are cheaper to build this way

KEY (CORRECT ANSWERS)

1.	D	11.	C
2.	A	12.	D
3.	A	13.	A
4.	B	14.	D
5.	C	15.	B
6.	D	16.	D
7.	C	17.	A
8.	C	18.	A
9.	D	19.	B
10.	B	20.	D

21. A
22. D
23. B
24. B
25. D

FUNDAMENTALS OF DIESEL ENGINES

CHAPTER 1

INTRODUCTION

The modern diesel engine is a result of internal combustion principles which were proposed by Sadi Cornot in the first part of the 19th Centry, and which were put into practice by Rudolf Diesel in 1895.

Actually, engines similar to modern diesels were operating before 1895. "Oil engines" appeared in several forms more than 30 years earlier. Oil engines used a separately heated "hot bulb" or precombustion chamber to facilitate compression ignition. They produced modest amounts of power and vast amounts of smoke, a characteristic not significantly improved upon by Dr. Diesel's designs. In 1872 George B. Brayton patented a low compression oil engine using a pilot light igniter. The engine was not successful, but the thermodynamic principles it employed led to the modern jet and gas turbine engines. In 1890 a Hornsby-Ackroyd oil engine was run on a test stand with a flat plate replacing its precombustion chamber. It ran on compression ignition for 6 hours, but the engine was never commercially developed.

Rudolf Diesel patented his combustion principle before he built an engine. In his patented diesel cycle, combustion was started by compression heat and continued at constant pressure during the full power stroke of the engine.

Dr. Diesel built his first engine to run on coal dust. To increase its theoretical efficiency, he used a compression pressure of 1500 psi and omitted the cooling system. The engine exploded, nearly killing its inventor. After recovering from his injuries, Diesel tried again, but used oil as the fuel, added a water jacket to the cylinder, and lowered the compression pressure approximately 550 psi. His third engine was successful and was demonstrated in the United States. Production rights were purchased by Adolphus Busch, who built the first engine for commercial use and installed it in his St. Louis brewery to drive a pump.

It was a few years before the diesel engine found its way from the Busch brewery to a ship. The first marine diesel engine dates from 1910. Because Dr. Diesel imposed his patented combustion cycle on all engines produced from his design, the early, true diesel engines were massive, low powered, and wasteful of fuel. To retain constant pressure throughout the power stroke, piston speeds had to be slow and fuel injection had to be prolonged.

After Diesel mysteriously disappeared while traveling to London in 1913, there were fewer constraints on diesel engine builders, and a semidiesel cycle began to evolve. In the modified cycle, all the fuel was injected at the top of the stroke, and pressure was allowed to fall off during the power stroke. More complete combustion resulted, and greater piston and rotational speed could be attained. The semi-diesel, which is the engine we use today, became light and powerful enough to become the surface propulsion engine of most World War I submarines. It began to supersede the oil engine as the principal type of large internal combustion engine and by the 1920's was in use in locomotives and passenger liners.

By World War II the diesel engine was the predominant means of marine propulsion.

After the true diesel cycle was abandoned, the evolution of the engine design was principally in shifting from air-pressure fuel injection to solid injectors and in developing two-cycle, supercharged designs that permit significant weight savings and size reduction for equivalent power. A contributing technological improvement was standardization of diesel fuel. Five diesel fuel grades were proposed in the late 1930's. One standard fuel with established viscosity and combustion simplifies the engine designer's job and permits more efficient and reliable engines. Some civilian engines run on various fuels, ranging from heavy oils to gases, however, it is more economical for others to have a single fuel in its supply system to take advantage of readily available or cheap fuels.

While present diesel engines are tremendously improved as compared with diesel engines built 20 and even 10 years ago, further progress undoubtedly will take place. The probable improvement will be a further increase in the engine speed along with more efficient combustion. However, improvements become more and more difficult as the present engines have almost reached the safe limits of high temperatures and stresses in various parts.

CHAPTER 2

BASIC PRINCIPLES

You must understand the basic principles and sciences, which include basic physics, engine performance and efficiency, engine mechanics, and the petroleum products used in diesel engines before you can fully comprehend what takes place in an operating diesel engine. This chapter covers the above material in depth and will further your understanding of diesel engines as well as help you to operate and troubleshoot diesel engines more effectively.

For your convenience and easy reference, the examples in this chapter will be numbered 2A, 2B, 2C, etc, and equations will be numbered (2.1), (2.2), (2.3), etc.

UNITS OF MEASUREMENT

All physical quantities can be expressed by one of three units distance (length), force (weight or pressure), and time. In the English system used in the United States, the standard units are the foot (ft), pound (lb), and second (sec).

Derived units are formed and developed from the three standard English units and are used to measure quantities encountered in engineering practice.

DERIVED UNITS

Area

Area is a measure of surface expressed as the product of the length and width, or of two characteristic lengths of the surface. Areas are expressed in square units, such as square feet (sq ft or ft^2).

Volume

Volume is a measure of space expressed as the product of area and depth, or of three characteristic lengths of the space. Volumes are measured in cubic units, such as cubic feet (cu ft or ft^3) or cubic inches (cu in. or $in.^3$).

Linear Motion

Linear motion is the length of the line along which a point or a body has moved from one position to another. Linear distance is measured in units of length, such as feet or inches.

Rotary Motion

Rotary motion is the movement of a point or body along a circular path. The position of a point or body rotating about a fixed point in a plane is expressed by the angle through which it has rotated. Thus, in figure 2-1, when point a has moved to b, remaining all the time at a constant length r from the fixed point o, the position of b is determined by the angle of rotation c. Angles are measured in degrees, 360° corresponding to one complete revolution.

COMPARATIVE UNITS

Velocity

Velocity is the distance traveled by a moving point in a unit of time, as second, minute, or hour. Velocity is computed by dividing the distance traveled by the time used for the travel:

$$\text{Velocity} = \text{distance} \div \text{time} \quad (2.1)$$

DIESEL ENGINES

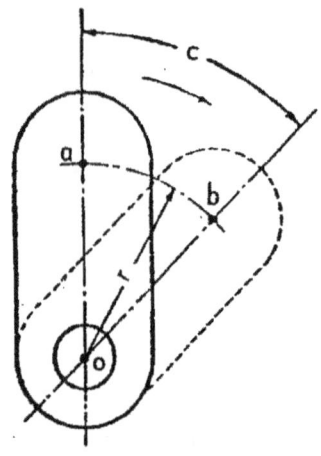

Figure 2-1.—Rotary motion.
256.151

In reference to the flow of fluids such as gas or water, the rate of flow is called velocity expressed in terms of feet per minute (ft/min) or feet per second (ft/sec). On the other hand, the term speed is applied in reference to the rotary motion of a mechanism. Thus, engine speed is said to be so many revolutions of its crankshaft per minute, and is designated as revolutions per minute (rpm).

Acceleration

Acceleration is a change in the velocity of a moving body within a unit of time. Acceleration may be uniform or varying. Acceleration is positive when the velocity increases and negative when the velocity decreases. Negative acceleration is called deceleration.

Acceleration is computed by dividing the change in velocity by the time during which this change takes place. If the acceleration is uniform, then this formula will give the actual acceleration. If the change in velocity is not uniform, then this formula will give the average acceleration. When the velocity is expressed in feet/minute, acceleration will be expressed in feet/minute per minute or feet/minute^2. If the velocity is expressed in feet/second, the acceleration will be expressed in feet/second per second or feet/second^2.

An example of constant acceleration is the acceleration of the earth's force of gravity which, for all technical calculations, can be set at 32.2 ft/sec^2.

Example 2C: A ship accelerates from dead in the water to 20 knots in 5 minutes. A speed of 20 knots is considered to be 2,000 feet per minute. What is the average acceleration in feet/sec^2? First, convert all factors into seconds:

$$2,000 \text{ ft/min} = 2,000 \div 60 = 33.33 \text{ ft/sec}$$

$$5 \text{ minutes} = 60 \times 5 = 300 \text{ seconds}$$

Average Acceleration = $\dfrac{\text{change in velocity}}{\text{change in time}}$

or

$$\frac{33.33}{300} - 0 = 0.11 \text{ ft/sec}^2$$

When the distance is expressed in feet and the time is expressed in minutes, the velocity will be expressed in feet per minute (ft per min or ft/min). If the time is expressed in seconds, the velocity will be expressed in feet per second (ft per sec or ft/sec).

Example 2A: A point traveled 1,800 ft in 2.5 min. Find its velocity.

Velocity = distance ÷ time

or

$$1,800 \div 2.5 = 720 \text{ ft/min}$$

Velocity may be uniform or varying. If the motion is uniform, i.e., if the velocity is constant, the above formula will give the actual velocity. If the motion, and hence also the velocity, is not uniform, as in the reciprocating motion of a piston in an engine cylinder, then the above formula will give the average velocity. The average piston velocity is referred to as piston speed. The velocity of a moving vehicle or aircraft is generally called speed and is expressed in miles per hour (mph).

Example 2B: Find the velocity in feet/minute of an automobile traveling at a speed of 50 mph. 1 mile = 5,280 ft; 1 hour = 60 min; speed = 50 mph; therefore

$$50 \times 5,280 \div 60 = 4,400 \text{ ft/min}$$

Chapter 2—BASIC PRINCIPLES

Pressure

Pressure may be defined as a force acting on a unit of area. Pressure may be exerted either by a solid body or by a fluid.

Example 2D: Determine the pressure on the subbase of a 1,800-lb engine whose contact area between the engine and the subbase consists of two strips, each of which is 2 in. wide and 40 in. long.

In this case the weight of the engine is a force pressing the engine against the subbase. The pressure (p) will be equal to the force (F) divided by the area (A):

$$p = F \div A \qquad (2.2)$$

or

$$p = \frac{1,800}{2(2 \times 40)} = 11.25 \text{ psi}$$

The force may be in pounds, and the area upon which the force is acting may be expressed in square inches or square feet. Accordingly, pressure may be in pounds per square foot (psf) or in pounds per square inch (psi).

In the case of contact between two solid bodies, the surfaces have a perfect uniform contact only in exceptional cases. The presence of uneven areas will give higher pressures at the high spots, and lower pressures, if any, at the places of depression. In such a case, the pressure determined, as in the above example, will give only the average value. However, when a force is transmitted by a fluid, either liquid or gas, the pressure between the fluid and the walls of the container will be uniform and equal in all directions, regardless of the shape of the walls.

Example 2E: Determine the pressure in an air compressor if the force acting upon the piston is 750 lb and the piston diameter is 3 in. The area of a 3-in. circle:

$$A = \pi r^2 = \pi(d \div 2)^2 = (\pi d^2) \div 4 = 3.14 \times 3^2 \div 4$$

$$= 7.07 \text{ sq in.}$$

and the pressure will be according to equation (2.2)

$$p = 750 \div 7.07 = 106 \text{ psi}$$

Specific Gravity

The ratio of the weight of a certain volume of a liquid to the weight of an equal volume of water is called specific gravity. For practical use, it is well to remember:

1,723 cu in. = 1 cu ft

1 cu ft of freshwater weighs 62.4 lb

1 gal = 231 cu in.

therefore, 1 gal weighs:

$$62.4 \times 231 \div 1,723 = 8.34 \text{ lb/gal}$$

Example 2F: Determine the weight of 1 gal of fuel oil which has a specific gravity of 0.84. The weight of the oil will be equal to the weight of the water times the specific gravity.

$$8.34 \times 0.84 = 7 \text{ lb/gal}$$

Work

Work is done when a force is moving a body through a certain distance. Work (W) is measured by the product of the force (F) multiplied by the distance (d) moved in the direction of the force.

$$\text{Work} = \text{force} \times \text{distance} \qquad (2.3)$$

or

$$W = F \times d$$

Work is expressed in ft-lb or in in.-lb.

Example 2G: Find the work necessary to raise the weight of 100 lb a distance of 2 3/4 ft.

$$100 \times 2.75 = 275 \text{ ft/lb}$$

Power

Power is the rate at which work is performed, or the number of units of work performed in one unit of time. Power is measured in foot-pounds/minute. In engineering calculations, 550 ft-lb/sec = 33,000 ft-lb/min and is called a horsepower.

$$\text{Power} = \text{work} \div \text{time}$$

or

$$P = W \div t$$

Example 2H: Determine the power required to do the work of example 2G if the work is to be performed (a) in 5 sec or (b) in 25 sec.

FOR CASE (a): The rate of performing the work is

$$275 \text{ ft-lb} \div 5 \text{ sec} = 55 \text{ ft-lb/sec}$$

Expressed in horsepower this is

$$\frac{55 \text{ ft-lb/sec}}{550 \text{ ft-lb/sec}} = 0.1 \text{ hp}$$

or since

$$55 \text{ ft-lb/sec} \times 60 \text{ sec/min} = 3{,}300 \text{ ft-lb/min}$$

then

$$\frac{3{,}300 \text{ ft-lb/min}}{33{,}300 \text{ ft-lb/min}} = 0.1 \text{ hp}$$

FOR CASE (b): The rate of performing the work is

$$275 \text{ ft-lb} \div 25 \text{ sec} = 11 \text{ ft-lb/sec}$$

so

$$\frac{11 \text{ ft-lb/sec}}{550 \text{ ft-lb/sec}} = 0.02 \text{ hp}$$

Electric Power

Electric power is measured in units called watts; 1,000 watts equal 1 kilowatt (kW). The conversion factors between hp and kW are

$$1 \text{ hp} = 0.746 \text{ kW or } 1 \text{ kW} = 1.341 \text{ hp}$$

Temperature

The temperature of a body is a characteristic which can be determined only by comparison with another body. When two bodies are placed in close contact, the one which is hotter will begin to heat the other and is said to have a higher temperature.

The scales of temperature are set arbitrarily. The two scales in general use are the Celsius, or centigrade scale, and the Fahrenheit scale. The temperature scale generally used in this country is the Fahrenheit scale. In this scale the two reference points are the temperature of melting ice, designated as 32°F, and the temperature of steam with the water boiling under normal barometric pressure, designated 212°F. The distance on the scale between these two points is divided into 180 equal parts called degrees. The scale is continued in both directions, above 212° and below 32°. Below 0°F the temperatures are designated by a minus (-) sign.

In theoretical calculations pertaining to gases, another scale, the absolute or rankine (R), is used. The unit of the rankine scale is the degree, the same as in the Fahrenheit scale, but the absolute zero is placed at -460°F. Thus, the relation between the absolute temperature (T) and the corresponding Fahrenheit temperature (t) is

degree rankine - degree Fahrenheit = 460

or

$$T = t + 460 \tag{2.4}$$

In technical calculations pertaining to gases, 60°F is the normal or standard temperature.

Gas Pressure Relationships

We have already discussed pressure. Additionally, as applied to gas, the pressure of a gas is often expressed by the height of the column of either water or mercury which balances the gas pressure in the space under consideration. The relationship between the gas and water or between the gas and mercury can be established as follows:

1 cu ft of freshwater at room temperature weighs 62.4 lb

Chapter 2—BASIC PRINCIPLES

or

a column of water 1 ft high acting upon an area of 1 sq ft is equal to a pressure of 62.4 psf

since

1 cu ft contains 1,728 cu in., the weight of 1 cu in. of water is 62.4 ÷ 1,728 = 0.0361 lb

therefore

a column of water 1 in. high, acting upon 1 sq in. will produce a pressure of 0.0361 psi.

To obtain a pressure of 1 psi, the column must be higher in the proportion of 1 ÷ 0.0361 = 27.70

or

27.70 in., or also 27.70 ÷ 12 = 2.309 ft.

Mercury is 13.6 times heavier than water. Therefore, a column of mercury must be shorter in this proportion

or

1 psi = 27.70 ÷ 12.6 = 2.036 in. mercury

conversely

1 in. mercury = 1 ÷ 2.036 = 0.491 psi.

GAGE AND ABSOLUTE PRESSURES.—Instruments measure the pressure of gases in respect to the pressure of atmospheric air, also called barometric pressure. Pressures measured thusly, are called gage pressures which usually indicate pounds per square inch gage (psig). The actual pressure exerted on the gas can be obtained by adding the barometric pressure to the gage pressure. This pressure is called absolute pressure and is indicated as pounds per square inch absolute (psia) and pounds per square foot absolute (psfa). If absolute pressure is designated p_a, gage pressure p_g, and barometric pressure b, then the relation can be written as

abs. pressure = gage pressure + barometric pressure

or

$$p_a = p_g + b \qquad (2.5)$$

The barometric pressure (b) is not constant because it changes with the altitude and weather conditions. Normal or standard barometric pressure at sea level is 29.92 in. of mercury

or

29.92 ÷ 2.036 = 14.70 psia

Volume is the space occupied by a body whether solid, liquid, or gas. If the body is a vapor or gas, its volume must be confined on all sides. In engines the volume of gas is usually confined by a cylinder that has one end closed by a stationary cylinder head and the other end closed by the head of a piston. The piston provides a gastight seal. When the piston changes position, the volume of the gas changes. When the piston approaches the cylinder head, the volume is being decreased and the gas is compressed; when the piston moves away from the cylinder head, the volume increases and the gas expands.

GAS PRESSURE, VOLUME, AND TEMPERATURE.—In gases the three measurable quantities—pressure, volume, and temperature—are called gas properties or characteristics. The three characteristics are connected by a simple relation, which for any gas can be written as

$$pV = WRT \qquad (2.6)$$

where p is the absolute pressure in pounds per square foot absolute, V is the volume in cubic feet, W is the weight of the gas in pounds, T is the absolute temperature in degrees rankine, and R is a constant called the gas constant. The numerical value of R is known for all gases. It is expressed in foot-pounds per pound per degree rankine. Equation (2.6) shows that if the three characteristics of a certain amount of gas are known, the weight can be found; or, if the weight is known, any one of the three characteristics can be found if the two others are measured.

DIESEL ENGINES

Example 2I: Find the weight of air contained in a 2-cu ft cylinder at a pressure of 100 psig with a temperature of 72°F and the gas constant of air of R = 53.3:

1. Find the absolute pressure by equation (2.5), assuming a normal barometric pressure (b) of 14.7 psia:

$$\text{pressure} = 100 + 14.7 = 114.7 \text{ psia}$$

or

$$p = 114.7 \times 144 = 16,500 \text{ psfa}$$

2. Find the absolute temperature by equation (2.4)

$$T = 72 + 460 = 532°R$$

3. Solving equation (2.5) for W and substituting the corresponding numerical values gives

$$W = pV \div RT = 16,500 \times 2 \div (53.3 \times 532)$$

$$= 1.16 \text{ lb}$$

Example 2J: Determine what will happen if the air in example 2I is heated to 150°F. The new absolute temperature is T = 150 + 460 = 610°R. The characteristic which will change is p. Solving equation (2.6) for p, and substituting the corresponding values gives

$$p = WRT \div V = 1.16 \times 53.3 \times 610 \div 2$$

$$= 18,900 \text{ psfa}$$

Converting 18,900 psfa to psia gives 18,900 ÷ 144 = 131.2 psia

The gage pressure will be according to equation (2.5)

$$P_g = 131.2 - 14.7 = 116.5 \text{ psig}$$

or an increase of 16.5 psi over the original pressure of 100 psig.

Energy

Energy of a body is the amount of work it can do. Energy exists in several different forms; a body may possess energy through its position, motion, or condition. Energy due to a position occupied by a body is called mechanical potential energy. An example of mechanical potential energy is a body located at a higher level, such as water behind a dam. When a body is moving with some velocity, it is said to possess energy of motion, or kinetic energy, such as a ball rolling upon a level floor. A third form of energy is internal energy, or energy stored within a body, either gas, liquid or solid, due to the forces between the molecules or atoms composing the body, such as in steam or gas under pressure. Chemical energy in fuel or in a charged storage battery is also classified as internal energy.

These three forms of energy, mechanical potential, kinetic, and internal, have in common the characteristic of being forms in which energy may be stored for future use.

Work can be classified as mechanical or electrical energy in the state of transformation or transfer. Work done by raising a body stores mechanical potential energy in the body due to the force of gravity; work done to set a body in motion stores kinetic energy; work done in compressing a gas stores internal energy in the gas; electrical work can be transformed into mechanical work by means of an electric motor and, after that, it may undergo other changes the same as mechanical work.

Heat, like work, is energy in the state of transfer from one body to another, due to a difference in temperature of the bodies.

UNITS OF ENERGY.—There are two basic independent units of energy:

1. The foot-pound (ft-lb) is the amount of energy as shown by work and is equivalent to the action of a force of 1 lb through a distance of 1 ft.

2. The British thermal unit (Btu) is the energy required to raise the temperature of 1 lb of pure water by 1°F at a standard atmospheric pressure of 14.70 psia.

Chapter 2—BASIC PRINCIPLES

The conversion factor from ft-lb to Btu's, often called the mechanical equivalent of heat, is

$$1 \text{ Btu} = 778 \text{ ft-lb}$$

There are two other energy units used in engineering calculations derived from the basic unit of foot-pounds:

3. The horsepower-hour (hp-hr) which is the transfer of energy at the rate of 33,000 ft-lb per min during 1 hr, or a total of 1,980,000 ft-lb, or, using the factor 778,

$$1 \text{ hp-hr} = 1{,}980{,}000 \div 778 = 2{,}544 \text{ Btu}$$

4. The kilowatt-hour (kW-hr) which is the transfer of energy at the rate of 1,000 watts per hour or 1.341 hp per hour which is equivalent to 44,253 ft-lb per min during 1 hr, or a total of 2,655,180 ft-lb or

$$1 \text{ kW-hr} = 2{,}655{,}180 \div 778 = 3{,}412 \text{ Btu}$$

KINETIC ENERGY.—Kinetic energy of a body is computed by

$$KE = 1/2(W \div g)v^2 \qquad (2.7)$$

where g is the acceleration due to gravity, 32.2 ft/sec^2 and v is the velocity of the body, ft/sec. Work done by kinetic energy is due to a change of velocity from an initial value of v_1 to a final value v_2.

Example 2K: Find the work done by 500 lb of exhaust gases discharged upon the blades of a supercharger turbine if the initial velocity of the gases were 9,000 ft/min and the exit velocity were 5,400 ft/min.

First the velocity must be changed to ft/sec:

$$v_1 = 9{,}000 \div 60 = 150 \text{ ft/sec}$$

$$v_2 = 5{,}400 \div 60 = 90 \text{ ft/sec}$$

By equation (2.7) the kinetic energies before and after the turbine are

$$KE_1 = 1/2(500 \div 32.2) \times 150^2 = 175{,}000 \text{ ft-lb}$$

$$KE_2 = 1/2(500 \div 32.2) \times 90^2 = 63{,}000 \text{ ft-lb}$$

and the work done

$$175{,}000 - 63{,}000 = 112{,}000 \text{ ft-lb}$$

ENERGY CONSERVATION.—The principle of conservation of energy states that energy may exist in many varied and interchangeable forms but may not be quantitatively destroyed or created. Thus, mechanical energy may be transformed into heat, or vice versa, but only in a definite relation as given before, 1 Btu = 778 ft-lb. Potential or internal energy may be changed to kinetic energy, etc.

Heat Flow

As stated before, heat is a form of energy in a state of change; it is expressed in Btu. Quantitatively, a flow of heat is determined by the change of temperature of a body—heat is conveyed if the temperature of the body rises and taken away if the temperature drops. A quantitative measurement of heat is possible only by comparison with the behavior of some other body selected as a standard. Since the Btu (heat unit) is determined with the aid of water, water is used as the standard to determine the behavior of all other substances in respect to a change of heat.

Specific Heat

The specific heat of a substance is the ratio of heat flow required to raise by 1°F the temperature of a certain weight of the substance to the heat flow required to raise by 1°F the temperature of an equal weight of water. Due to the definition of 1 Btu, the specific heat of water is unity, or 1 Btu/lb-deg F, and numerically the specific heat of a substance is equal to the heat flow, in Btu, required to raise by 1°F the temperature of 1 lb of the substance. Denoting the specific heat by c, the heat flow Q required to raise the temperature of W lb of a substance from t_1 to t_2 degree F is:

Heat = Weight (of body) X specific heat

X temperature difference

or

$$Q = Wc(t_2 - t_1) \qquad (2.8)$$

In general, specific heat varies with the temperature, and for gases depends also upon conditions of pressure and volume. For many calculations, a mean value of specific heat can be used.

Example 2L: Find the heat which is transferred to 53 gal of lubricating oil when its temperature rises from 70° to 165°F. The specific heat of the oil is 0.5 Btu/lb-deg F and its specific gravity is 0.925.

1 gal of oil weighs 8.34 X 0.925 = 7.71 lb

53 gal weigh 53 X 7.71 = 408 lb

Therefore by equation (2.8) the heat transferred

$$Q = 408 \times 0.5(165 - 70) = 19,380 \text{ Btu}$$

Heat Transfer

Generally speaking, heat is transferred by three methods: conduction, radiation, and convection.

Conduction is energy transfer by actual contact from one part of a body having a higher temperature to another part of it or to a second body having a lower temperature.

Radiation is energy transfer through space from a hotter body to a colder body.

Convection is not a form of energy transfer. Convection designates a process in which a body and the energy in it are moved from one position to another without change of state. An example of convection is the movement of heated air from one part of a room to another.

Basic principle of heat flow is that heat can flow from one body to a second body only if the temperature of the first body is higher than the temperature of the second body.

ENGINE MECHANICS

The term "engine mechanics" is used to cover various factors such as piston and crankshaft travel, piston speed, inertia, torque and speed factor. These factors are important because they play a large part in limiting the capabilities of a diesel engine.

PISTON AND CRANK TRAVEL

The movements of the piston are transmitted to the crankshaft by means of a connecting rod and the crank. By these two members the forward and back motion of the piston, called reciprocating motion, is transformed into rotary motion. For all practical purposes, the travel of the crankpin can be considered as a uniform motion along a circle described with the radius R equal to the length of the crank throw.

For convenience of presentation, figure 2-2 shows the motion of a piston along a horizontal line. If the connecting rod, instead of being L inches long, were infinitely long, then at all positions of the crank, the connecting rod could be considered to remain parallel to the cylinder centerline m-c, figure 2-2. In this case, at any position 1-c of the crank, the travel of the small end of the connecting rod from top center position m along the centerline would be equal to the distance o-s, cut off by the crank circle and the perpendicular 1-s, drawn through the position of the crankpin.

The actual position of the small end of the rod, when it is L inches long, and of the piston can be found by putting one leg of a compass at point 1 and swinging the compass with a radius equal to L to the intersection p with the horizontal centerline. The distance m-p will be the piston travel when the crank has traveled the

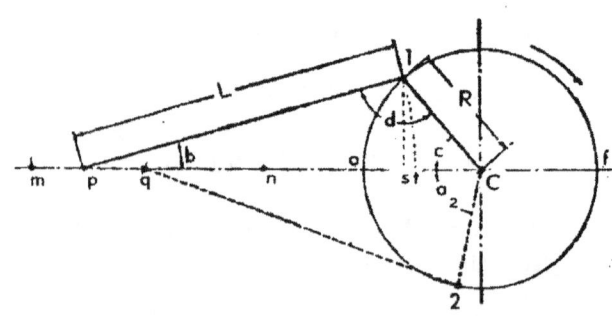

256.152

Figure 2-2.—Crank and piston travel.

Chapter 2—BASIC PRINCIPLES

angle a. On the other hand, putting one leg of a compass at point p and swinging the other leg to intersect the centerline at t will give the same distance o-t = m-p. The additional travel s-t is caused by the definite length L, or by the angularity of the connecting rod, and is due to the connecting rod's being inclined at an angle b instead of being parallel when it has an infinite length.

Thus, the angularity of the connecting rod during the first 20° of crank motion from the left or top center increases the length of travel of the piston as compared with an infinite connecting rod. Conversely, the angle of crank travel is smaller than with an infinite connecting rod. Thus, for the midposition of the piston the crank angle a_2 is smaller than 90°. Evidently the total piston travel or stroke m-n = o-r = 2R.

PISTON SPEED

While the crankpin travel is uniform and has a constant velocity, the piston travel is not uniform and the piston speed constantly varies. At each dead center, the piston comes to a standstill, its speed becomes zero; as the piston begins to move, the speed gradually increases and reaches a maximum when the angle a (fig. 2-2), formed by the crank and the cylinder centerline, is equal to 90°. After this position, the piston speed begins to decrease and at the dead center again becomes zero.

For many calculations, the average or mean piston speed must be known or the constant speed at which the piston must move to travel the same distance in the same time as it travels at the actual variable speed must be known. Using our definition of velocity, this speed is expressed as the distance traveled divided by the time used for the travel. Piston speed is expressed in ft/min. The distance traveled by the piston in one revolution is evidently two strokes. The piston stroke is usually measured in inches. Divide the strokes by 12 to convert to feet, multiply by the number of rpms, and divide 12 by 2 because the piston travels down as well as up:

stroke X rpm ÷ 6 = the distance traveled in 1 min and at the same time, according to the definition of velocity, this will be the mean piston speed, usually called simply piston speed

or

$$\text{Piston speed} = \text{stroke} \times \text{rpm} \div 6 \quad (2.9)$$

Example 2M: Find the piston speed of an 8 1/2 X 10 1/2 engine running at 750 rpm. According to equation (2.9):

Piston speed = 10.5 X 750 ÷ 6 = 1,313 ft/min

In diesel engines now in use by the Navy, the piston speed at rated rpm varies from 1,000 to approximately 2,000 ft/min.

INERTIA

Inertia is the resistance of a body to a change of motion—the tendency of an object to remain at rest if it is stationary or to continue to move if it is moving. Inertia as such cannot be measured directly; however, it can be expressed in terms of the force which must be applied to a body in order to change its velocity. As with any force, inertia forces are expressed in pounds. Since a change in velocity is defined as acceleration or deceleration, inertia may also be defined as being equal to that force which must be applied to a body in order to impart to it a certain acceleration or deceleration, either to speed it up or to slow it down, as the case may be. Numerically, the force of inertia F is equal to the weight of a body W, divided by the acceleration of the force of gravity, g = 32.2, and multiplied by the acceleration a, which is imparted to the body:

Inertia force = (weight ÷ 32.2) X acceleration

or

$$F = (W \div g)a \quad (2.10)$$

Example 2N: Determine the force of inertia of a body, which weighs 12 lb and moves uniformly with a velocity of 15 ft/sec, that is required to stop the body in 2 seconds. The

DIESEL ENGINES

acceleration, or since in this case it is negative, the deceleration per second is

$$a = 15 \div 2 = 7.5 \text{ ft/sec}$$

And the negative acceleration force of F is

$$F = (12 \div 32.2) \times 7.5 = 2.8 \text{ lb}$$

Therefore, if a steady force of 2.8 lb is applied to the body against its motion, the body will be brought to rest at the end of 2 seconds.

Equation (2.10) and example 2N show that the force of inertia of a body is not a fixed but a variable quantity. The force of inertia of a body is dependent on the acceleration that is applied to the body or, in other words, is dependent on the rate of change of the velocity of the body. The lesser the time in which a change takes place and the higher the required acceleration, the greater becomes the force of inertia.

TORQUE

Torque is the effect which rotates or tends to rotate a body. To produce rotation of a free body, there must be two equal and opposite forces acting along parallel lines but at separate points of the body. These two forces form a "couple." The perpendicular, or shortest, distance between the lines of action of the forces is called the arm of the couple. The magnitude, or moment, of the couple is expressed as the product of one of the forces multiplied by the length of the arm of the couple.

When a body rotates about the point of application of one of the forces of a couple, as on a fixed pivot, the arm of the couple is known as the lever, and the turning moment is called the torque. If the lever is fastened to a rotating shaft, it is called a crank. Figure 2-3 shows a force F, acting perpendicularly to a crank having a length $\int$ from the center of rotation 0 of a rotating shaft. The torque T, acting on this shaft is

$$\text{Torque} = \text{Force} \times \text{lever}$$

or

$$T = F \times \int \quad (2.11)$$

Torque is measured in pound-foot (lb-ft) or pound-inch (lb-in.).

SPEED FACTOR

Engines are often divided into several classes according to their speed capacity. Some are classified as low-speed, others as medium-speed, and still others as high-speed. However, unless a definite yardstick is used, the designations remain vague. There have been attempts to use either the engine speed (rpm) or its piston speed (ft/min) as a measure of speed capacity, but neither of these two methods can give correct indications. Rotative speed, as such, is not suitable as a speed characteristic because it does not take into consideration the size of the engine. A 6-cylinder X 3 1/2 X 4 1/2 X 900 rpm engine is not a high-speed engine because this type engine normally operates at speeds up to 2,000 rpm and higher. On the other hand, 8 1/2 in. X 10 1/2 in. diesel engines usually operate at speeds not exceeding 750 rpm and, even at this lower speed, have many features common with high-speed engines.

The same is true, only in reverse, with respect to piston speeds. In a large engine a relatively high piston speed, 1,800 ft/min or

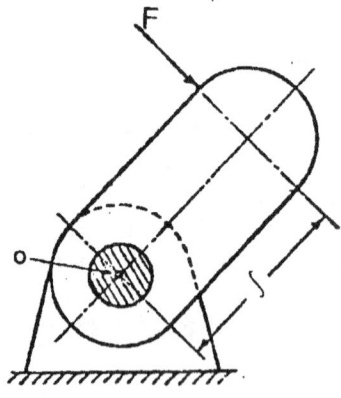

256.153

Figure 2-3.—Torque.

Chapter 2—BASIC PRINCIPLES

more, may be obtained with a relatively low rpm; in a small high-speed engine the piston speed is not high.

A good speed characteristic, called speed factor, is obtained as a product of rpm and piston speed. For the sake of obtaining smaller, more easily remembered figures, the product is divided by 100,000 thus

$$\text{Speed factor} = \frac{\text{rpm} \times \text{piston speed (ft/min)}}{100,000} \quad (2.12)$$

The figures obtained for various existing diesel engines lie between the limits of 1 and slightly less than 81. According to this data, all engines can be divided into four classes, in each class the high limit being obtained by multiplying the low limit by 3:

1. Low-speed engines with a speed factor of 1 to 3
2. Medium-speed engines with a speed factor of 3 to 9
3. High-speed engines with a speed factor of 9 to 27
4. Superhigh-speed engines with a speed factor of 27 to 81

Example 2O: Find the speed factor and speed classification of a 16 X 8 1/2 X 10 1/2 X 750 engine. As found in example 2M, the piston speed is 1,313 ft/min, and therefore, by equation (2.12):

$$\text{Speed factor} = \frac{750 \times 13,313}{100,000} = 9.85$$

According to the four classes of engines, an engine having a speed factor over 9 but under 27 is classified as a high-speed engine.

Classification of an engine in one of the above-named groups according to its speed factor has a particular value for purposes of designing the engine. Knowledge of the speed group to which an engine belongs is also of value to the engine operator: the higher the speed classification of an engine, (1) the more attention the operator should give to maintaining the engine in its best possible running condition by observing every detail given in the manufacturer's instruction book and (2) the more careful he should be when inspecting or overhauling the engine.

ENGINE PERFORMANCE AND EFFICIENCY

To understand the various factors that influence engine performance and efficiency, you must have a thorough knowledge of the internal-combustion process. Once you understand the combustion process, you will appreciate more easily the parts played by such factors as engine design, engine operating conditions, fuel characteristics, fuel injection, ignition, pressures and temperatures, and compression ratios.

This section provides some of the information necessary for a better understanding of many of the factors that affect engine performance and efficiency. You should:

1. Know how the power that an engine can develop is determined by limiting factors.
2. Learn how heat losses, efficiency of combustion, volumetric efficiency, and the proper mixing of fuel and air limit the power which a given engine cylinder can develop.
3. Become familiar with the factors that cause overloading of an engine and unbalance between engine cylinders.
4. Know the symptoms, causes, and effects of cylinder load unbalance, and know what is necessary if an equal load is to be maintained on each cylinder.
5. Know what is meant by engine efficiency, and know how the various types of efficiencies and losses are used in analyzing the internal-combustion process.
6. Be familiar with the factors which may cause the various efficiencies to increase or decrease, and the way in which these variations affect engine performance.

POWER LIMITATIONS

The amount of power that an engine can develop is limited by factors that are chiefly a result of design. These limiting factors are mean effective pressure, length of piston stroke, cylinder bore, and piston speed. This latter is itself limited by the frictional heat generated and by the inertia of moving parts.

DIESEL ENGINES

Mean Effective Pressure

The average pressure exerted on the piston during each power stroke is referred to as mean effective pressure and is determined from a formula or by means of a planimeter. There are two kinds of mean effective pressure: indicated mean effective pressure (imep), which is developed in the cylinder and can be measured; and brake mean effective pressure (bmep), which is computed from the brake horsepower (bhp) delivered by the engine.

Length of Stroke

The distance a piston travels between dead centers (TDC, BDC) is known as the length of stroke and is one of the factors that determines the piston speed. The shorter the length of stroke, the faster the engine can turn without placing excessive strain on rods and bearings. On the other hand, a slower engine can develop more power if it has a longer stroke.

Cylinder Bore

Bore is used to identify the diameter of the cylinder. The diameter must be known in order to compute the area of the piston crown. It is upon this area that the pressure acts to create the driving force. This pressure is calculated and expressed for an area of 1 square inch.

The ratio of length of stroke to cylinder bore is fixed in engine design. In most slow-speed engines the stroke is greater than the bore.

Revolutions Per Minute

The speed at which the crankshaft rotates is measured in rpm. Since the piston is connected to the shaft, the rpm, along with the length of the stroke, determines piston speed. During each revolution, the piston completes one up-stroke and one down-stroke; therefore, piston speed is equal to rpm times twice the length of the stroke. As described previously, this speed is usually expressed in feet per minute (fpm).

HORSEPOWER COMPUTATION

The power developed by an engine is dependent on the type of engine as well as the engine's speed. REMEMBER that a cylinder of a single-acting, 4-stroke cycle engine will produce one power stroke for every two crankshaft revolutions, while a single-acting, 2-stroke cycle engine produces one power stroke for each revolution.

Indicated Horsepower

The power developed within a cylinder is calculated by measuring the imep and engine speed. (The rpm of the engine is converted to the number of power strokes per minute.) With the bore and stroke known (available in engine manufacturers' technical manuals), the horsepower can be computed for the type engine involved. This power is called indicated horsepower (ihp) because it is obtained from the pressure measured with an engine indicator. Power loss due to friction is NOT considered in computing ihp.

Using the factors which influence the engine's capacity to develop power where

P = Mean indicated pressure, in psi

L = Length of stroke, in feet

A = Effective area of the piston, in square inches

N = Number of power strokes per minute

33,000 = Unit of power (1 horsepower), or footpounds per minute

the general or standard equation for calculating ihp is

$$ihp = \frac{P \times L \times A \times N}{33,000}$$

Example 2P: Assume that a 12-cylinder, 2-stroke cycle, single-acting engine has a bore of 8 1/2 inches and a stroke of 10 inches. Its rated speed is 744 rpm. With the engine running at full load and speed, the imep is measured and found

Chapter 2—BASIC PRINCIPLES

to be 105 psi. What is the indicated horsepower developed by one cylinder of the engine?

In this case

$$P = 105; L = \frac{10}{12}; A = 3.1416 \left(\frac{8.5}{2}\right)^2; N = 744$$

or for one cylinder

$$ihp = \frac{105 \times \frac{10}{12} \times 3.1416 \left(\frac{8.5}{2}\right)^2 \times 744}{33,000} = 111.9$$

or for a 12-cylinder engine

$$ihp = 12 \times 111.9 = 1343$$

Brake Horsepower (bhp)

This power, sometimes called shaft horsepower, is the amount available for useful work. Because of the various power losses that occur during engine operation, bhp is less than indicated horsepower. To obtain the brake or shaft horsepower developed by an engine and delivered as useful work, deduct the sum total of all mechanical losses from the total indicated horsepower.

CYLINDER PERFORMANCE LIMITATIONS

The factors that limit the power, which a given cylinder can develop, are piston speed and mean effective pressure. As stated earlier, the piston speed is limited by the inertial forces set up by the moving parts and frictional heat; in the case of the mean effective pressure, the limiting factors are:

1. Heat losses and efficiency of combustion.
2. Volumetric efficiency, or the amount of air charged into the cylinder and the degree of scavenging
3. Mixing of the fuel and air

The manufacturer prescribes the limiting mean effective pressures, both brake and indicated, which should never be exceeded.

In a direct-drive ship, the mean effective pressures developed are determined by the rpm of the power shaft. In electric-drive ships, the horsepower and bmep can be determined by a computation based on readings from electrical instruments and on generator efficiency.

CYLINDER LOAD BALANCE

To ensure a balanced, smooth-operating engine, its general mechanical condition must be properly maintained so that the power output of the individual cylinders is within the prescribed limits at all loads and speeds. To have a balanced load on the engine, each cylinder must produce its share of the total power developed. If the engine is developing its rated full power, or nearly so, and one cylinder or more is producing less than its share, obviously the remainder of the cylinders will become overloaded.

Using the rated speed and bhp, it is possible to determine for each individual cylinder a rated bmep which cannot be exceeded without overloading the cylinder. If engine rpm drops below the rated speed, then the cylinder bmep generally drops to a lower value. The bmep should never exceed the normal mean effective pressure (mep) at lower engine speed. Usually, it should be somewhat lower if the engine speed is decreased.

Some engine manufacturers design the fuel systems so that rated bmep cannot be exceeded to any extent. By installing a positive stop to limit the maximum throttle or fuel control, the maximum amount of fuel that can enter the cylinder is regulated and, therefore, the maximum load of the cylinder is kept within the rated bmep.

Some engines are rated as lower than those for industrial use, in order to meet emergency situations. The economical speed for most of these diesel engines is approximately 90% of the rated speed. For this speed the best load conditions have been found to be from 70% to 80% of the rated load or output. On this basis, if an engine is operated at an 80-90 combination (80% of rated load at 90% rated speed), the parts will give a longer life, and the engine will remain cleaner and in better operating condition.

Diesel engines do not operate well at exceedingly low bmep such as that occurring at idling speeds. You may be aware that idling an engine tends to gum up parts associated with the combustion spaces. Operating an engine at idling speeds for long periods will require cleaning and overhauling much sooner than operating at 50% to 100% of load.

SYMPTOMS OF UNBALANCE

Evidence of an unbalanced condition existing between the cylinders of an engine may be indicated by black exhaust smoke, high exhaust temperatures, high temperatures in lubricating oil and cooling water, excessive heat, or excessive vibration or unusual sound.

BLACK EXHAUST SMOKE

When the exhaust emits black smoke, it is not possible to determine immediately whether the entire engine or just one of the cylinders is overloaded. To determine which cylinder is overloaded, open the indicator cock on individual cylinders and check the color of the exhaust.

HIGH EXHAUST TEMPERATURES

When the temperatures of exhaust gases from individual cylinders become higher than normal, an overload within the cylinder is indicated. Higher than usual temperature of the gases in the exhaust header indicates that all cylinders are probably overloaded. A frequent check on the pyrometer will indicate whether each cylinder is firing properly and carrying its share of the load. Any sudden change in the exhaust temperature of any cylinder should be investigated immediately. The difference in exhaust temperatures between any two cylinders should not exceed the limits prescribed in the engine manufacturer's technical manual.

HIGH LUBRICATING OIL AND COOLING WATER TEMPERATURES

If the temperature gages for the lubricating oil and cooling water systems show an abnormal rise in the temperature, an overloaded condition may exist. The causes of an abnormal temperature in these systems should be determined and corrected immediately if engine efficiency is to be maintained.

EXCESSIVE HEAT

In general, excessive heat in any part of the engine may indicate overloading. An overheated bearing may be the result from overloading the engine as a whole.

EXCESSIVE VIBRATION OR UNUSUAL SOUND

If all cylinders are not developing an equal amount of power, the forces exerted by individual pistons will be unequal. When this occurs, the unequal forces may cause an uneven turning moment to be exerted on the crankshaft, and vibrations will be set up. Through experience, you can learn to tell by the vibrations and sound of an engine when a poor distribution of load exists. Use every opportunity possible to observe engines running under all conditions of loading and performance.

CAUSES OF UNBALANCE

An engine must be kept in excellent mechanical condition if unbalance is to be prevented. A leaky valve or fuel injector, leaky compression rings, or any other such mechanical difficulties will make it impossible for you to balance the load unless you secure the engine and dismantle at least a part of it. In other words, an engine must be placed in proper mechanical condition before the load can be balanced.

To obtain equal load distribution between individual cylinders, the clearances, tolerances, and general condition of all parts that affect the cycle must be maintained so that very little, if any, vibration exists between individual cylinders. In this connection, unbalance will occur unless the following are as nearly alike as possible for all cylinders:

1. Compression pressures
2. Fuel injection timing
3. Quantity and quality of fuel injected
4. Firing pressures
5. Valve timing and lift

Chapter 2—BASIC PRINCIPLES

When unbalance occurs, correction usually involves repair, replacement, or adjustment of the affected part or system. Before any adjustments are made to eliminate unbalance, it must be determined beyond all doubt that the engine is in proper mechanical condition. When an engine is in good mechanical condition, few, if any, adjustments will be required. However, after an overhaul in which piston rings or cylinder liners have been renewed, considerable adjustment may be necessary. Until the rings become properly seated, some lubricating oil will leak past the rings into the combustion space. This excess oil will burn in the cylinder, giving an incorrect indication of fuel oil combustion. If the fuel pump is set for normal compression and the rings have not seated properly, the engine will become overloaded. As the compression rises to normal pressures, there will be an increase in the power developed, as well as in the pressure and temperature under which the combustion takes place. Therefore, when an overhaul has been completed, the engine instruments must be carefully watched until the rings are seated and adjustments are made as necessary. Frequent compression tests will serve as a helpful aid in making the necessary adjustments. Unless an engine is equipped so that compression can be readily varied, the engine should be operated under light load until you are sure that the rings are properly seated.

EFFECT OF UNBALANCE

From the preceding discussion you can readily see that, in general, the result of unbalance will be overheating of the engine. The clearances established by the engine designer allow for sufficient expansion of the moving parts when the engine is operating at the designed temperatures, but an engine operating at temperatures in excess of those for which it was designed is subject to many casualties. Excessive expansion soon leads to seizure and burning of the engine parts. If the temperatures rise above the flashpoint of the lubricating oil vapors in the crankcase, an explosion may result. High temperature may destroy the oil film between adjacent parts, and the resulting increased friction will further increase the temperature.

Since power is directly proportional to the mean effective pressure developed in a cylinder, any increase in mean effective pressure will cause a corresponding increase in power. If the mean effective pressures in the individual cylinders vary, power will not be evenly distributed among the cylinders.

The quality of combustion obtained is dependent on the heat content of the fuel, and the amount of heat available for power is dependent on temperature. Temperature varies directly as the pressure; therefore, a decrease in pressure will result in a decrease in temperature, and in poor combustion. The results of poor combustion will be lowered thermal efficiency and reduced engine output.

Cylinder load balance is essential to obtain the desired efficiency and performance of an engine. To avoid the harmful effects of overloading and unbalancing of load, the load on an engine should be properly distributed among the working cylinders; no cylinder, or the engine itself, should ever be overloaded.

In general, load balance in an engine can be maintained if the following procedures are observed:

1. Maintain the engine in proper mechanical condition.
2. Adjust the fuel system according to the manufacturer's instructions.
3. Operate the engine within the temperature limits specified in appropriate instructions.
4. Keep cylinder temperatures and pressures as evenly distributed as possible.
5. Train yourself to recognize the symptoms of serious engine conditions.

ENGINE EFFICIENCY

Engine efficiency is the amount of power developed compared to the energy input which is measured by the heating value of the fuel consumed. In other words, the term "efficiency" is used to designate the relationship between the result obtained and the effort expended to produce the result.

DIESEL ENGINES

The term "compression ratio" is frequently used in connection with engine performance and the various types of efficiencies. From your study of the first part of this chapter, you will recall that compression ratio is the ratio of the volume of air above the piston when it is at the bottom dead center position to the volume of air above the piston when it is at the top dead center position.

The principal efficiencies considered in the internal-combustion process are cycle, thermal, mechanical, and volumetric.

CYCLE EFFICIENCY

The efficiency of any cycle is equal to the output divided by the input. The efficiency of the diesel cycle is considerably higher than the otto or constant-volume cycle because of the higher compression ratio and because combustion starts at a higher temperature. In other words, the heat input is at a higher average temperature. Theoretically, the gasoline engine using the otto cycle could be more efficient than the diesel engine if equivalent compression ratios could be used. However, in practice, engines operating on the otto cycle cannot use a compression ratio comparable to those of diesel engines because the fuel and air are drawn into the cylinder together and compressed. If comparable compression ratios were used, the fuel would fire or detonate before the piston reached the correct firing position.

Since temperature and amount of heat content which is available for power are proportional to each other, the cycle efficiency is actually computed from measurements made of the temperature. The specific heat of the mixture in the cylinder is either known or assumed and, when combined with the temperature, the heat can be calculated at any instant.

THERMAL EFFICIENCY

Thermal efficiency may be regarded as a measure of the efficiency and completeness of combustion of the fuel or, more specifically, the ratio of the output or work done by the working substance in the cylinder in a given time to the input or heat energy of the fuel supplied during the same time. Generally, two kinds of thermal efficiency are considered for an engine: indicated thermal efficiency and overall thermal efficiency.

Indicated Thermal Efficiency

Since the work done by the gases in the cylinder is called indicated work, the thermal efficiency determined by its use is often called indicated thermal efficiency. If all the potential heat in the fuel could be delivered as work, the thermal efficiency would be 100%. Because of the various losses, this percentage is not possible in actual installations.

If the amount of fuel injected is known, the total heat content of the injected fuel can be determined from the heating value, or Btu per pound, of the fuel; the thermal efficiencies for the engine can then be calculated. From the mechanical equivalent of heat (778 foot-pounds = 1 Btu and 2545 Btu = 1 hp-hr), the number of foot-pounds of work contained in the fuel can be computed. If the amount of fuel injected is measured over a period of time, the rate at which the heat is put into the engine can be converted into potential power. Then, if the indicated horsepower developed by the engine is calculated as previously explained, the indicated thermal efficiency (ite) can be computed as:

Indicated thermal efficiency

$$= \frac{\text{Indicated hp} \times 2545 \text{ Btu per hr per hp}}{\text{Rate of heat input of fuel in Btu per hr}} \times 100 \quad (2.14)$$

Example 2Q: Assume that the same engine used as an example in computing indicated horsepower consumes 360 lb (approximately 50 gallons) of fuel per hour, and the fuel has a value of 19,200 Btu per pound. What is the indicated thermal efficiency of the engine?

The work done per hour when 1343 ihp are developed is 1343 × 2545 or 3,417,935 Btu. The heat input for the same time is 360 × 19,200, or 6,912,000 Btu. Then, by equation (2.14) the indicated thermal efficiency is

$$\text{ite} = \frac{1343 \times 2545}{360 \times 19,200} \times 100$$

$$= \frac{3,417,935}{6,912,000} \times 100 = 49.4\%$$

Chapter 2—BASIC PRINCIPLES

Overall Thermal Efficiency

The other type of thermal efficiency—overall thermal efficiency—considered for an engine is a ratio similar to indicated thermal efficiency, except that the useful or shaft work (brake horsepower) is used. Therefore, overall efficiency (often called brake thermal efficiency) is computed as:

$$\text{overall thermal efficiency} = \frac{\text{brake horsepower}}{\text{heat input of fuel}} \times 100 \quad (2.15)$$

Converting these factors into the same units (Btu), the equation is written as power output in Btu divided by fuel input in Btu.

Example 2R: If the engine used in example 2Q delivers 900 brake horsepower (determined by the manufacturer), what is the overall thermal efficiency of the engine?

$$1 \text{ hp-hr} = 2545 \text{ Btu}$$

$$900 \text{ bhp} \times 2545 \text{ Btu per hp-hr}$$

$$= 2{,}290{,}500 \text{ Btu output per hr}$$

Substituting factors already known, overall thermal efficiency is computed as follows:

$$\text{overall thermal efficiency} = \frac{2{,}290{,}500}{6{,}912{,}000} = 0.331, \text{ or } 33.1\%$$

Compression ratio influences the thermal efficiency of an engine. Theoretically, the thermal efficiency increases as the compression ratio is increased. The minimum value of a diesel engine compression ratio is determined by the compression required for starting; this compression is, to a large extent, dependent on the type of fuel used. The maximum value of the compression ratio is not limited by the fuel used, but is limited by the strength of the engine parts and the allowable engine weight per brake-horsepower output.

MECHANICAL EFFICIENCY

Mechanical efficiency is the rating that shows how much of the power developed by the expansion of the gases in the cylinder is actually delivered as useful power. The factor that has the greatest effect on mechanical efficiency is friction within the engine. The friction among moving parts in an engine remains practically constant throughout the engine's speed range. Therefore, the mechanical efficiency of an engine will be highest when the engine is running at the speed at which maximum brake horsepower is developed. Since power output is brake horsepower, and the maximum horsepower available is indicated horsepower, then

$$\text{mechanical efficiency} = \frac{\text{brake hp}}{\text{indicated hp}} \times 100 \quad (2.16)$$

During the transmission of indicated horsepower through the piston and connecting rod to the crankshaft, the mechanical losses which occur may be due to friction, or they may be due to power absorbed. Friction losses occur because of friction in the various bearings, or between piston and piston rings and the cylinder walls. Power is also absorbed by valve and injection mechanisms and by various auxiliaries, such as the lubricating oil and water circulating pumps and the scavenge and supercharge blowers. As a result, the power available for doing useful work (bhp) is less than indicated power.

The mechanical losses which affect the efficiency of an engine may be called frictional horsepower (fhp) or the difference between ihp and bhp. The fhp of the engine used in the preceding examples, then, would be 1343 ihp - 900 bhp = 443 fhp, or 33% of the ihp developed in the cylinders. Then, using the equation for mechanical efficiency, the percentage of power available at the shaft is computed as:

$$\text{mechanical efficiency} = \frac{900}{1343} = 0.67 \text{ or } 67\%$$

When an engine is operating under part load, it has a lower mechanical efficiency than when operating at full load. The explanation of this is that most mechanical losses are almost independent of the load and, therefore, when load decreases, ihp decreases relatively less than bhp. Mechanical efficiency becomes zero when an engine operates at no load because then bhp = 0, but ihp is not zero. In fact, if bhp is zero and the expression for fhp is used, ihp is equal to fhp.

To show how mechanical efficiency is lower at part load, assume the engine used in preceding examples is operating at 3/4 load. Brake horsepower at 3/4 load is 900 X 0.75 or 675. Assuming that fhp does not change with load, fhp = 443. The ihp is, by expression, the sum of bhp and fhp.

$$ihp = 675 + 443 = 1118$$

$$\text{mechanical efficiency} = 675 \div 1118$$

$$= 0.60 \text{ or } 60\%$$

This is appreciably lower than the 67% indicated for the engine at full load.

VOLUMETRIC EFFICIENCY

The term volumetric efficiency applies to 4-stroke engines. It is an indication of the efficiency of the air intake system. An engine would have 100% volumetric efficiency if an amount of air exactly equal to piston displacement could be drawn into the cylinder. This is not possible, except by supercharging, because the passages through which the air must flow offer a resistance, the force pushing the air into the cylinder is only atmospheric, and the air absorbs heat during the process. Therefore, volumetric efficiency is determined by measuring (with an orifice or venturi-type meter) the amount of air taken in by the engine, converting the amount to volume, and comparing this volume to the piston displacement.

$$\text{volumetric efficiency} = \frac{\text{volume of air admitted to cylinder}}{\text{volume of air equal to piston displacement}} \times 100$$

(2.17)

SCAVENGE EFFICIENCY

The concept of volumetric efficiency does not apply to 2-stroke cycle engines. Instead, the term "scavenge efficiency" is used, which shows how thoroughly the burned gases are removed and the cylinder filled with fresh air. As in the case of a 4-stroke cycle engine, it is desirable that the air supply be sufficiently cool. Scavenge efficiency depends largely upon the arrangement of the exhaust, scavenge air ports, and valves.

ENGINE LOSSES

As the heat content of a fuel is transformed into useful work, during the combustion process, many different losses take place. These losses can be divided into two general classifications: thermodynamic and mechanical. The net useful work delivered by an engine is the result obtained by deducting the total losses from the heat energy input.

Thermodynamic Losses

Thermodynamic losses of this nature are a result of: loss to the cooling and lubricating systems; loss to the surrounding air; loss to the exhaust; and loss due to lack of perfect combustion.

Heat energy losses from both the cooling water system and the lubricating oil system are always present. Some heat is conducted through the engine parts and radiated to the atmosphere or picked up by the surrounding air by convection. The effect of these losses varies according to the part of the cycle in which they occur. The heat of the jacket cooling water cannot be taken as a true measure of heat losses since all this heat is not absorbed by the water. Some heat is lost to the jackets during the compression, combustion, and expansion phases of the cycle; some is lost (to the atmosphere) during the exhaust stroke; and some is absorbed by the walls of the exhaust passages.

Heat losses to the atmosphere through the exhaust are unavoidable because the engine cylinder must be cleared of the hot exhaust gases before the next air intake charge can be made. The heat lost to the exhaust is determined by the temperature within the cylinder when exhaust begins. The amount of fuel injected and the weight of air compressed within the cylinder are controlling factors. Improper timing of the exhaust valves, whether early or late, will result in increased heat losses. If early, the valve releases the pressure in the cylinder before all the available work is obtained; if late, the

Chapter 2—BASIC PRINCIPLES

necessary amount of air for complete combustion of the next charge cannot be realized although a small amount of additional work may be obtained. Proper timing and seating of the valves is essential to maintain heat loss to the exhaust at a minimum.

Heat losses due to imperfect or incomplete combustion have a serious effect on the power that can be developed in the cylinder. Because of the short interval of time necessary for the cycle in modern engines, complete combustion is not possible; but heat losses can be kept to a minimum if the engine is kept in proper adjustment. It is often possible to detect incomplete combustion by watching for abnormal exhaust temperatures and changes in the exhaust color and by being alert for unusual noises in the engine.

Mechanical Losses

There are several kinds of mechanical losses, but all are not present in every engine. The mechanical or friction losses of an engine include bearing friction; piston and piston ring friction; pumping losses caused by operation of water pumps, lubricating pumps, and scavenging air blowers; power required to operate valves; etc. Friction losses cannot be eliminated, but they can be kept to a minimum by maintaining the engine in its best mechanical condition. Bearings, pistons, and piston rings should be properly installed and fitted, shafts must be in alignment, and lubricating and cooling systems should be at their highest operating efficiency.

Remember that the total of these mechanical losses must be deducted from ihp of the engine in order to determine actual bhp.

PETROLEUM PRODUCTS

FUELS

Except in an emergency, the fuels burned in the internal-combustion engines must meet the specifications prescribed. Thus, the problem of selecting a fuel which has the required properties is not your responsibility. Your primary responsibility is to follow the rules and regulations dealing with the proper use of fuels. Strict adherence to prescribed safety precaution is required. Also, every possible precaution must be taken to keep fuel as free from impurities as possible.

Fuels are generally delivered clean and free from impurities. However, the transfer and handling of fuel increase the danger of fuel's becoming contaminated with foreign material which interfers with engine performance. Foreign substances such as sediment and water cause wear, gumming, and corrosion in the fuel system. Foreign material in fuel also causes an engine to operate erratically with a power loss. For these reasons, the necessity for periodic inspection, cleaning, and maintenance of fuel handling and filtering equipment must be kept constantly in mind.

Even though proper handling and use is your prime responsibility with respect to fuel, a knowledge of fuels and their characteristics will make problems encountered in engine operation and maintenance more readily understood.

DIESEL ENGINE FUEL OIL

In the past, fuel normally used in diesel engines was diesel fuel oil, but other fuels such as JP-5 and some distillate fuels have been authorized for use in diesel engines when it would be a logistic advantage. At present, most ships carry a distillate fuel oil for boilers and JP-5 for diesel engines. Because of the increased concern, and need to know, to control environmental pollution distillate fuel will be used for both types of propulsion plants.

Some distillate fuel burns more completely and cleaner, leaving fewer carbon deposits. This not only helps reduce air pollution, but reduces the time spent cleaning, such as burners and firesides in the boiler and eliminates the need for carrying different types of fuel.

Because of the differences in the combustion processes and in the fuel systems of diesel and gasoline engines, the fuels for these engines must be refined to meet different requirements. In general, diesel engines require a fuel which is particularly clean; otherwise, the closely fitted parts of the injection equipment will wear rapidly and the small passages which create the fuel spray within the cylinders will become clogged. The composition of diesel fuel oil must be such that it can be injected into the cylinders in a fine mist of fog. Ignition qualities must be such that the fuel will ignite properly and burn rapidly when it is injected into the cylinders.

The self-ignition point of a fuel is a function of temperature, pressure, and time. In a diesel engine that is operating properly, the intake air is compressed to a high pressure (thus increasing the temperature), and the injection of fuel starts a few degrees before the piston reaches TDC. The fuel is ignited by the heat of compression shortly after the fuel injection starts, and combustion continues throughout the injection period. Combustion is much slower than in a gasoline engine, and the rate of pressure rise is relatively small.

After injection, the first effect on the fuel is a partial evaporation with a resultant chilling of the air in the immediate vicinity of each fuel particle. However, the extreme heat of compression rapidly heats the fuel particles to the self-ignition point and combustion begins. The fuel particles burn as they mix with the air, the smaller particles burning rapidly, and the larger particles taking more time to ignite because heat must be transferred into them to bring them to the self-ignition point.

There is always some delay between the time that fuel is injected and the time that it reaches the self-ignition point. This delay is commonly referred to as "ignition delay," or "lag." The duration of the ignition delay is dependent on the characteristics of the fuel, the temperature and pressure of the compressed air in the combustion space, the average size of the fuel particles, and the amount of turbulence present in the space. As combustion progresses, the temperature and pressure within the space rise; thus, the ignition delay of fuel particles injected late in the combustion process is less than in those injected earlier. The delay period between the start of injection and the start of self-ignition is sometimes referred to as the first phase of combustion in a diesel engine. The second phase of combustion includes ignition of the fuel injected during the first phase, and the spread of the flame through the combustion space, as injection continues. The resulting increases in temperature and in pressure reduce the ignition lag for the fuel particles entering the combustion space during the remainder of the injection period.

Remember that only a portion of the fuel has been injected during the first and second phases. As the remainder of the fuel is injected, the third and final phase of combustion takes place. The increase in both temperature and pressure during the second phase and progression into the third phase are sufficient to cause most of the remaining fuel particles to ignite, with practically no delay, as they come from the injection equipment. The rapid burning during the final phase of combustion causes an additional, rapid increase in pressure, which is accompanied by a distinct and audible knock. A knock so caused is characteristic of normal diesel operation, particularly at light loads.

The knock that occurs during the normal operation of a diesel engine should not be confused with "detonation." Detonation in a diesel engine is generally an instantaneous explosion of a greater than normal quantity of fuel in the cylinder, instead of only a portion of the fuel charge (as in the gasoline engine). Whether combustion is normal or whether detonation occurs is determined by the amount of fuel that ignites at one time, the greater the pressure rise and the more severe the knock. Detonation in a diesel engine is generally caused by too much delay in ignition. The delay can be the result of poor injector timing or cold combustion spaces—the greater the delay, the greater the amount of fuel that accumulates in the cylinder before ignition. When the ignition point of the excess fuel is reached, all of this fuel ignites simultaneously, causing extremely high pressures in the cylinder and an undesirable knock. Thus, detonation in a diesel generally occurs at what is normally considered the start of the second phase of combustion, instead of during the final phase, as in a gasoline engine. Detonation in a diesel engine may occur when the engine is not warmed up sufficiently, when fuel injection is timed too late or too early, or when leaking injection valves permit excessive fuel to accumulate in the cylinder.

Even though diesel fuel must have the ability to resist detonation, it must ignite spontaneously at the proper time under the

Chapter 2—BASIC PRINCIPLES

pressure and temperature conditions existing in the cylinder. The ease with which a diesel fuel oil will ignite and the manner in which it burns determine the ignition quality of the fuel. The ignition quality of a fuel is determined by its cetane rating, or CETANE VALUE. The cetane value of a fuel is a measure of the ease with which the fuel will ignite. The cetane rating of any given fuel is identified by its cetane number—the higher the cetane number, the less the lag between the time the fuel enters the cylinder and the time it begins to burn.

The cetane rating of a diesel fuel is determined in a manner similar to that used to determine the octane value of gasoline. However, the hydrocarbons used for the reference fuel are cetane and alpha-methyl-napthaline. Cetane has an excellent ignition quality (100) and alpha-methyl-napthaline has a very poor ignition quality (zero). By comparing the performance of a reference fuel with that of a fuel whose ignition quality is unknown, the unknown cetane rating or number can be determined. The cetane number represents the percentage of pure cetane in a reference fuel which will just match the ignition quality of the fuel being tested—the higher the cetane number, the quicker burning the fuel, and the better the fuel from the standpoint of ignition and combustion.

ENGINE LUBRICANTS

Lubrication is as important to successful engine operation as air, fuel, and heat are to combustion. Lubrication is frequently considered one of the most important factors in efficient engine operation. It is important that the proper type of lubricant be used, that the lubricant be supplied to the engine parts in the proper quantities at the proper temperature, and that provisions be made to remove any impurities that enter the system.

It is essential to the operation of an engine that the contacting surfaces of all moving parts of an engine be kept free from abrasion and that friction and wear be kept to a minimum. If sliding contact is made by two dry metal surfaces under pressure, excessive friction, heat, and wear will result. Friction, heat, and wear can be greatly reduced if metal-to-metal contact is prevented by a clean film of lubricant between the metal surfaces. The necessary film between the bearing surfaces in naval machinery is provided by either a specified oil or grease.

OILS

A lubricating oil with the necessary properties and characteristics will: (1) provide a film of proper thickness between the bearing surfaces, under all conditions of operation; (2) remain stable under changing temperature conditions; and (3) prevent corrosion of the metal surfaces. If the lubricating oil is to meet these requirements, the engine temperature during operation must NOT be allowed to exceed a specified limit.

In addition to preventing metal-to-metal contact, the lubricating oil is required to: (1) form a seal between the piston rings and the cylinder wall, (2) aid in engine cooling, and (3) aid in keeping the inside of the engine free of sludge.

A direct metal-to-metal moving contact has an action comparable to a filing action. The filing action is due to minute irregularities in the surfaces, and the severity of the action depends on the finish of the surfaces and the force with which the surfaces are brought into contact, as well as on the relative hardness of the materials used. Lubricating oil fills the minute cavities in bearing surfaces, thereby preventing high friction losses, rapid wear of engine parts, and many other operating difficulties. Lack of a proper oil film results in seized, or frozen, pistons, wiped bearings, and stuck piston rings.

Lubricating oil assists in cooling the engine by transferring or carrying away heat from localized hot spots in the engine. The principal parts from which oil absorbs heat are the bearings, the journal surfaces, and the pistons. In some engines the oil carries the heat to the sump where the heat dissipates in the mass of oil. However, most modern internal-combustion engines use a centralized pressure-feed lubrication system. This type of system incorporates an oil cooler or heat exchanger where the heat from the oil is transferred to the circulating water of the cooling system.

Causes of Sludge

Almost any type of gummy or carbonaceous material that accumulates in lubricating oil is called sludge. Most engine lubricating oils have some natural ability for preventing conditions that may cause sludge to form and for carrying sludge that does form in a finely suspended state until it is removed by filtering equipment. Chemicals are added to some oils to improve their ability to prevent and to remove sludge.

The formation of sludge is greatly reduced if the lubricating oil has the proper stability. Proper stability is essential if a strong oil film, or body of oil, is to be maintained under varying temperature conditions. Stability of the oil should be such that a proper oil film is maintained throughout the entire operating temperature range of the engine. Such a film will ensure sufficient oiliness, or film strength, between the piston and the cylinder wall so that partly burned fuel and exhaust gases cannot get by the piston rings to form sludge.

Various factors may tend to cause sludge to form in an engine. Carbon from the combustion chambers or from the evaporation of oil on a hot surface, such as on the underside of a piston, will cause the formation of sludge. Gummy, partially burned fuel, which gets past the piston rings, or an emulsion of lubricating oil and water, which may enter the lubricating oil system, will also tend to cause sludge.

Effects of Sludge

Sludge in the lubricating oil system of an engine is harmful for several reasons. In addition to carbon and gummy material, sludge may contain abrasive ingredients, such as dust from the atmosphere; rust caused by water condensation in the engine; and metallic particles resulting from wear of engine parts. Sludge in engine lubricating oil causes premature wear of parts and eventual breakdown of the engine. Sludge may clog the oil pump screen or collect at the end of the oil passage leading to a bearing, thereby preventing sufficient oil's reaching the parts to be lubricated. Sludge will coat the inside of the crankcase, act as insulation, blanket the heat inside the engine, raise the oil temperature, and induce oxidation. Sludge will accumulate on the underside of the pistons and prevent proper heat transfer, thereby raising piston temperatures. Sludge in lubricating oil also contributes to piston ring sticking.

OIL CHARACTERISTICS AND TESTS

Lubricants are tested for viscosity, pour point, flashpoint, fire point, autogenous ignition point, neutralization number, demulsibility, and precipitation number. The lubricants must meet the following requirements.

1. They must have a suitable viscosity at the operating temperature of the bearing being lubricated.
2. They must form durable boundary films on the metal rubbing surfaces.
3. They must not chemically attack the journal or the bearing metals.
4. They must not change chemical composition with use.

Chapter 9 contains more information on lubricating oil systems, purification of oil, testing, and handling of oils.

GREASES

Greases are used in certain places where oil will not provide proper lubrication. Operating temperatures, the rate at which lubrication must be supplied, and the design of the equipment may make the use of oil impractical. At points where oil will not provide proper lubrication, machinery manufacturers have installed fittings, either pressure type or the cup type for applying grease of the proper type and grade. The location of grease fittings and the type of grease required are shown on machinery lubrication charts and in manufacturers' technical manuals. It is important that you follow lubrication instructions, since some greases are of the type developed for general use and others are developed for special purposes. Maintenance problems involving lubrication will be more

Chapter 2—BASIC PRINCIPLES

readily understood if you are familiar with the principal factors related to the composition and classification of greases.

SUMMARY

In this chapter we have dealt with the basic principles related to diesel engines. A knowledge of basic physics associated with diesel engines not only helps you in understanding internal workings of an engine, but can also be very useful to you in troubleshooting diesel engines.

A thorough understanding of engine mechanics in diesel engines allows you to see how various stress factors such as piston speed, torsion and inertia play an important part in limiting the capabilities of a diesel engine.

Although there are limits to what a diesel engine can do, the operator's knowledge of engine performance and how to get maximum efficiency from an engine are extremely important in getting maximum endurance and reliability from diesel-driven vehicles. Various losses affect engine performance and efficiency. Some are inherent and cannot be removed. Other losses can be overcome, thereby adding to better overall engine operation.

The correct selection, use, testing and handling of petroleum products are vital to long diesel engine life and good overall performance. Knowledge of petroleum products forms an integral part of diesel engine technology.

CHAPTER 3

RECIPROCATING INTERNAL-COMBUSTION ENGINES

There are many similarities in the appearance of small diesel engines and the larger gasoline engines. Some basic design considerations are common to both types of reciprocating engines. Valve gear is required on both, and the basic crank and piston arrangements are similar although the diesel engine components are heavier and stronger. In this chapter we shall explore the specific functions that occur in the diesel engine. The principal functional difference between the diesel and gasoline engine is that the diesel engine has its fuel forcibly injected into the top of the cylinder, while the gasoline engine takes in a mixture of air and gasoline vapor which it ignites at the top of the cylinder with a spark ignition system.

In this chapter we shall discuss only diesel engines, but we shall make some comparisons with gasoline engines.

Modern designs permit more powerful and lighter weight diesel engines. Diesel engines in service range from 5 horsepower up to 3000 horsepower engines for ship propulsion. Within this range diesel engines vary greatly in appearance, size, number of cylinders, cylinder arrangement, and details of construction.

Some designs of diesel engines reflect major differences in principles of operation, which we shall discuss in this chapter.

Three basic engine designs are used—

They are the in-line type, the V-type, and the opposed-piston type.

IN-LINE TYPE ENGINE

The in-line type is the simplest arrangement with all cylinders parallel and in line, as shown in figure 3-1. This construction is limited in respect to its length. The longer the engine, the more difficult it is to make a sufficiently rigid frame and crankshaft.

In-line diesel engines rarely have more than six cylinders, and those engines which have more require special designs which usually add to the weight of the engine.

The in-line design is normally used for engines that have no more than eight cylinders.

V-TYPE ENGINE

The V-type engine (figure 3-2) with two connecting rods attached to each crankpin permits the entire length to be reduced by one-half, thus making it much more rigid with a stiff crankshaft. This is a common arrangement

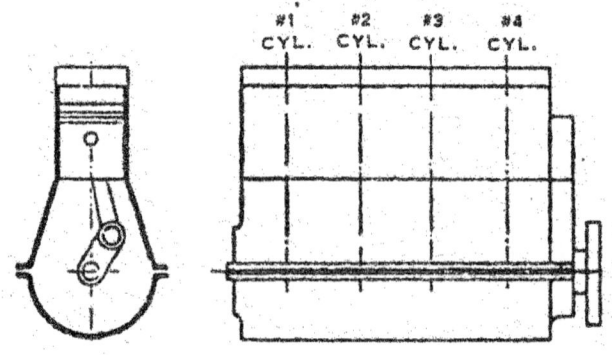

256.4

Figure 3-1.—In-line type diesel engine.

Chapter 3—RECIPROCATING INTERNAL-COMBUSTION ENGINES

(upper and lower) are required for transmission of power. Both shafts contribute to the power output of the engine. In most opposed-piston engines, crankshafts are connected by a vertical drive (figure 3-3).

ENGINE DESIGNATION

Engines are designated by the number of cylinders, bore, stroke, and speed, if

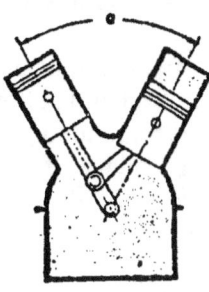

Figure 3-2.—V-type diesel engines.

256.5

for engines with 8 to 16 cylinders. Cylinders lying in one plane are called a bank, and the angle a between the banks may vary from 30° to 120°, the most common angle being between 40° and 75°.

OPPOSED-PISTON ENGINE

Engines of the opposed-piston type are not to be confused with engines of the "flat" or 180° V-type. Flat engines have two rows of cylinders in a horizontal plane with one crankshaft, located between the rows, which serves both rows of cylinders. This type engine is single-acting and is sometimes referred to as a horizontal-opposed engine (the term is based on cylinder arrangement). With respect to combustion-gas action, the term OPPOSED-PISTON identifies those engines which have TWO PISTONS and ONE COMBUSTION SPACE in each cylinder. The pistons are arranged in "opposed" positions; that is, crown to crown, with the combustion space in between (figure 3-3). When combustion takes place, the gases act against the crowns of both pistons, driving them in opposite directions. Thus, the term "opposed" not only signifies that, with respect to pressure and piston surfaces, the gases act in "opposite" directions, but also classifies the piston arrangement within the cylinder.

In modern engines that have the opposed-piston arrangement, two crankshafts

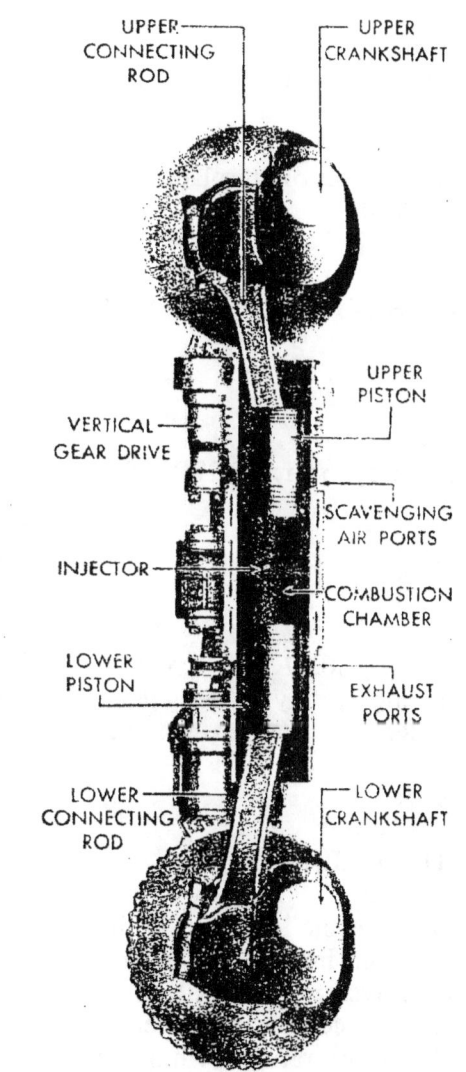

75.8
Figure 3-3.—Opposed-piston type diesel engine.

135

the engine operates at a definite speed, in the order named. Thus a 6-cylinder X 3 3/4 in. X 5 in. X 1,500 rpm (often written simply as 6 X 3 3/4 X 5 X 1,500) designation means an engine with 6 cylinders, a 3/4-in. bore, 5-in. stroke, that is normally operated at 1,500 rpm.

Another designation is by PISTON DISPLACEMENT, or, for short, by displacement. To find the engine displacement, multiply the piston area times the piston stroke times the number of cylinders. (Engine displacement is not concerned with engine speed.) In English units, displacement is expressed in cubic inches. Sometimes the displacement is indicated as the number of cylinders and the displacement of only one cylinder.

Example: Find the piston displacement of an 8 X 8 X 10 X 720 naval engine.

Piston area: $\pi r^2 = 3.14159 \times \frac{(8)^2}{(2)} = 50.27$ sq. in.

Stroke: 10 in.

Displacement of one cylinder: 50.27 X 10 = 502.7 cu in.

Number of cylinders: 8

therefore

Total displacement = 50.27 X 10 X 8 = 4,021.6 cu. in. or the engine may be designated as 8-503 to avoid decimal fractions in the designation.

CYCLES OF OPERATION

The operation of an engine involves (1) the admission of fuel and air into a combustion space and (2) the compression and ignition of the charge. The resulting combustion releases gases and increases the temperature within the space. As temperature increases, pressure increases and forces the piston to move. The piston movement is transmitted to a rotating shaft. The rotary motion of the shaft is used to perform work; thus, heat energy is transformed into useful mechanical energy. In order for the process to be continuous, the expanded gases must be removed from the combustion space, a new charge must be admitted, and then the process must be repeated.

In the process of engine operation, beginning with the admission of air and fuel and following through to the removal of the expanded gases, a series of events or phases take place. The term "cycle" identifies the sequence of events that takes place in the cylinder of an engine for each power impulse transmitted to the crankshaft. These events always occur in the same order each time the cycle is repeated.

The mechanics of engine operation is sometimes referred to as the MECHANICAL (or operating) CYCLE of an engine, while the heat process, which produces the forces that move engine parts, may be referred to as the COMBUSTION CYCLE. A cycle of each type is included in a cycle of engine operation.

MECHANICAL CYCLES

In the preceding paragraphs, we emphasized the events taking place in a cycle of engine operation. Little was said about piston strokes except that a complete sequence of events will occur during a cycle regardless of the number of strokes made by the piston. The number of piston strokes occurring during any one series of events is limited to either two or four, dependent on the design of the engine. Thus, we have a 4-stroke cycle and a 2-stroke cycle. These cycles are known as the mechanical cycles of operation.

The terms "4-stroke" and "2-stroke" identify a cycle of events; also, both types of mechanical cycles are used in both four- and two-stroke cycle reciprocating engines. You should be familiar with the principal differences in these cycles. The relationship of the events and piston strokes occurring in a cycle of operation involves some of these differences.

Relationship of Events and Strokes in a Cycle

You have learned that a piston stroke is the movement of a piston between its limits of

Chapter 3—RECIPROCATING INTERNAL-COMBUSTION ENGINES

travel. Now we shall discuss the cycles of engine operation.

An engine operating on a 4-stroke cycle involves four piston strokes—INTAKE, COMPRESSION, POWER, and EXHAUST. An engine operating on a 2-stroke cycle involves two piston strokes—POWER and COMPRESSION.

In figure 3-4, the strokes are named to correspond to the events which occur in particular strokes. However, six events are listed for diesel engines (there are five events for gasoline engines), so it is evident that more than one event takes place during some of the strokes, especially in the 2-stroke cycle. Even so, it is common practice to identify some of the events as strokes of the piston because such events as intake, compression, power, and exhaust in a 4-stroke cycle involve at least a major portion of a stroke and, in some cases, more than one stroke. The same is true of power and compression events and strokes in a 2-stroke cycle. Such relationship between events and strokes ignores other events which are also taking place during the cycle of operation. This feature of the event-stroke relationship sometimes leads to confusion when one studies the operation of an engine or deals with maintenance problems involving the timing of fuel injection systems.

4-STROKE CYCLE.—To point out the relation between events and strokes, our discussion will cover the events which occur during a specific stroke, the duration of an event with respect to a piston stroke, and the cases where one event overlaps another. The relationship of events and strokes can be shown best by a graphic presentation of the changing situation occurring in a cylinder during a cycle of operation. Figure 3-4 illustrates these changes for a 4-stroke cycle diesel engine.

The relationship of events and strokes is more readily understood if the movements of a piston and its crankshaft are considered first. In figure 3-4A, the travel of a piston during two piston strokes, is shown along with the rotary motion of the crank. The positions of the piston and crank at the start and end of a stroke are marked "top" and "bottom," respectively. If these positions and movements are marked on a circle (figure 3-4B), the piston position at the top of a stroke is located at the top of the circle. When the piston is at the bottom of a stroke, the piston position is located at the bottom center of the circle. Top center and bottom center are two terms which you will encounter frequently when discussing the timing of fuel injection systems. Note in both A and B of figure 3-4 that top center and bottom center identify points where the piston changes its direction of motion. In other words, when the piston is at top center, upward motion has stopped and downward motion is ready to start or, with respect to motion, the piston is "dead." The points which designate changes in direction of motion for a piston and crank are frequently called TOP DEAD CENTER (TDC) and BOTTOM DEAD CENTER (BDC).

If the circle illustrated in figure 3-4C is broken at various points and "spread out," the events of a cycle and their relationship to the strokes can be shown, including how some of the events of the cycle overlap. TDC and BDC should be kept in mind since they identify the start and end of a STROKE, and they are the points from which the start and end of EVENTS are established.

By following the strokes and events as illustrated, you will see that the intake event starts before TDC, or before the actual down stroke (intake) starts, and continues on past BDC, or beyond the end of the stroke. The compression event starts when the intake event ends, but the upstroke (compression) has been in process since BDC. The injection and ignition events overlap with the latter part of the compression event, which ends at TDC. The fuel continues to burn until a few degrees past TDC. The power event or expansion of gases ends several degrees before the down (power) stroke ends at BDC. The exhaust event starts when the power event ends and continues through the complete upstroke (exhaust) and past TDC. Note that the exhaust event overlaps with the intake event of the next cycle. The details on why certain events overlap and why some events are shorter or longer with respect to strokes will be given later in this text.

From the preceding discussion, you can see why the term "stroke" is sometimes used to identify an event which occurs in a cycle of

DIESEL ENGINES

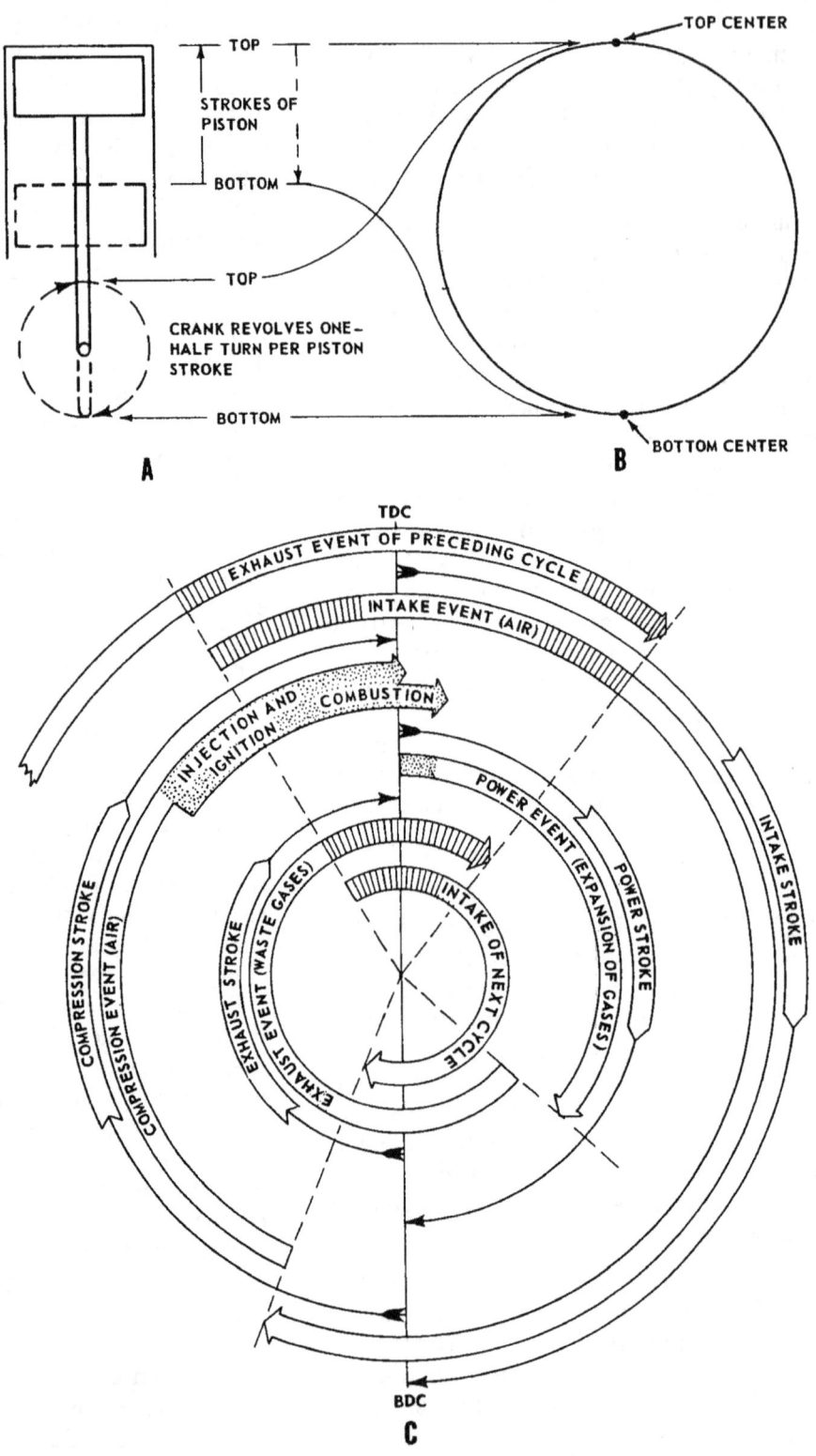

Figure 3-4.—Relationship of events and strokes in a 4-stroke cycle diesel engine.

Chapter 3—RECIPROCATING INTERNAL-COMBUSTION ENGINES

operation. However, it is best to remember that a stroke involves 180° of crankshaft rotation (or piston movement between dead centers) while the corresponding event may take place during a greater or lesser number of degrees of shaft rotation.

2-STROKE CYCLE.—The relationship of events to strokes in a 2-stroke cycle diesel engine is shown in figure 3-5. Comparison of figures 3-4 and 3-5 reveals a number of differences between the two types of mechanical or operating cycles. These differences are not too difficult to understand if you remember that four piston strokes and 720° (180° per stroke) of crankshaft rotation are involved in the 4-stroke cycle, while only half as many strokes and degrees are involved in a 2-stroke cycle. The five cross-sectional illustrations in figure 3-5 will help you to associate the event with the relative position of the piston. Even though the two piston strokes are frequently referred to as power and compression, we shall refer to them as the "downstroke" (TDC to BDC) and "upstroke" (BDC to TDC) to avoid confusion when reference is made to an event.

Starting with the admission of air, (1) in the circle in figure 3-5, we find that the piston is in the lower half of the downstroke and that the exhaust event (6) is in process. The exhaust event (6) started a number of degrees before scavenging. Both exhaust and scavenging start several degrees before the piston reaches BDC. The overlap of these events is necessary so that the incoming air (1) can aid in clearing the cylinder of exhaust gases. Note that the exhaust event stops a few degrees before the intake event stops, but several degrees after upstroke of the piston has started. (The exhaust event in some 2-stroke cycle diesel engines ends a few degrees after the intake event ends). When the scavenging event ends, the cylinder is charged with the air which is to be compressed. The compression event (2) takes place during the major portion of the upstroke. The injection event and ignition (3) and combustion (4) occur during the latter part of the upstroke. (The point at which injection ends varies with engines. In some engines, it ends before TDC; in others, a few degrees after TDC). The intense heat (approximately 1000°F) generated during the compression of the air ignites the fuel-air mixture, and the pressure resulting from combustion forces the piston down. The expansion (5) of the gases continues through a major portion of the downstroke. After the force of the gases has been expended, the exhaust valve opens (6) and permits the burned gases to enter the exhaust manifold. As the piston moves downward, the intake ports are uncovered (1), and the incoming air clears the cylinder of the remaining exhaust gases and fills the cylinder with a fresh air charge (1); thus, the cycle of operation has started again.

Now, what is the difference between the 2- and 4-stroke cycles? From the standpoint of the mechanics of operation, the principal difference is the number of piston strokes taking place during the cycle of events. A more significant difference is that a 2-stroke cycle engine delivers twice as many power impulses to the crankshaft for every 720° of shaft rotation. (See fig. 3-6.)

COMBUSTION CYCLES

To this point, we have given greater consideration to the strokes of a piston and the related events which take place during a cycle of operation than we have to the heat process involved in the cycle. However, the mechanics of engine operation cannot be discussed without dealing with heat. Such terms as ignition, combustion, and expansion of gases, all indicate that heat is essential to a cycle of engine operation.

The two most common combustion cycles associated with reciprocating internal-combustion engines are the otto cycle and the diesel cycle. Since the otto cycle pertains to gasoline engines, we shall discuss only the diesel cycle in this chapter.

Relationship of Temperature, Pressure, and Volume

To illustrate the relationship of temperature, pressure, and volume in an engine, let us consider what takes place in a cylinder fitted with a reciprocating piston (figure 3-7).

DIESEL ENGINES

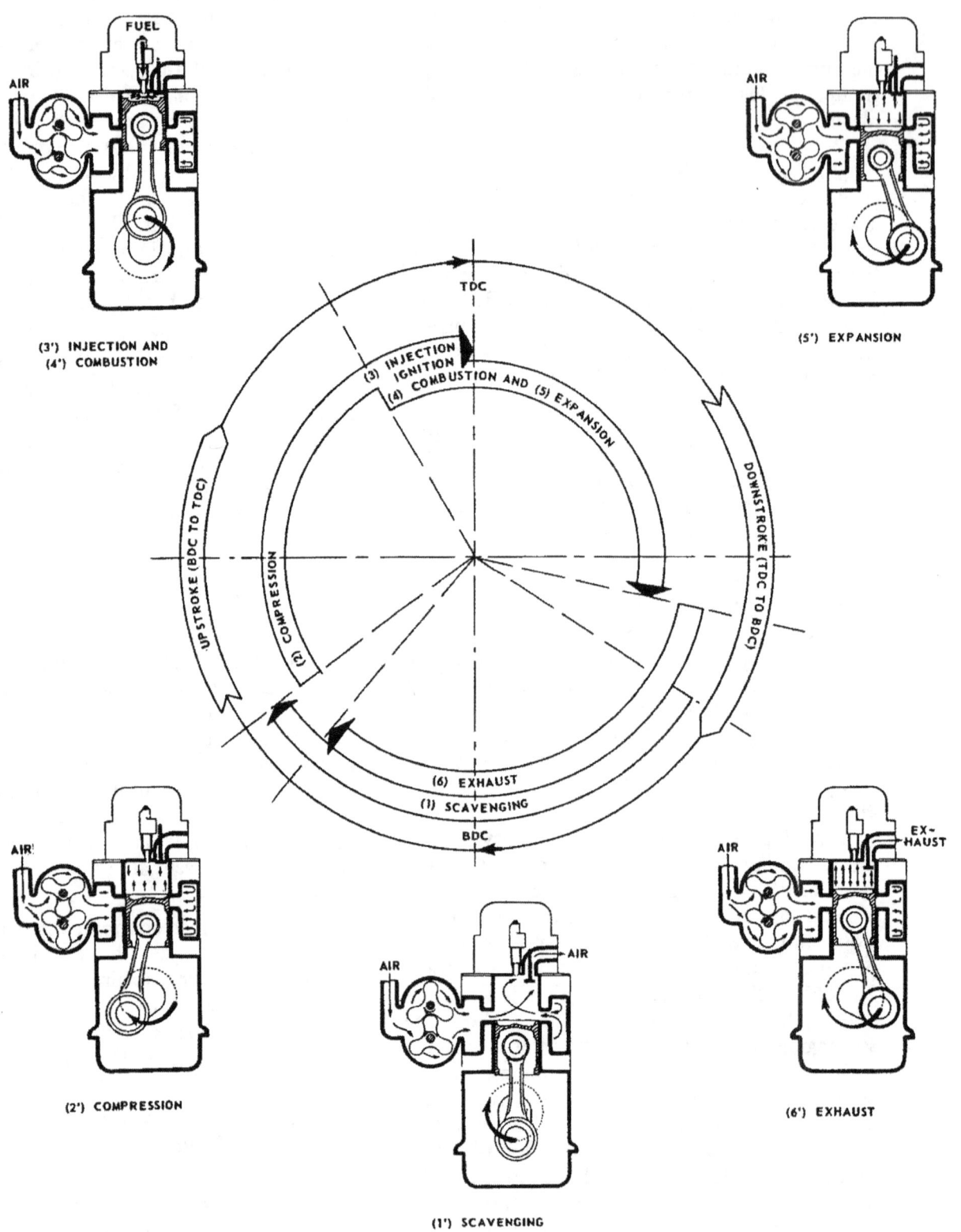

Figure 3-5.—Strokes and events of a 2-stroke cycle diesel engine.

54.20A

Chapter 3—RECIPROCATING INTERNAL-COMBUSTION ENGINES

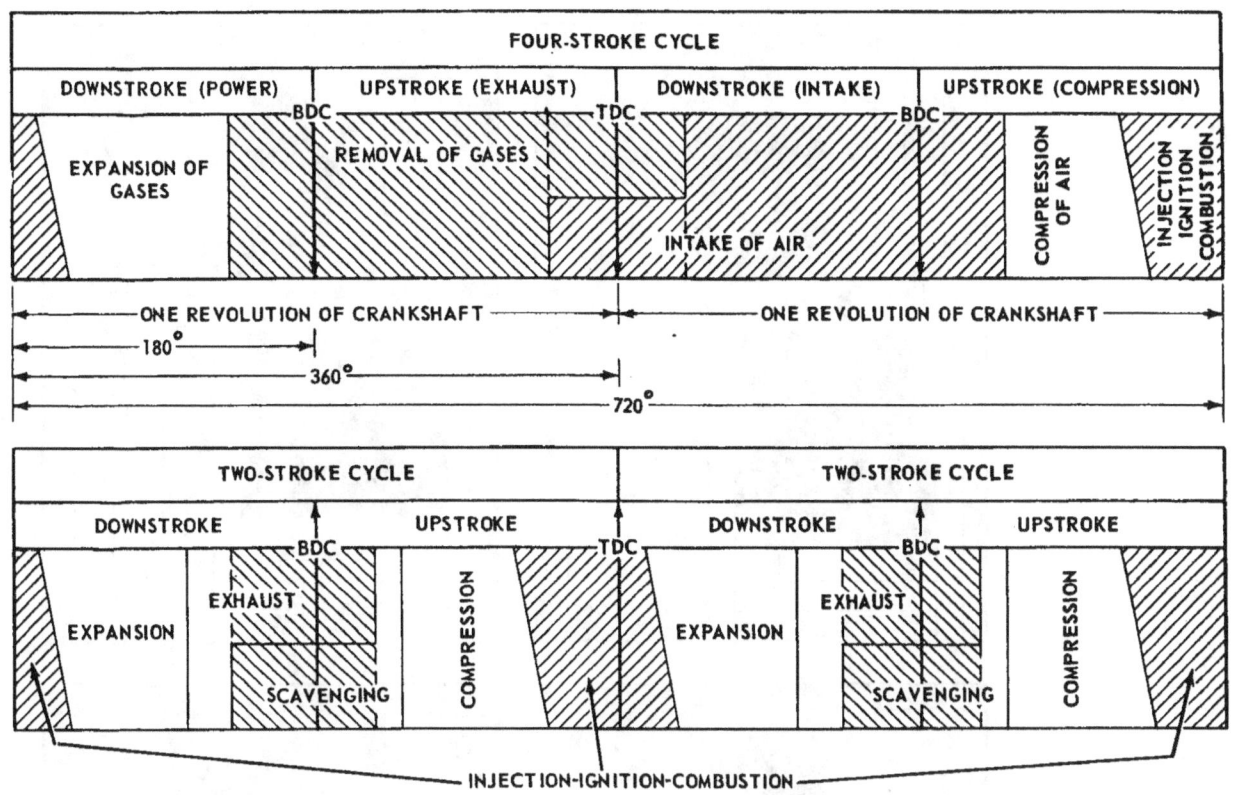

Figure 3-6.—Comparison of the 2- and 4-stroke cycles.

Instruments indicate the pressure within the cylinder as well as the temperature inside and outside the cylinder. Assume that the air in the cylinder is at atmospheric pressure and that the temperatures, inside and outside the cylinder, are approximately 70° as in figure 3-7A.

If the cylinder is an airtight container and a force pushes the piston toward the top of the cylinder, the entrapped charge will be compressed. As the compression progresses, the VOLUME of the air DECREASES, the PRESSURE INCREASES, and the TEMPERATURE RISES as in figure 3-7B and C. These changing conditions continue as the piston moves, and as the piston nears TDC, (figure 3-7D), we find that there has been a marked decrease in volume, and that both pressure and temperature are much greater than at the beginning of compression. Note that temperature has gone from 70° F to approximately 1,000°F. These changing conditions indicate that mechanical energy, in the form of force applied to the piston, has been transformed into heat energy in the compressed air. The temperature of the air has been raised sufficiently to cause ignition of fuel when the fuel is injected into the cylinder.

Further changes take place after ignition. Since ignition occurs shortly before TDC, there is little change in volume until the piston passes TDC. However, there is a sharp increase in pressure and temperature shortly after ignition takes place. The increased pressure forces the piston downward. As the piston moves downward, the gases expand, or increase in volume, and pressure and temperature decrease rapidly. The changes in volume, pressure, and temperature, described and illustrated in figure 3-7, are representative of the changing conditions in the cylinder of a modern diesel engine.

DIESEL ENGINES

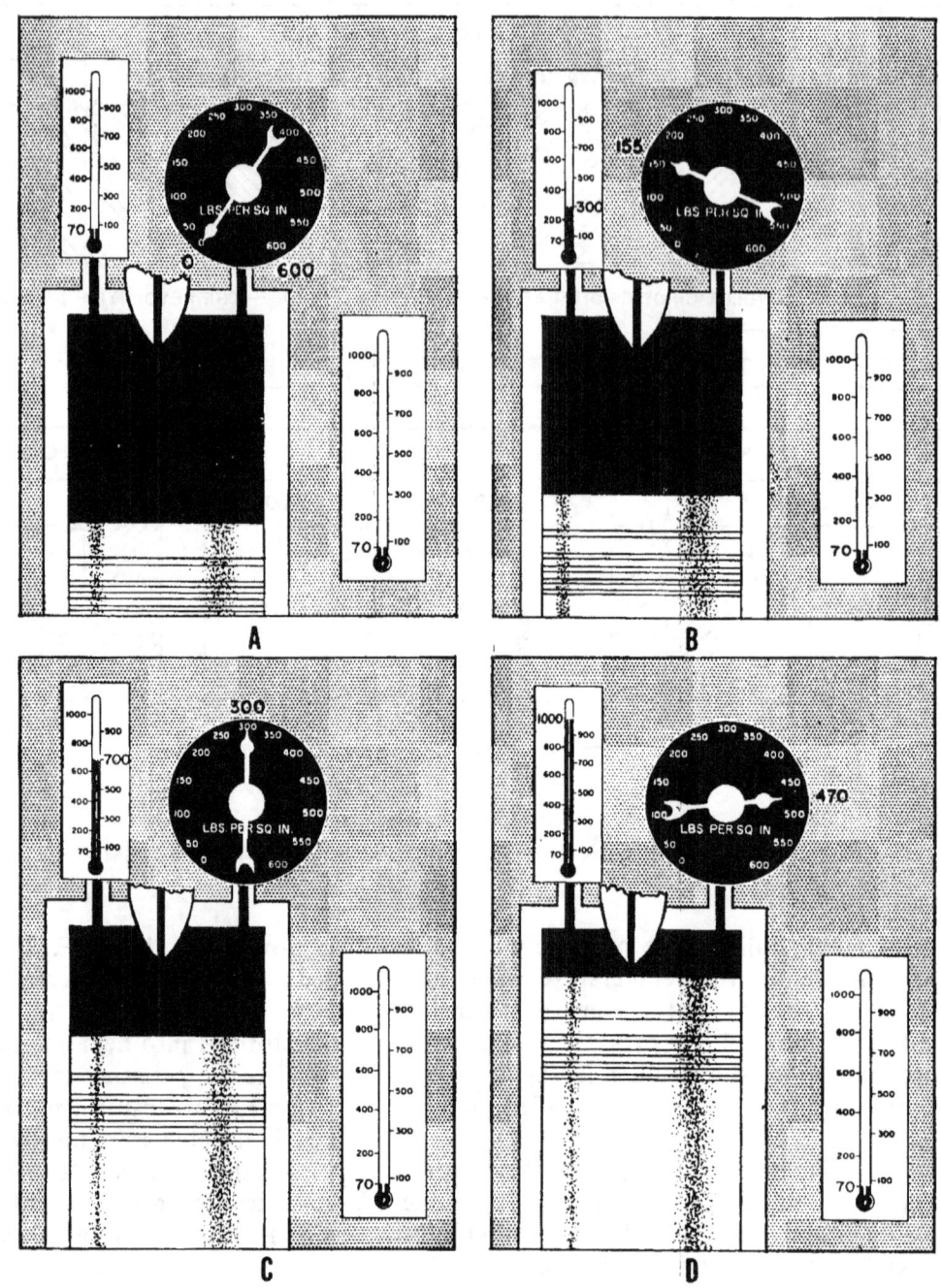

Figure 3-7.—Volume, temperature, and pressure relationship in a cylinder.

The changes in volume and pressure in an engine cylinder can be illustrated by diagram similar to that shown in figure 3-8. Such a diagram is made by devices which measure and record the pressures at various piston positions during a cycle of engine operation. Diagrams which show the relationship between pressures and corresponding piston positions are called PRESSURE-VOLUME DIAGRAMS or INDICATOR CARDS.

Chapter 3—RECIPROCATING INTERNAL-COMBUSTION ENGINES

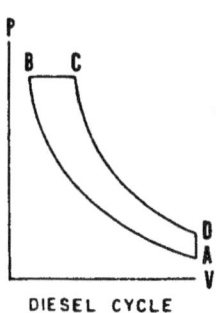

Figure 3-8.—Pressure-volume diagram for theoretical combustion cycles.

On diagrams which provide a graphic representation of cylinder pressure as related to volume, the vertical line P on the diagram (figure 3-8) represents pressure and the horizontal line V represents volume. When a diagram is used as an indicator card, the pressure line is marked off in units of pressure and the volume line is marked off in inches. Thus, the volume line shows the length of the piston stroke which is proportional to volume. The distance between adjacent letters on each of the diagrams (figure 3-8), represents an event of a combustion cycle; that is, compression of air, burning of the charge, expansion of gas, and removal of gases.

True Diesel (Constant-Pressure) Cycle

The true diesel cycle may be defined as one in which combustion, induced by compression ignition, theoretically occurs at a constant pressure. (See figure 3-8.) Adiabatic (without loss or gain of heat) compression (line AB) of the air increases its temperature to a point when ignition occurs automatically as the fuel is injected. Fuel injection and combustion are so controlled that constant-pressure combustion (line CD) and constant volume rejection of the gases (line DA) are assured.

In the true diesel cycle, the mixture of fuel and compressed air burns in a process that is relatively slow compared with the quick, explosive-type combustion process of the gasoline engine. As injected fuel penetrates the compressed air, some ignites, and the rest of the fuel charge feeds the fire. The expansion of the gases keeps pace with the change in volume caused by piston travel; thus combustion is said to occur at CONSTANT PRESSURE (line BC in figure 3-8).

Actual Diesel Combustion Cycles

The preceding discussion covered the theoretical combustion cycle which serves as the basis for modern diesel engines. In actual operation, modern engines operate on modifications of the theoretical cycle. However, characteristics of the true cycles are incorporated in the actual cycles of modern engines, which we shall discuss in the following examples representing the actual cycle of operation in diesel engines.

The actual diesel combustion cycle is one in which the combustion phase, induced by compression ignition, begins on a constant-volume basis, where pressure increases, and ends on a constant-pressure basis. The actual cycle is used as the basis for the design of practically all modern diesel engines and is referred to as a MODIFIED DIESEL CYCLE, or semi-diesel cycle.

MODIFIED 4-STROKE DIESEL COMBUSTION CYCLE.—An example of a pressure-volume diagram for a modified 4-stroke diesel engine is shown in figure 3-9. Note that the volume line is divided into 16 units, indicating a 15:1 compression ratio. The higher compression ratio accounts for the increased temperature necessary to ignite the charge. Fuel is injected at point c and combustion is represented by line cd.

Combustion in the actual diesel cycle takes place with volume practically constant for a short time, during which period there is a sharp increase in pressure, until the piston reaches a point slightly past TDC. Then, combustion continues at a relatively constant pressure, dropping slightly as combustion ends at d.

143

DIESEL ENGINES

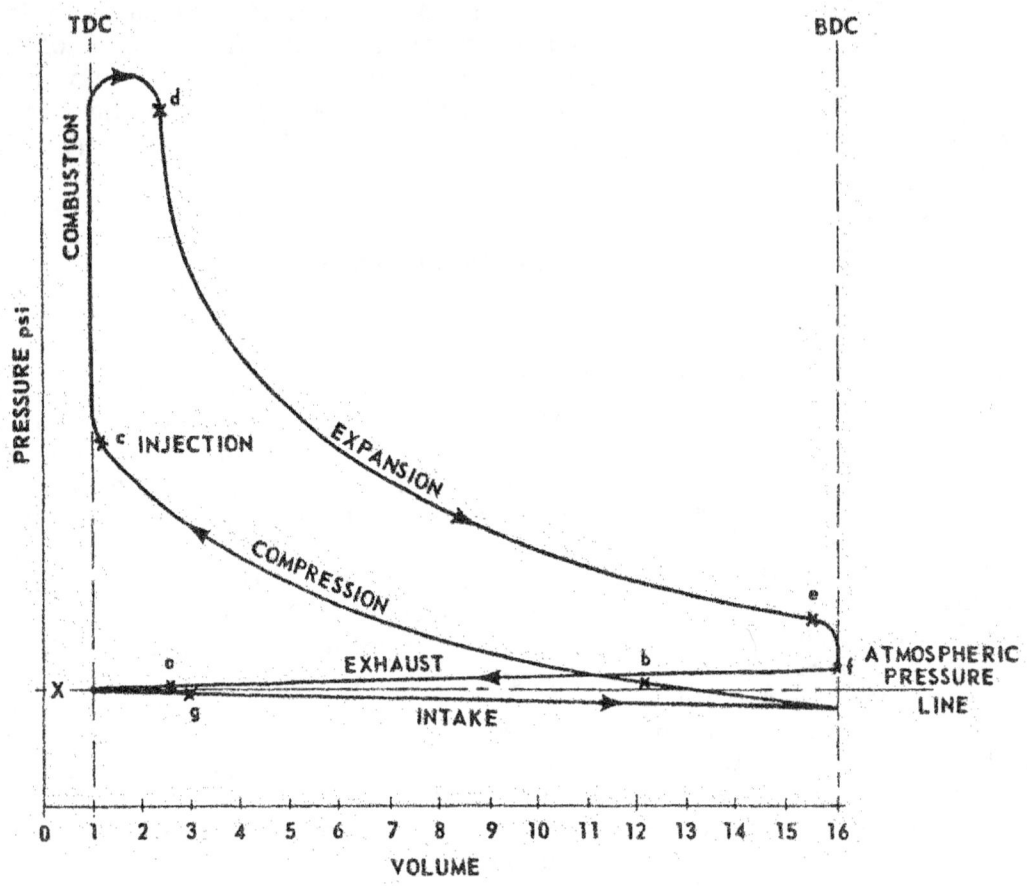

Figure 3-9.—Pressure-volume diagram, diesel 4-stroke cycle.

54.19C

MODIFIED 2-STROKE DIESEL COMBUSTION CYCLE.—Pressure-volume diagrams for diesel engines that operate on the 2-stroke cycle will be similar to those just discussed, except that separate exhaust and intake curves will not exist because intake and exhaust occur during a relatively short interval of time near BDC and do not involve full strokes of the piston as in the 4-stroke cycle. Thus, a pressure-volume diagram for a 2-stroke modified diesel cycle will be similar to a diagram formed by f-b-c-d-e-f in figure 3-9. The exhaust and intake phases will take place between e and b with some overlap of the events. (See fig. 3-5).

The preceding discussion has pointed out some of the main differences between diesel engines used in naval service. In brief, these differences involve engine designs, designations, and principles.

SUMMARY

In summary, the three major diesel engine designs used are the in-line type, the V-type, and the opposed-piston type.

Diesel engines are designated by number of cylinders, bore, stroke, and rpm, or by the cubic inch displacement per cylinder or for the total engine.

You should also remember that all diesel engines have a cycle of four events: intake, compression, power and exhaust. The events vary with piston strokes in a two-stroke cycle or

Chapter 3 – RECIPROCATING INTERNAL-COMBUSTION ENGINES

four-stroke cycle engine, but these events always occur in the same order. The relationship of temperature, pressure and volume plays an important part in the actual operation of a diesel engine. As the volume in a cylinder decreases due to piston movement, the pressure and temperature increase until sufficient temperature is reached (approximately 1,000°F) to ignite the fuel injected into the cylinder. Combustion then takes place and continues at a relatively constant pressure, until the beginning of the exhaust event.

BASIC FUNDAMENTALS
OF HYDRAULICS AND ELECTRICITY

TABLE OF CONTENTS

	Page
INTRODUCTION	1
HYDRAULICS	1
HYDRAULIC RADIUS	5
ELECTRICITY	18

BASIC FUNDAMENTALS OF HYDRAULICS AND ELECTRICITY

There are similarities between fluids and electricity which help us to understand the fundamental of both. For example, we have the following units of measurement:

	Fluid	*Electricity*
Pressure	pounds per square inch (psi) or feet of water	electromotive force (emf) E or volts
Flow	gallons per minute (gpm) or cubic feet per second (cfs)	amperes (amp)
Resistance to flow	head loss feet of fluid or psi	resistance (ohms)
Quantity	gallons or cubic feet (gal) or (cf)	kilowatt hours (KWH)

Hydraulics

This is the name given to that branch of science which deals with fluids at rest and in motion. The former is sometimes spoken of as hydrostatics and the latter as hydrodynamics. We are concerned here mainly with water at rest and in motion. Many of the same principles apply to air and gases.

Consideration will be given to water moving or flowing through pipes, channels and pumps and ways of measuring the quantity flowing in a given time. We must be careful of units, the basic ones being:

Length in feet	ft
Area in square feet	sq ft or ft^2
Rate: gallons per minute	gpm.
million gallons per day	mgd
cu ft per second	cfs or sec ft
Weight: 1 gallon of water	8.34 lb
1 cu ft water	62.4 lb
Speed or velocity of flow in feet per second	ft/sec

Head. The precise meaning of the term *head* is the amount of energy possessed by a unit quantity of water at its given location. Ordinarily, the energy is expressed in *foot-pounds,* and the unit quantity of water considered is one pound. The head, then, is expressed in foot-pounds of energy per pound of water, or,

$$\frac{ft \times lb}{lb} = ft$$

Thus, all heads can be expressed in feet. Water may contain energy due to (a) its elevation, (b) its pressure, or (c) its velocity. These energies are called elevation (or static) head, pressure head, and velocity head, respectively. In addition, operators often have occasion to refer to *pump head,* which is the energy required for a pump to move one pound of water, and to *friction head,* which is the energy lost due to friction within the fluid and against the walls of the pipe or channel.

Elevation (or static) head. Elevations must be expressed as the vertical distance from some base level, or reference plane, such as mean sea level, the surface of the ground, or some other arbitrarily chosen level.
Then, for example, water that is 100 ft above the reference plane, has 100 ft-lbs of energy, and its elevation head is 100 ft.

Pressure head. Pressures are expressed in terms of force per unit area, such as pounds per square inch or pounds per square foot. One square foot contains 144 square inches. Therefore, a pressure of 1 lb/in^2 = 144 lb/ft^2, since every square inch is subjected to a force of one pound.

To calculate the energy per pound of water, we must consider the number of pounds of water in a unit volume, which is called the "density" of the water. The density of water is 62.4 lb/ft^3. Then if the pressure of the water is 1 lb/in^2 (often written 1 psi), the "pressure head" is

$$\frac{144 \text{ lb}/ft^2}{62.4 \text{ lb}/ft^3} = 2.3 ft$$

or
1 psi = 2.3 ft pressure head

By the same kind of calculation, a water pressure of 40 psi equals

$$\frac{40 \times 144 \text{ lb}/ft^2}{62.4 \text{ lb}/ft^2} = 92.3 ft \text{ pressure head}$$

or
40 X 2.3 = 92.3 ft pressure head

Velocity head. The energy of motion is called kinetic energy, and is calculated by the relationship

$$\text{Energy} = \frac{mv^2}{2g}$$

where m represents the mass of the moving object, v its velocity, and g the force which gravity exerts on a mass of one pound.

In everyday speech, we are accustomed to expressing both force and mass in pounds. However, this causes confusion when energy calculations are attempted, because the force exerted by gravity is not numerically equal to the mass in pounds. That is to say, force and mass cannot properly be expressed in the same units.

One way of avoiding this difficulty is to speak of the force of gravity in terms of the acceleration it produces when it acts upon a unit mass. One of the fundamental laws of physics is that force equals mass times acceleration. Thus, the force on a unit mass of one pound is numerically equal to the acceleration.

Acceleration is the rate at which velocity changes. If an automobile goes from zero miles per hour to sixty miles per hour in two minutes, we can say that its average change of speed was thirty miles per hour in each minute, or thirty miles per hour per minute. Likewise, if water moving ten feet per second speeds up to fifteen feet per second, and the time required for the change of speed is one second, we could say that it accelerated five feet per second per second. Accelerations are often expressed in feet per second. The units can then be written ft/sec. This is equivalent to writing $\frac{ft}{sec \times sec}$ or $\frac{ft}{sec^2}$

When gravity acts upon a free-falling body, it produces an acceleration of 32.2 ft/sec^2. This value of g can be used in the equation for calculating velocity head. If we consider, for example one pound of water moving with a velocity of 10 ft/sec, its velocity head is calculated as follows:

$$\text{Energy} = \frac{1 \text{ lb} \times 10 \text{ ft/sec} \times 10 \text{ ft/sec}}{2 \times 32.2 \text{ ft/sec}^2} = 1.5 \text{ ft-lb}$$

$$\text{Velocity head} = \frac{1.5 \text{ ft-lb}}{1 \text{ lb}} = 1.5 \text{ ft}$$

In the first of these two equations we multiplied by the weight of the water. In the second we divided by the weight of the water. Since these two operations cancel each other, the velocity head can be calculated by leaving out the weight in the first place:

$$\text{Velocity head} = \frac{v^2}{2g}$$

Friction head. Friction head equals the loss of energy due to friction within the liquid and friction against the walls of the pipe or channel. When we are dealing with water, the friction within the liquid is relatively small, and most of the energy is lost due to friction against the walls. Therefore, the friction loss depends mostly upon the characteristics of the material of which the pipe or channel is made and its surface smoothness. The usual procedure for estimating friction head losses is to use a table in an engineering handbook which gives directly the friction loss per foot of a particular kind of pipe or channel.

Pump head. The pump head equals the ft-lb of energy given to each pound of water passing through the pump.

Pumping. Pumps are used to move liquids to a higher level or to increase the rate of flow. Figure (1) and Figure (2) show two typical pumping conditions. To understand these figures it is necessary to know that in a liquid at rest the pressure at any point is equal to the weight of the liquid above the point, plus the weight of the atmosphere above the surface of the liquid. Both, must be expressed in the same units.

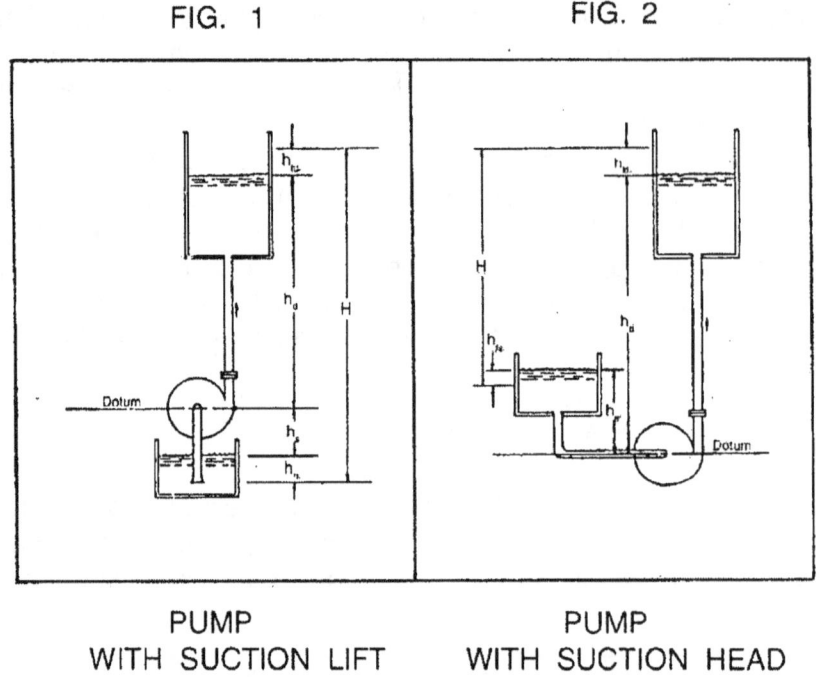

PUMP WITH SUCTION LIFT   PUMP WITH SUCTION HEAD

These units are usually pounds per square inch (psi) or feet of water. Since most pumping problems involve difference in pressure, the atmospheric pressure may be neglected and gauge pressures (psig) or height in feet may be used. Total head in feet at a point can be expressed as the height of a column of water whose weight would produce a certain pressure at that point. Psi X 2.31 = head in feet.

FIG. 3

OPEN CHANNEL   CIRCULAR CONDUIT

HYDRAULIC RADIUS

For Figure 1— Pump operating with a suction lift:

$$H = h_d + h_s + h_{fd} + h_{fa} + \frac{V_d^2}{2g} \quad \frac{V_s^2}{2g}$$

For Figure 2 — Pump operating with suction head:

$$H = h_d + h_s + h_{fd} + h_{fa} + \frac{V_d^2}{2g} \quad \frac{V_s^2}{2g}$$

Where —
- H = Total head in feet (formerly called total dynamic head) at which the pump operates.
- h_d = Static discharge head in feet, or the vertical distance between the pump datum and liquid surface in the receiving tank. The pump datum is at the center line for horizontal pumps and at the entrance eye of the impeller for vertical pumps.
- $h.$ = Static suction head or lift in feet or vertical distance between pump datum and liquid surface in the suction well.
- h_{fd} = Friction head in discharge in feet or the head necessary to overcome friction in valves, fittings, etc. in the discharge piping.
- h_{fs} = Friction head in suction in feet
- g = 32.2 ft/sec² = Acceleration due to gravity.

$\frac{V_d^2}{2g}$ and $\frac{V_s^2}{2g}$ discharge nozzle and suction nozzle of the pump. When the nozzles are of the same diameter these values are equal and cancel out. Velocity head represents energy which the pump must deliver to the liquid but which is not measured by a pressure gage. It is the head required to give to the liquid the velocity "V" in feet per second.

The relationship between the volume of water flowing per unit of time, the velocity of the moving water and the size of pipe or channel through which the flow takes place may be expressed by the equation:

$$Q = AV$$

Where
- Q = rate of flow or volume per unit time (usually expressed as cubic ft/sec (cfs)
- A = Area through which water is flowing, measured at right angles in the direction of flow (usually expressed in sq ft)
- V = Average velocity of flow or distance traveled per unit of time (usually expressed as ft/sec)

There are three general types of problems using the equation $Q = AV$. These are as follows:

1. The water in an open channel has been observed to flow a distance of 180 feet in 2 minutes. The dimensions of the channel are 2 feet wide and 18 inches deep. Compute the rate of flow

$$V = \frac{180}{2 \text{ min}} = \frac{90 \text{ ft}}{\text{min}} = \frac{1.5 \text{ ft}}{\text{sec}}$$

$$A = 2 \text{ ft} \times 18 \text{ in} \times \frac{\text{ft}}{12 \text{ in}} = 3.0 \text{ sq ft}$$

then

$$Q = AV = 3.0 \text{ sq ft} \times \frac{1.5 \text{ ft}}{\text{sec}} = 4.5 \text{ cfs}$$

2. A meter shows water flowing through a 12 inch diameter pipe at the rate of 2 mgd. To determine the velocity of the water

$$Q = \frac{2,000,000 \text{ gal}}{\text{day}} \times \frac{\text{cu ft}}{7.5 \text{ gal}} \times \frac{\text{day}}{24 \text{ hr}} \times \frac{\text{hr}}{60 \text{ min}} \times \frac{\text{min}}{60 \text{ sec}} = 3.08 \text{ cfs}$$

$$A = \pi r^2 = 3.1416 \times 6 \text{ in} \times 6 \text{ in} \times \frac{\text{sq ft}}{144 \text{ sq ft}} = 0.79 \text{ sq ft}$$

then $V = Q/A = \dfrac{3.08 \text{ cu ft}}{0.79 \text{ sq ft} \times \text{sec}} = 3.9 \dfrac{\text{ft}}{\text{sec}}$

3. Baffles are to be placed in a coagulation tank so that the velocity of flow between baffles is 0.3 ft/sec. The depth of flow in the tank is 8 feet and the rate of flow through the tank is 2 mgd. Find the distance, w between baffles.

$$Q = 2 \text{ mgd} \times 1.55 \frac{\text{cfs}}{\text{mgd}} = 3.08 \text{ cfs}$$

V=0.3 ft/sec
let the distance between baffles equal w

then $A = 8 \times w = \dfrac{Q}{V} = 3.08 \dfrac{\text{cu ft}}{\text{sec}} \times \dfrac{\text{sec}}{0.3 \text{ ft}}$

$$W = \frac{3.08 \text{ cu ft / sec}}{8 \text{ ft} \times 0.3 \text{ ft / sec}} = 1.28 \text{ ft}$$

Pipe Friction. The h_{fd} and h_{fs} in the preceding paragraphs are those portions of the total head necessary to overcome friction between the fluid and the walls of the suction and discharge piping. The values of these terms depend upon the length of the pipeline, its diameter, the velocity of the flowing liquid and the condition of the internal walls of the pipe, usually called the roughness factor. These influences are expressed in the formula

h_f = Friction head = $f \dfrac{L}{d} \dfrac{V^2}{2g}$

Where f = roughness factor
       L = length of pipe
       d = diameter

$\dfrac{V^2}{2g}$ = velocity head

Tables are available for the value of f, which varies with both V and d in this formula. The value of f is fractional, varying from .04 for small V and d to .01 for large values of V and d. Another formula derived from this basic one expresses the roughness factor as a whole number known as the C value in the Hazen & Williams formula. Tables and a special slide rule have been developed for solving pipe problems by this formula. The value of C varies from 140 for very smooth large pipe to a low of 40 or less for badly corroded or dirty pipe. See Figure 4 (Flow Chart for value "C" equals 100)

FIG. 4

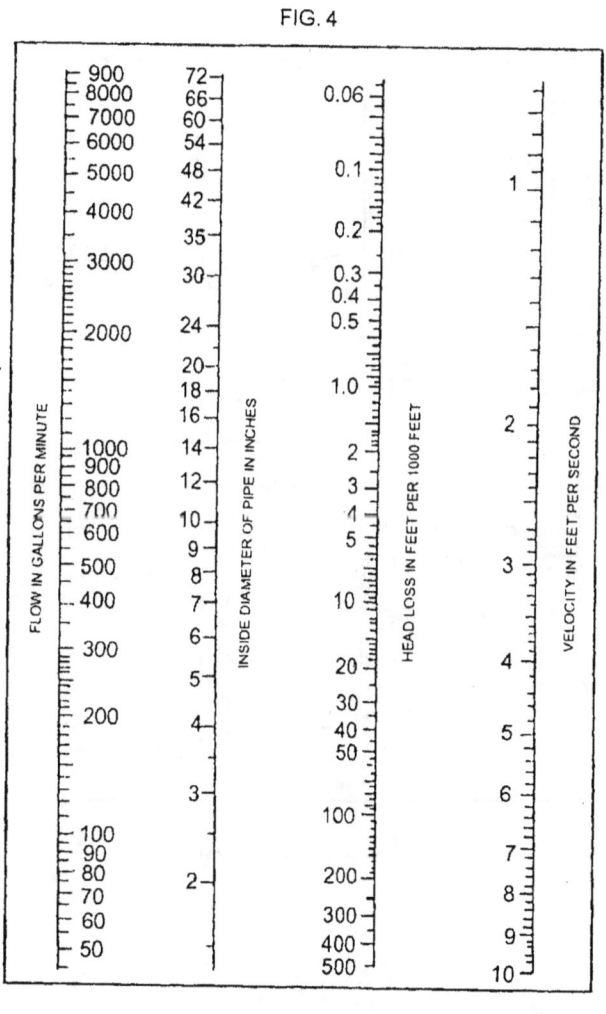

FLOW CHART
"C" 100
Based on the Hazen-Williams Formula

FIG. 5

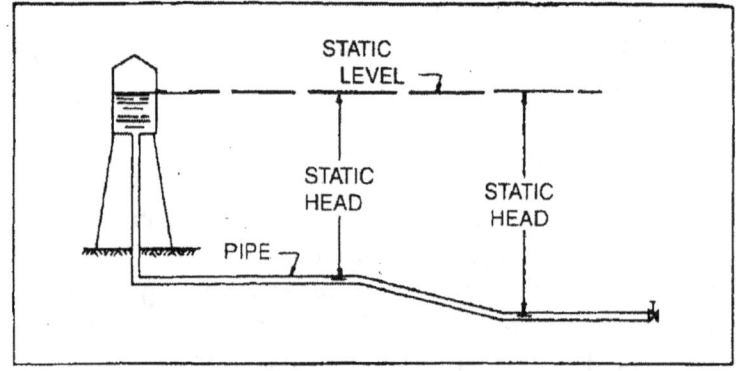

STATIC HEAD

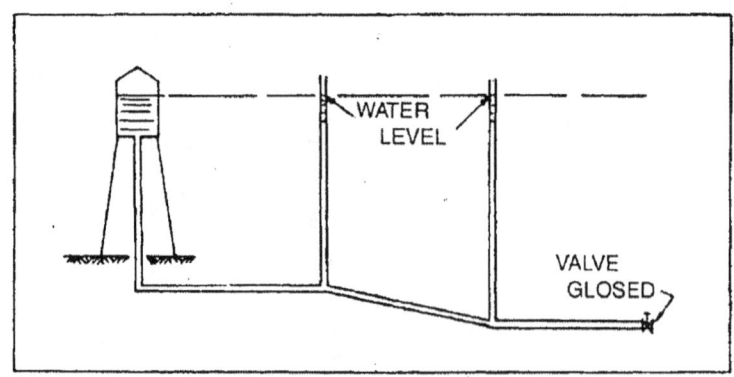

WATER LEVEL, NO FLOW IN PIPE

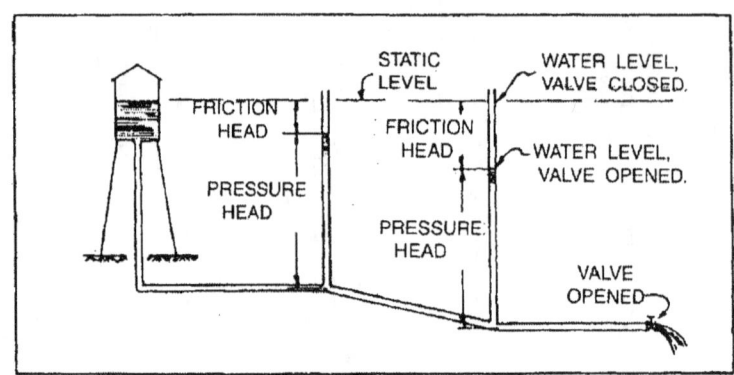

PRESSURE HEAD

If vertical open pipes are attached in a pipe line as shown in Figure 6, the water level in the pipes will stand at a level even with the elevation of the water in the storage tank. If the outlet valve is opened to permit water to flow, the level of the water in the vertical pipes will drop. The drop in the level or loss in head is the "friction head" and represents the energy lost by friction of the water flowing through the pipe.

Power Requirements for Pumping. Work must be done to move liquid against the total heads (H) indicated in Figures 8 and 9. The unit of work is the foot pound which is the amount of work or energy required to lift one pound a vertical distance of one foot. The common unit of power or rate of doing work is horsepower (hp). One horsepower is equal to 33,000 ft. lbs. per minute. In electrical units, one horsepower is equivalent to 746 watts.

The power required to drive a pump can be computed as follows:
Work done by the pump (or water horsepower) = Whp

$$Whp = \frac{lbs. \text{ of water raised per minute} \times H}{33,000}$$

$$= \frac{gpm \times 8.34 \times H}{33,000} = \frac{gpm \times H}{3,960}$$

Example: The sum of the elevation, pressure, velocity and friction heads is 100 ft. What would be the work done by the pump or the horsepower required (water horsepower) if 50 gallons per minute is pumped?

$$Whp = \frac{gal/min \times lbs/gal \times ft\ lbs/lb}{ft\text{-}lbs/min}$$

= 1.26 horsepower

Since all the power delivered by the driving unit cannot be converted to useful work, the ratio between output and input is called pump efficiency.

Power required to drive the pump, or "brake horsepower" is computed by this formula:

$$bhp = \frac{whp}{pump\ eff} = \frac{gpm \times 8.33 \times H}{33,000 \times pump\ eff} = \frac{gpm \times H}{3960 \times pump\ eff}$$

If the efficiency (eff) of the pump is 65%

$$\frac{1.26}{0.65} = 1.94 \text{ horsepower must be delivered to the pump.}$$

Again since motors are not 100% efficient

$$Motor\ hp = \frac{whp}{pump\ eff \times motor\ eff}$$

$$= \frac{gpm \times H}{3960 \times pump\ eff \times motor\ eff}$$

If the motor efficiency is 80%

$$\frac{1.26}{0.65 \times 0.80} = 2.425$$

horsepower must be delivered to the motor in order to pump 50 gpm against a total head of 100 feet.

Flow in Open Channels. Flow in open conduits and in partially filled pipes is affected by the same factors as in pipes flowing full. These factors determine the slope required for an open channel to maintain a certain flow and velocity. The velocity, is actually determined by the slope of the water surface, but this is usually also the slope of the bottom of the channel and the water flows at a constant depth. The slope of the water surface is called the hydraulic gradient. The friction between water and the conduit walls depends upon the roughness of the surface, but the formula for it is different because the liquid now has a free surface and the length of contact depends upon the shape of the channel and the depth of flow. These factors are combined in the " hydraulic radius," which is found by dividing the cross-sectional area of the flowing water by the distance around that area along the walls of the channel. This distance is called the "wetted perimeter" of the channel (see Figure 3). Thus,

Hyd Rad $r = \dfrac{A}{W}$ feet (figure 3)

From these considerations, there has been developed the Chezy formula:

$v = C\sqrt{rs}$ feet per sec

where C = coefficient based on roughness, slope and value of r.

s = slope of the hydraulic gradient or water surface in open channels, usually expressed as ft per foot or ft per thousand feet. Thus, a slope of .004 indicates a drop of four feet in a thousand foot length.

The two principal formulas for determining C, the Kutter and the Manning formulas, depend largely upon values of "n" which is the coefficient of friction. These values have become quite well known for various types of surfaces and materials. Thus $n=.013$ is commonly used for design of vitrified tile pipes and for large diameter pre-cast concrete pipes.

Tables and diagrams have been published from which velocities, rates of flow and slopes can be determined for various diameters of pipes and values of "n".

Weirs. There are numerous ways of measuring flowing water, but three devices most commonly used are weirs, Venturi meters, and Parshall flumes.

The weir consists of rectangular opening or V notch opening with sharp edges. The weir is set vertically so that the flow passes over it tnd falls away from it.

FIG. 6

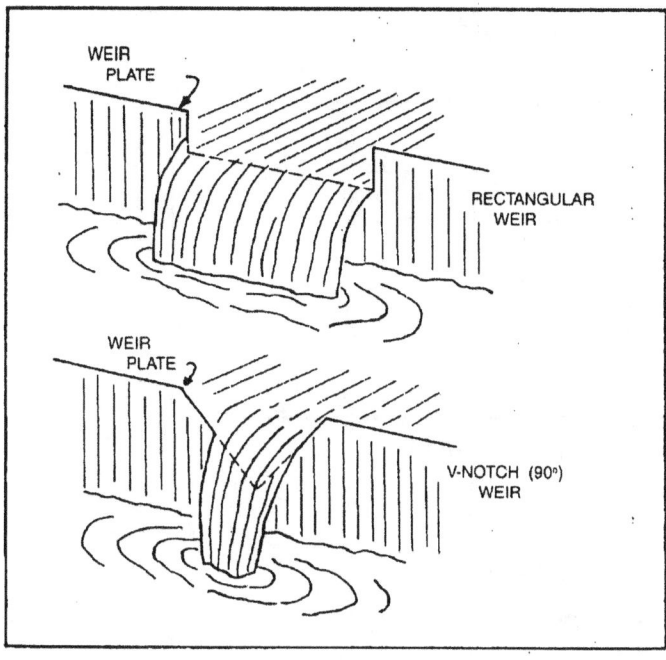

WEIRS

It is only necessary to measure the height of water above the crest of the weir at a point sufficiently upstream which avoids the curve of the water surface over the weir. In placing a weir, two points must be considered. First, the weir should be installed in the channel so that the velocity of the water approaching the weir is relatively low. Second, the "head" on the weir is not the depth of water as it passes over the weir proper but is the difference in elevation between the edge of the weir and the water upstream a short distance. In Figure 7 both of these points are illustrated. By using the head measurement the flow is determined from the formula:

Rate of flow $Q - 3.33 \, L \, h \sqrt{h}$ cfs (for a suppressed weir) and

$$Q = 3.33 \, (L - \frac{h}{5}) \, h \, \sqrt{h} \text{ cfs (for a contracted weir)}$$

where h = the height of horizontal water surface above crest of weir, L= horizontal length of weir.

The V notch weir is more accurate than the rectangular weir for small flows. For a 90 degree notch, the formula is: (Figure 8)

$Q = Ch^2 \sqrt{h}$ cfs where

C is a coefficient depending upon the material of the weir and the range of head. Values of C are given in handbooks for various materials and heads. The V notch weir is suitable for measuring flows from 10 to 3,500 gpm.

Another formula which may be used with a V notch weir with

90° angle is

$Q = 2.5 h^{5/2}$

where   Q = rate of discharge in cfs
            h = "head" on weir in feet (Figure 8)

Using the chart. (Figure 8)
  If h is measured to be 0.20 feet then Q = .045cfs
            = 21 gpm

FIG. 7

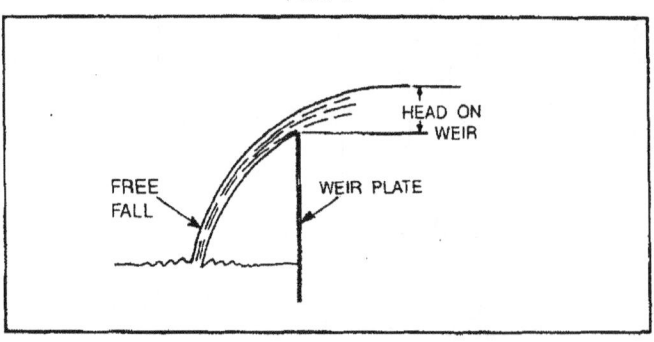

HEAD ON WEIR

FIG. 8

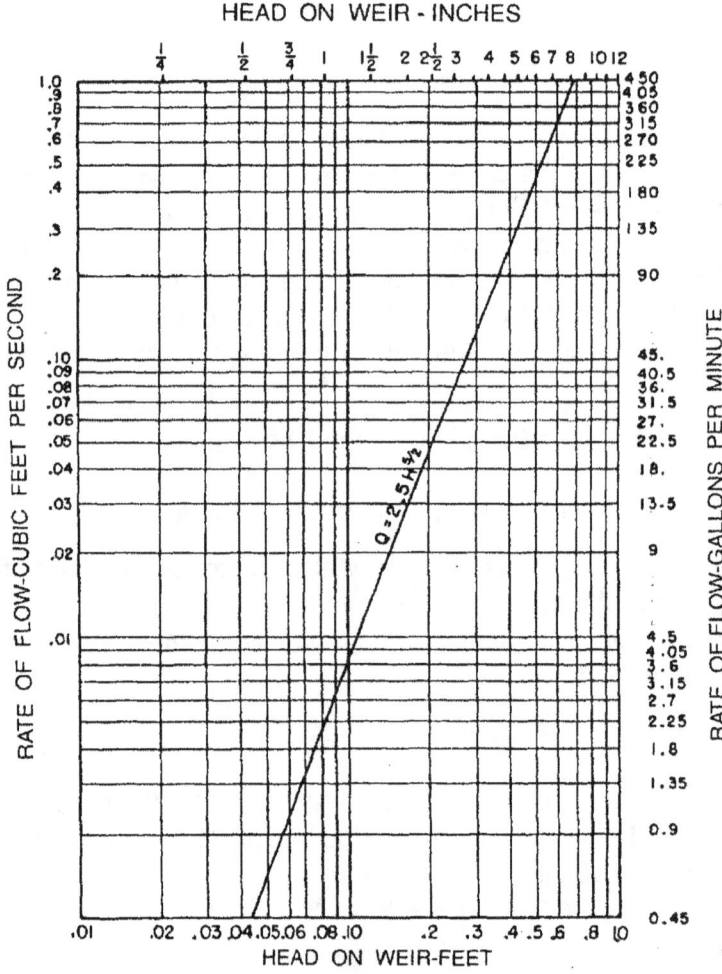

90° V-NOTCH WEIR FORMULA-Q=2.5H5/2

Venturi Meter. This type of flow measuring device is installed in a pipe line and consists of a throat carefully machined to a given inside diameter, a converging section which tapers from the pipe diameter to the throat and a diverging section from the throat to the pipe diameter. (See Figure 9) Taps are provided for measuring pressure head at points just before convergence and at the throat. The only measurement necessary to compute the flow is the difference in pressure head between the two tap points. Figure 10 shows graphically how pressure and velocity heads change in the Venturi Meter.

Parshall Flume. This type of flow measuring device was developed for measuring irrigation water in open channels where there may be debris and silt and where little loss of head can be permitted.

FIG. 9

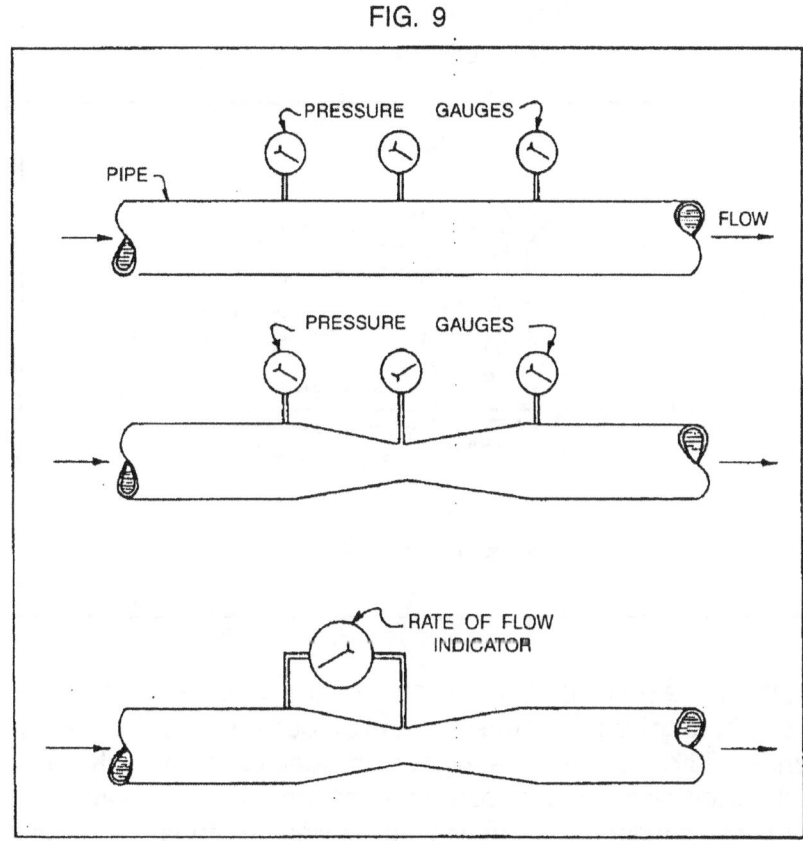

VENTURI TUBE

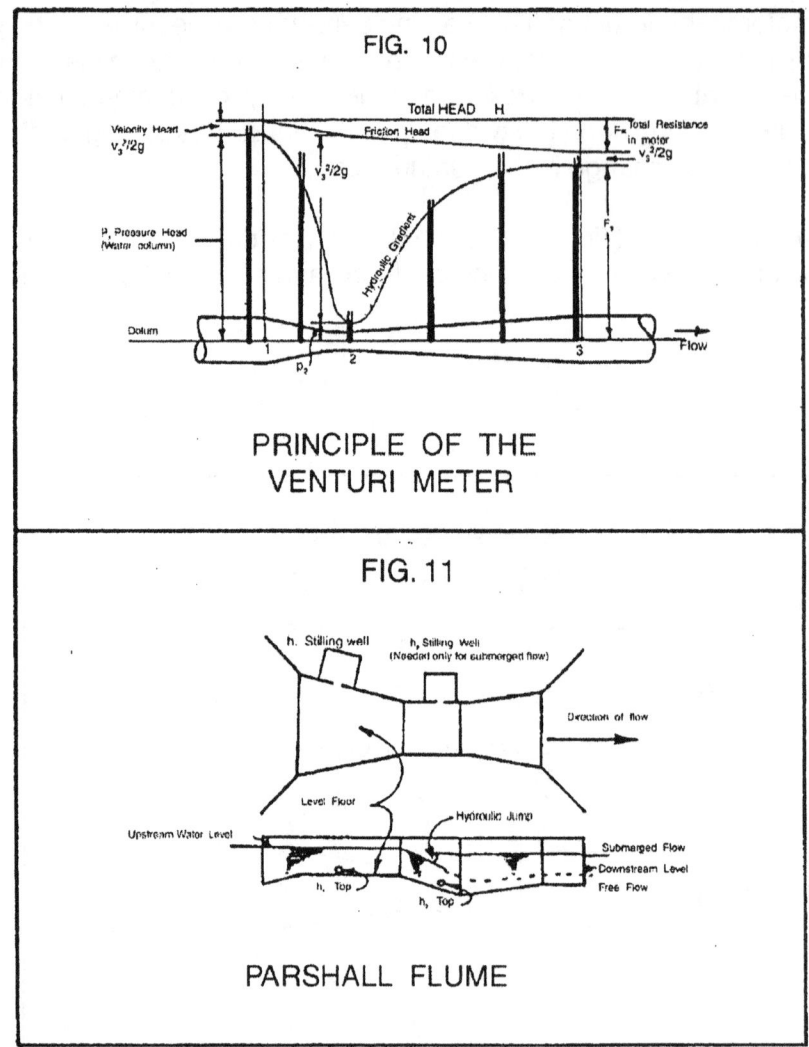

FIG. 10 — PRINCIPLE OF THE VENTURI METER

FIG. 11 — PARSHALL FLUME

In principle, the flume is similar to the Venturi meter. It has an inlet section with sides converging slowly to a throat of fixed dimensions and an outlet section diverging more rapidly to the original channel width. For the usual non-submerged condition only measurement of the depth of water at a fixed distance upstream from the throat is necessary to determine the flow. The flume may be constructed of almost any building material. For greatest accuracy the throat is often made to accurate dimensions from corrosion resistant metal. Figure 11 illustrates the Parshall Flume.

Magnetic Flow Meter. Bach of the previously described flow measuring devices involves an appreciable loss of head. A new development consists of a non-magnetic tube of the same internal diameter as the pipe line across which a magnetic field is established. Water flowing through the magnetic field produces a voltage proportional to the velocity. This voltage is converted by electrical and mechnical means to indicate and record the rate of flow.

An important operating and maintenance requirement of any flow measuring device is that pressure connecting stilling wells, floats and float tubes must be kept clean.

Rate of Flow Controllers. These are used to maintain flows at constant rates. Generally, all of the newer models depend on the Venturi principle to control a movable diaphragm or a pilot valve. This in turn actuates a main valve so as to control the size of an opening so that the desired amount of water is passed. Figure 12 shows a section through one type of controller. Actually this particular type of controller has two valves on the vertical stem and two valve seats but, for simplification, only one has been shown.

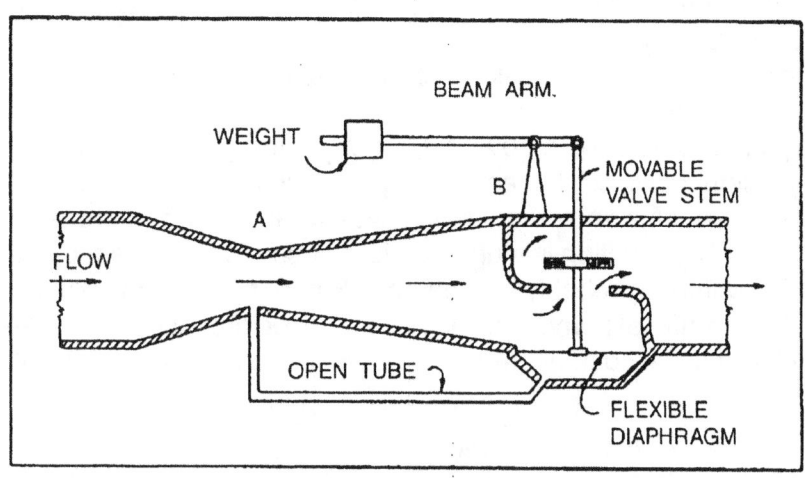

RATE OF FLOW CONTROLLER

The weight is placed at the desired point on the beam arm which corresponds to a certain rate of flow through the valve. At this particular rate of flow the unit pressure at point "A" will be less than the unit pressure at point "B". The unit pressure at point A is transferred, by means of the small open tube, to the compartment below the flexible diaphragm. The downward total pressure on the diaphragm is then greater than the upward total pressure. This results in a tendency for the valve stem to move downward. This tendency is counteracted by the weight at the proper location on the beam arm. At the desired rate of flow everything is in balance.

Pumps. Pumps have many uses in waterworks practice. Though there are many types, practically all water pumps may be classified into two general categories: displacement pumps and velocity pumps.

Displacement pumps employ some mechanical means (plungers, pistons, gears or cams) for forcing specific volumes of water through the units. Velocity pumps impart a high velocity to water and convert the velocity head into pressure head which forces the water through the apparatus.

Either type of pump raises the pressure on inlet side to a higher pressure on the outlet side. The specific means for bringing this about are quite different for the two types. Displacement type pumps, when operating at a particular speed, will take specific unit volumes of water and mechanically force the water out of the pump at a certain rate without regard to conditions beyond the pumping unit. When the resistance to flow beyond the pump is increased, the pressure will be increased. The only limit is the available horsepower and the physical strength of the discharge pipe or the pump. In other words, if something goes wrong on the discharge side of the pump to stop the flow, something may have to "give" and serious damage may result.

This is not the case with a velocity pump. A velocity pump merely causes the water to move with a very high velocity within the pump, usually in a circular direction. Under most conditions the amount of water which passes through the pump depends upon the resistance to flow on the discharge side. If the resistance is too great, for example if a valve is closed, the pump will continue to operate. This will produce the maximum pressure obtainable from that particular pump and speed of operation, but no wa.ter will pass through the pump. Probably no damage will result unless the pump is allowed to run until it over heats.

Displacement pumps may be subdivided into two general types-reciprocating and rotary. The reciprocating type, equipped with either plungers or pistons, includes direct acting, single or duplex, steam pumps, crank and flywheel pumps, and plunger pumps. Rotary pumps may be either cam, screw or gear types.

Velocity pumps may be subdivided into several general types including centrifugal, propeller, mixed flow, and turbine units.

Displacement pumps have certain advantages over velocity types. In displacement pumps the quantity of liquid delivered does not vary with the discharge head; they are easily primed; many act like air pumps and prime themselves when the suction head is low. They will operate smoothly on high suction lifts up to 25 feet or so. For high heads and small quantities the reciprocating pump is probably still the best. For many applications, the velocity pump, particularly the centrifugal pump, has displaced the reciprocating pump. Advantages of velocity pumps are lower initial cost, generally higher efficiency and easier installation and maintenance.

FIG. 13

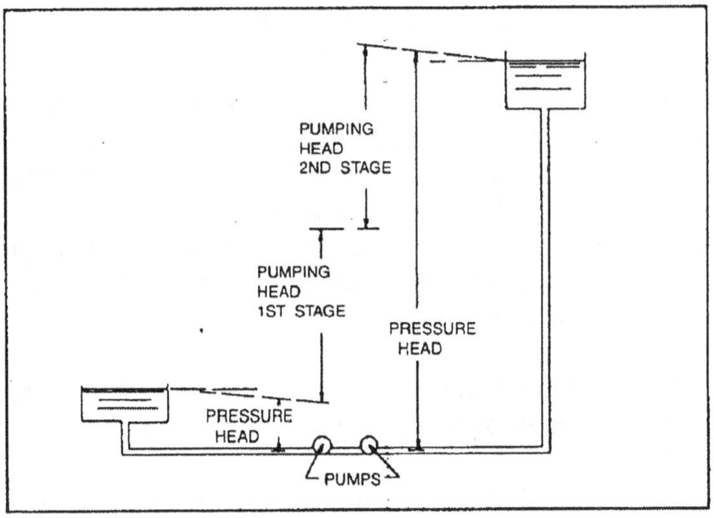

TWO STAGE PUMPING

Centrifugal Pumps. In the centrifugal pump, pressure is developed almost entirely by centrifugal force. Water enters at the center of an impeller which is rotated at high speed. Pressure is exerted and water moves to the outside. A specially shaped casing around the impeller discharges the water through a single opening to discharge line. There are various types of impellers. These include the open type which is commonly" used for pumping sewage and the closed type which is commonly used for pumping clear water. The water may enter at one side of the impeller in the side suction pump or on both sides in the double suction pump. Two or more pumps are used in stages when pumping against high heads. More than one stage can be obtained by using several impellers mounted on a single shaft. Also, two individual pumps can be mounted on a single shaft, driven by one motor, when the head conditions are high. The application of a multistage layout is illustrated in Figure 13.

Centrifugal pumps may be operated with suction lifts. With all but minimum lifts, priming arrangements may be required.

The performance and operating characteristics are given on a pump curve sheet supplied by the manfacturer for each pump. On Figure 14 the curves show the discharge in gallons per minute (gpm) of the pump at various heads, the pump efficiency under different head-discharge conditions and the brake horsepower under various head-discharge conditions. As the head increases the discharge decreases until the shut-off head is reached.

FIG. 14

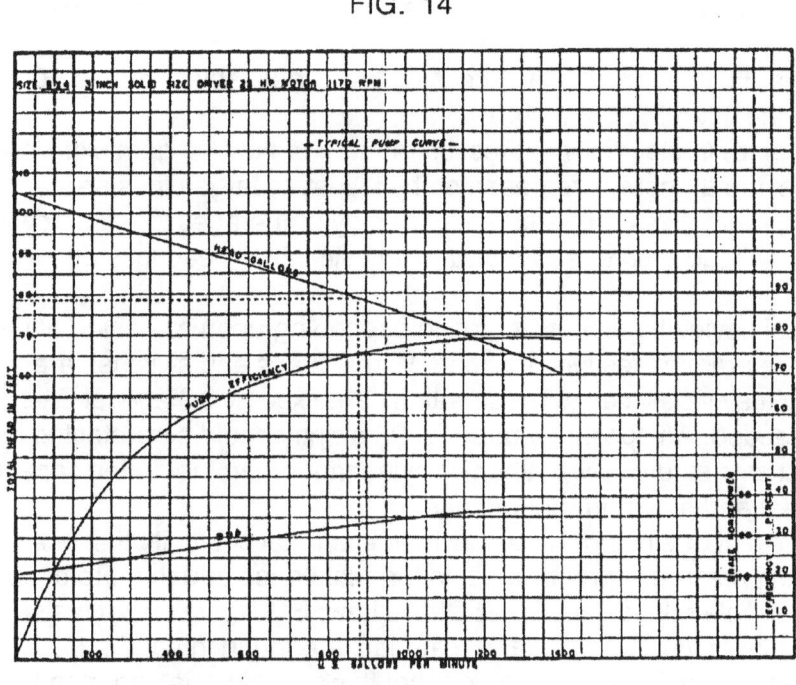

TYPICAL PUMP CURVE

On the pump curves, Figure 14, dotted lines indicate how values can be read from these curves. The pump for which these curves were prepared, when operated at 1170 revolutions per minute (rpm), will deliver 880 gpm at a total head of 79 feet. The brake horsepower (bhp) of the pump is 23 and the pump efficiency 75%. For a motor with an efficiency of 92 percent, the mhp (motor horsepower) should be 25. (Refer to power requirement for pumping). The shutoff head at which no water is delivered is 105 feet.

Large centrifugal pumps usually operate at slow speeds to minimize wear and maintenance costs.

The other velocity pumps have, in general, similar operating characteristics. They may vary considerably in construction and have different applications to water pumping problems. Propeller types are usually limited to low heads and the turbine type, with several stages, is most often used as a deep well pump.

Electricity

Electrical Units. The volt, as indicated in the introduction to this chapter, expresses electrical pressure just as feet, head or psi expresses water pressure. It is represented by the symbol "E", or sometimes emf, the abbreviation for electro-motive force.

For years, standard voltages have been 110, 220, 440, 2,200, 4,400 and 13,200. In water plants the voltage seldom exceeds 440. Higher voltages are used primarily for transmission lines. In some places the 110 and 220 standards have been replaced by 120 and 208. High voltages require proper equipment to prevent leaks (short circuits), and must be respected for personal-safety. Even pressures as low as 110 volts can be fatal.

Proper equipment should be used for the voltage furnished. If the average voltage is 120 on lighting circuits, then 120 and not 110 volt lamps should be used. They will last about three times as long.

For motors over 50 hp, voltages in excess of 440 is desirable. For 5 to 50 hp motors, economy dictates the use of 220 and 440 volts.

The ampere (amp) in electricity expresses the rate of flow, as gpm expresses water flows. In equations, the ampere is represented by I. Just as large pipes are required for large flows of water, large wire sizes are required for hea.vy amperages to keep down the losses due to resistance. Voltage drop due to resistance is similar to head loss due to friction in a pipe line.

Every electrical device has a current rating depending upon its design and resistance to flow. In motors the current varies with the load. Wires, fuses and switches are rated as to the current which they may safely carry. These ratings are fixed by a National Electric Code and should not be exceeded. An appliance rated for 25 amps should be protected by a fuse of that capacity to act as a safety valve. When carrying more than their rated capacity, wires and appliances overheat and may burn out or cause fires.

The ohm is the unit of electrical resistance. In electrical circ-cuits the loss of voltage, voltage drop, or loss in pressure is proportional to the resistance and the rate of current flow. Thus we have the simple relation known as Ohm's Law: $E = RI$. Values of resistance R for unit lengths or conductors of various sizes and materials are found in handbooks.

Direct and Alternating Currents. If the current flows first in one and then the other direction, it is known as alternating current and the number of times per second that it flows in each direction determines the number of cycles. A current that flows in any one direction 60 times per second is called 60 cycle. This is the standard for alternating current in this country.

Transformers are used to increase or decrease voltage. They consist of two stationary coils of wire insulated from each other but wound around a common iron core. Current flowing through the primary coil induces a current in the secondary with a voltage related to the number of turns of wire on the primary and secondary coils.

The Watt (W) is the unit of electrical power (P) and is most commonly used as a thousand watts or the kilowatt (KW). The mechanical unit of power or horsepower (HP) is equivalent to 746 watts. For rough computation it can be remembered that horsepower is approximately equivalent to three-quarters of a KW. Since the efficiency of many small motors is about 75%, one kilowatt in-put is roughly equivalent to one HP out-put.

For direct current:

$P = E I$. By substitution for E,

$P = R I^2$, or by substitution for I

$$P = \frac{E^2}{R}$$

From these expressions it can be seen that power varies directly with both current and voltage if resistance is not considered, but as the square of either one when resistance is considered.

The "kilowatt hour" is the unit of cost for electricity. As the term indicates, it is the average power requirement in KW multiplied by the time in hours over which it is used.

The "single phase circuit" or two-wire system shown in Figure 15 is the simplest circuit. Figure 15 shows a single phase, three-wire system that can furnish two voltages. The three phase (three-wire) is the standard system for large motors. There are two different arrangements of leads from generators or transformers known as delta, Figure 16 and Y shown in Figure 16. Lighting circuits can be taken off as shown. However, unless motors are small, it is better to separate power and lighting circuits to avoid dimming of the lights when motors start.

Circuit protection is provided by fuses enclosed in some type of flame-proof case. They are not always suitable and more complicated thermal relays, air circuit breakers or oil breakers, are required to allow a heavy flow of current for a short time before acting. To allow for a heavy flow, these devices are needed with large motors. A special oil is used in circuit breakers. No other should be used. When a circuit breaker operates frequently, cause should be investigated and corrective steps taken. Protective devices should never be "jumped."

Grounding is extremely important and must be maintained.

Most alternating current "motors" are either of the induction or synchronous type. Synchronous motor speed is determined by the formula,

$N = 120 F/P$ when

N = revolutions of motor per minute (rpm)
F = frequency, cycles per second
P = number of poles
For 60 cycles, $N = 7200/P$

Thus, the fewer the poles, the faster the speed and the smallest possible number of poles is two. Since there must be an even number of poles, the greatest synchronous speed possible for 60 cycles is 3,600 r.p.m. Other possible speeds are 1,800 r.p.m., 1,200 r.p.m., 900 r.p.m., 450 r.p.m. and so forth. The synchronous motor operates accurately at the given speed. This is valuable for clocks and timing devices. However, the synchronous motor has definite poles which must be excited or magnetized by some source of direct current. Synchronous motors have low starting torque (or power), which makes them unsatisfactory for many loads. For this reason it is fortunate that centrifugal pumps can usually be started with small load. Synchronous motors are sometimes used because of their favorable power factor on extremely large pumps.

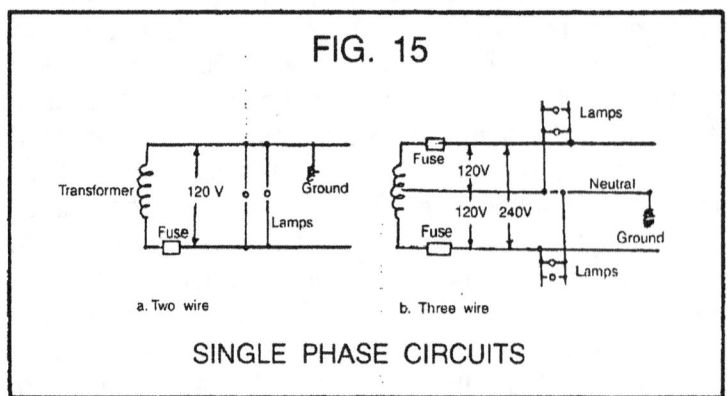

ELECTRIC CIRCUITS

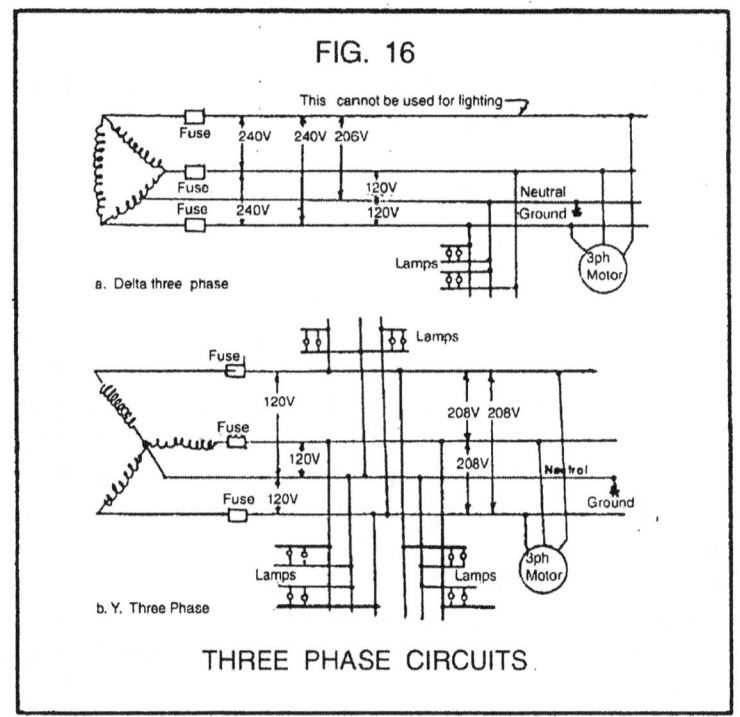

Induction motors. These motors have no poles which need excitation, and can be operated at variable speeds. They are sometimes called squirrel cage motors, because the rotor is made up of bars parallel to the shaft. Without a load, this type of motor will run at a speed close to the synchronous speed. As the load increases, the speed is reduced until at full load the speed is from 2% to 4% less than the synchronous speed. If the load is sufficiently increased, the motor will stop, or "pull out".

Induction motors require relatively small starting currents. Maintenance calls for keeping air ducts and windings of the motor clean. Oil in bearings should be flushed and changed at least once per year. The smaller motors require no special starting devices, and may be started directly across the line. Larger motors usually require reduced voltage for starting.

Variable speed is obtained in an induction motor by having a wound rotor, in whose circuit an external resistance may be added.

Thus a manufacturer can build a motor with external controls to give any speed and power which is required.

"Motor ratings", as well as the ratings for other electrical equipment, are based upon the temperature rise which will occur during operation continuously at normal full load and proper voltage. This rise is usually limited to 40 or 45 degrees centigrade. Thus, a motor may run hot to the touch and still be within its safe rating. A thermometer should be used to check the temperature on small motors. Large motors usually have temperature measuring devices built into them.